SAVANNAH SAMPLER COOKBOOK

Margaret DeBolt

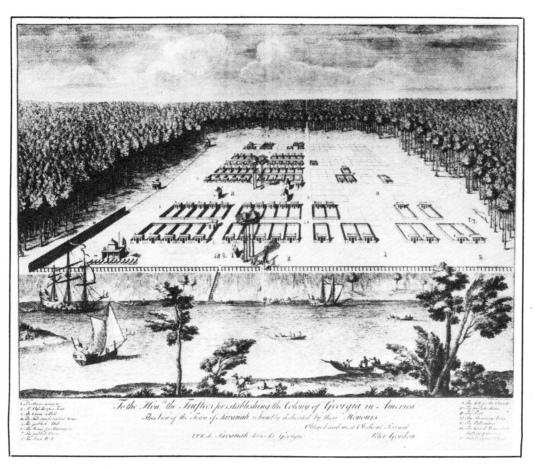

"A view of Savannah as it stood on the 29th of March, 1734,"
Peter Gordon called this drawing which he presented to the
London trustees of the thirteenth colony. Note that General
Oglethorpe's town plan has changed little since, except for
expansion. The Gordon journal is now part of the Wymberly
Jones DeRenne Georgia Collection at the University of Georgia.

SAVANNAH SAMPLER COOKBOOK

By Margaret Wayt DeBolt

With Emma R. Law, Food Consultant

A division of Schiffer Publishing Ltd.
77 Lower Valley Road
Atglen, PA 19310

A collection of the best of Low Country cookery and restoration recipes, old and new, including favorites from the *Savannah News-Press*.

ABOUT THE COVER

This charming cross-stitch design of the famous Davenport House on East State Street was completed by Becky Clark-Braddy of the Yarn Basket, 1 West Liberty Street, as the first of her Savannah Sampler series of historic Savannah places. Built by Isaiah Davenport about 1820, the Georgian town house was saved from demolition for a parking lot by Historic Savannah Foundation, Inc., in 1955. Now a house museum, its restored rooms and garden are open to the public.

Cover photography by Nancy Finke

Design by Mike Brewer

Published by Whitford Press
A Division of Schiffer Publishing, Ltd.
77 Lower Valley Road
Atglen, PA 19310 USA
Please write for a free catalog.
This book may be purchased from the publisher.
Please include $2.95 postage.
Try your bookstore first.

Library of Congress Cataloging in Publication Data:

DeBolt, Margaret Wayt, 1930-
Savannah sampler cookbook.
Includes index.
1. Cookery, American—Georgia. 2. Savannah
—History. 3. Savannah—Social life and
customs. I. Law, Emma Rylander, joint author.
II. Title
TX715.D3113   641.5'9758'724   78-1078
ISBN: 0-915442-49-3

Printed in the United States of America

This book is affectionately dedicated to the good cooks of Savannah and the South...past and present.

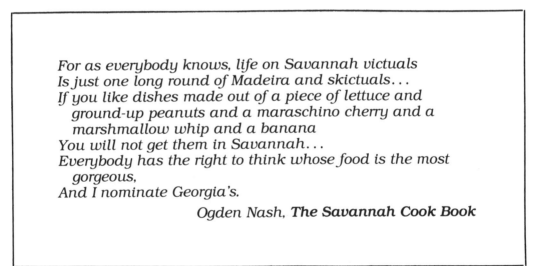

For as everybody knows, life on Savannah victuals
Is just one long round of Madeira and skictuals...
If you like dishes made out of a piece of lettuce and
    ground-up peanuts and a maraschino cherry and a
    marshmallow whip and a banana
You will not get them in Savannah...
Everybody has the right to think whose food is the most
    gorgeous,
And I nominate Georgia's.

Ogden Nash, **The Savannah Cook Book**

HIGH CALLING

The object of this book is to meet some of the most imperative needs of Southern housekeepers. The first thought of every woman when she assumes the duties of a home should be her kitchen, as the health, happiness, and prosperity of a family depend largely upon the character of the food eaten and upon the wisdom and economy of the housewife.

Mrs. Emma Rylander Lane,
Some Good Things To Eat, *1898*

FOOD & FOLKLORE

Good cooks will serve a bit of folklore and local history and family anecdotes along with their souffle or gumbo or pecan pie or smothered quail or hot cornbread, for folklore and history and family are fitting accompaniments for Georgia's traditional fine foods.

Kathryn Tucker Windham,
Treasured Georgia Recipes, *1973*

CONTENTS

POEM IN PRAISE OF PRACTICALLY EVERYTHING

By Johnny Mercer

To write about Georgia...how to start?
The indolent, proud, gentle-mannered heart
The oriole perched on a cattail stalk
The oyster-shell road and the field-hand walk
The basket of clothes balanced on the head
The lattice-work cool of the boat house shed
The heat of a blackberry afternoon
A moss-covered oak on the rising moon.

The breeze through the porch screen—as soft as a sigh
With heat lightning off in the distant sky
And rocking chair talk like a lullaby...

The seersucker suits and the "Whatcha say!"
The stop for a coke and the time of day
The firm-breasted girls walking Bull Street squares
The toss of the head for the prying stares...
The taffeta dresses and country club nights
The drink in the car, and the stag-line fights
The laugh floating over the moonlit lawn
And the barber-shop songs in the drunken dawn...
The open house Christmas that lasts for weeks
The arm-around singing, the quickly-kissed cheeks...

To write about Georgia...what to say?
Just put down the pencil and quote Benet—
"Georgia, Georgia, careless yield
The watermelons ripe in the field..."

Peaceful and lazy and too good to last
A "maybesome" future—But oh, what a past!
You gave me a childhood not many could know
And I blow you a kiss from the bald-head row.

Great-grandson of Confederate Brigadier General Hugh W. Mercer, composer Johnny Mercer began his theatrical career in his native city of Savannah with the local Little Theatre. He went on to New York and over 1,500 songs and four Oscars before his death in California in 1976. He is buried in Savannah.

"RESTORATION RECEIPTS"

Savannah, Georgia's oldest and most picturesque city, was founded as the last of the thirteen English colonies by the London philanthropist and military leader James Oglethorpe in 1733. Its history has included famine, fever, naval blockades, armed conflict, two military occupations, fires, earthquakes, hurricanes, and financial depressions as well as years of prosperity and splendor.

The cotton gin was invented near Savannah in 1793. The city's namesake, the *S. S. Savannah*, was the first steamship to cross the Atlantic, in 1819. Presidential visitors range from George Washington in 1791 to the present Georgia-born President, Jimmy Carter. John and Charles Wesley served here as young Episcopalian clergymen; Robert E. Lee was once stationed at Fort Pulaski. Illustrious native daughters and sons include Girl Scout founder Juliette Gordon Low, novelist Flannery O'Connor, poet Conrad Aiken, and Oscar-winning composer Johnny Mercer.

Present-day Savannah has won national acclaim for its restoration movement, in which the architectural gems of the past and a unique system of tree-sheltered squares co-exist with modern tourism, shipping, military bases, and industry.

Just as today's Savannah is an intriguing blend of tradition and progress, the foods of the city reflect a varied heritage. Here the English inheritance of roast beef and puddings, trifles and great (fruit) cakes have mingled with German sweets and sours, Scottish breads, Irish stews, African okra and benne seed dishes, and the Indian ways with seafood, corn, and wild game.

The "receipts" of the plantation period, the gumbos and beaten biscuits, barbecues and pecan pies, have been passed among the generations as carefully as the family silver and china once hidden from the soldiers who marched through Savannah with General William Tecumseh Sherman. They have been rediscovered with delight by tourists and those who have chosen to make the New South their home.

Whether served in a restored town house overlooking an azalea-bordered square, at one of Savannah's many historic restaurants, on renovated River Street with its reclaimed cotton warehouses turned boutiques, or at an informal Tybee Beach picnic or oyster roast, authentic Southern cuisine is memorable both for its time-tested flavor and the friendliness with which it is presented. Thus are converts made. The story is told of one retired Maine sea captain who was offered a glass of the insidious **Chatham Artillery Punch**, and then another. At this point he arose earnestly but unsteadily to declare to a startled assembly: "I'm here to say I can lick any Yankee in the house!"

This book was originally conceived as a collection of the best recipes from the *Savannah News-Press*, a publication dating back to 1850 and including author Joel Chandler Harris of "Uncle Remus" fame among its former editors. Like the Dixie moppet Topsy, *Savannah Sampler Cookbook* "just growed" to include contributions from acquaintances and relatives. Emma Rylander Law, the friend who has generously consented to act as food consultant in the project, made available her own remarkable collection spanning a distinguished career as home economist, dietician, and Madison Avenue food consultant, as well as family recipes from Burke County.

Historic perspective has been provided by the inclusion of vintage recipes from fragile Southern cookbooks long out of date, including two from Savannah. Private collections hereto unpublished have been generously made available, such as those of Mrs. Sophie Meldrim Shonnard and the late Helen Kehoe Crolly. Cosmopolitan present-day Savannah has been represented by a variety of ethnic recipes. Restaurants such as The Pirates' House and The Pink House have shared their specialties. Some of the modern recipes, for whole wheat bread and other from-scratch baking, express a contemporary interest in natural foods and nutrition. . .one which seems to go full-circle with our oldest recipes.

The result, we hope, is as varied as Savannah itself. "Restoration Receipts," one friend has called this book: a blending of the old and the new. It is also a three-year project which has been an act of love.

Margaret Wayt DeBolt

PRACTICAL SUGGESTIONS
FOR USING THIS BOOK

Although every effort has been made to make directions as clear as possible, this collection is necessarily intended for those with some knowledge of cooking terms and procedures. Novices are advised to invest first of all in a basic cookbook for detailed illustrations of cooking skills.

In trying a new recipe, check seasonings with reference to your own preference: in this area, all suggestions are only approximations. Oven recipes should also be timed initially in accordance with the peculiarities of your own equipment.

Although we have tried to be explicit about can and package sizes, they are constantly changing. Do the best you can! If you find a package which varies only an ounce or two from what we suggest, it probably won't make any difference. By the same token, when we say a stick (¼ pound) of butter, we are obviously not referring to the new whipped margarine with six sticks to the package!

"Flour" means unsifted, regular, all-purpose flour unless otherwise stated.

"One egg" refers to the large size, unless otherwise stated.

Baking powder is the double-acting variety.

Sugar is the white, granulated variety unless otherwise noted. Confectioner's sugar refers to the 10x variety.

Oven temperatures refer to a pre-heated oven, unless otherwise stated. (Don't put a chilled glass casserole in one unless it is of the type guaranteed to withstand such sudden changes in temperature.)

Shortening is vegetable shortening, unless otherwise stated.

Scissor-cutting with kitchen shears is the best way to mince, snip, chop, or dice dried fruit. Dip blades in warm water occasionally if they become sticky.

Margarine can be substituted for butter. However, there will be a slight difference in flavor. (Do *not* cook with whipped, diet margarines!)

Eggs give better results in cookery if they are at room temperature. However, they separate more easily when first removed from the refrigerator. Cover, and let them come to room temperature before using. Room temperature whites will give a larger volume when whipped.

We have not greased tube pans if they are of the slip-bottom variety: this gives a better volume. A sharp, thin knife will easily cut the cake away from the sides. Remove the bottom, and cut underneath to release. If tube pan is not a slip-bottom type, grease bottoms only. Never grease an angel food pan.

Muffin cups should be greased only on the bottoms. This is also true of loaf pans: a better volume is the result.

Cakes are "done" when tops have begun to brown, sides shrink from the pans, and tops spring back when gently pressed with tips of fingers. Large or loaf cakes may also be tested by piercing the middle well with a wooden pick. If the pick comes out clean, cake is "done."

Above all, have fun in the kitchen! Be creative; try out different flavor combinations to find out what is best for you and your family. Learn to adapt the ideas in new cookbooks, even if you don't use the whole recipe. Confidence will grow with success.

Good luck!

Great care has been taken in the preparation of this book to give to the public only such recipes as have been thoroughly tested and found reliable. The fact that these are "Home Recipes" used by the house-keepers of the Old South, gives the book an additional value. Many of the recipes have never been published before, but now, through the courtesy of friends, we are allowed to offer them to the public.

Favorite Recipes From Savannah Homes, 1904

APPETIZERS
&
BEVERAGES

The first printed plan of Savannah, 1734.

Courtesy of Georgia Historical Society

SAVANNAH, THE HOSTESS CITY

The Indian mica Tomochichi welcomed James Oglethorpe and the first settlers with a barbecue and campfire dancing. President George Washington was greeted with pageantry and entertainment in Johnson Square. President James Monroe had a cruise on the *S. S. Savannah* in 1819, and a party in his honor at the elegant Scarbrough house on West Broad Street. President William Howard Taft kept a parade waiting while he ate venison and waffles at the home of Juliette Gordon Low in 1909.

Savannah has always been famous for its hospitality. It is a tradition which endures today with several annual events eagerly awaited by residents and knowledgeable visitors.

One of these is Georgia Week, "The Ogeechee Mardi Gras." It is sponsored by Historic Savannah Foundation, Inc., to mark the founding of the last English colony in America on February 12, 1733. Its highlight is a pageant re-enacting that event, directed by the Little Theatre. School children parade in the squares in colonial garb, bands play on River Street, community groups have food and crafts booths, and a carnival atmosphere prevails.

March 17 brings the largest St. Patrick's Day parade south of New York City, a tradition dating to 1824. The day begins with church services and green grits (one year it was even a green Savannah River!). It continues with school bands, marching societies, floats, and merry-making sponsored by the St. Patrick's Day Parade Committee.

Later is the Savannah Tour of Homes and Gardens, sponsored by the Women of Christ Episcopal Church and Historic Savannah Foundation, Inc. This event is timed to coincide with the height of breath-taking azalea bloom on Victory Drive and through the squares, and the spring flowering of Low Country gardens. Once a year some of the city's most beautiful and historic private homes are open to the public, as well as more modest ones in the process of restoration, famous house museums, and some plantation homes.

New in 1976, and so successful it has become an annual late April event, was "Night In Old Savannah." The three-day feast of ethnic foods, music, and entertainment in Johnson Square is sponsored by the Girl Scout Council of Savannah, the first in the United States. A spirit of community fun prevails with such attractions as the Preservation Hall Jazz Band of New Orleans, bagpipers, a Chinese dragon weaving through the squares, French can-cans, and street theatre.

The annual Savannah Arts Festival, sponsored by the Savannah Art Association, is held at the historic Central of Georgia Train Shed on West Broad Street, now the Savannah Visitors Center. It was once the site of the 1779 Siege of Savannah, and now of the proposed Bicentennial Battle Park.

June brings the Blessing of the Fleet in Thunderbolt, a Savannah suburb named for a bolt of lightning in pioneer days, and now noted for its shrimping industry and marinas. During the weekend gaily-decorated shrimp vessels vie for the prize of most colorful craft, seafood is enjoyed, and arts and crafts stalls line River Road. Later in the summer comes The Great Ogeechee Raft Race, with some unlikely craft afloat in the river near Savannah.

Every "First Saturday" is a mini-festival on River Street. Sidewalk vendors, bands, and specials in the crafts shops lend a lively note to the monthly celebration on Georgia's oldest and newest street, where a seven-million-dollar restoration and park improvement program was completed in the summer of 1977. The same spirit is exhibited at Thunderbolt on the third weekend of each month, with everything from art exhibits to shrimp boat tours. Any excuse for a party!

Autumn brings holiday carnivals, bazaars, and festivals from many church and community groups. There is the annual Greek Pastry Sale at the Hellenic Community Center and the Day on the Island house tour and luncheon sponsored by Isle of Hope Methodist Church on the second Thursday in October. October also means the Coastal Empire Fair.

In the mild Southern winter, the holiday season is a round of open houses, church and cultural activities, and the Downtown Neighborhood Association house tour, when traditional decorations are at their most beautiful. Then there are the New Year's parties, and it all begins again. . . .

ASPARAGUS DIP

Yield: about 1 cup

1 14½-ounce can asparagus spears, drained
½ cup commercial sour cream
¼ teaspoon hot pepper sauce
¼ teaspoon dried dill weed
½ teaspoon Beau Monde seasoning

Combine all ingredients in blender. Blend until smooth. Chill. Serve with chips, crisp raw vegetables, or an assortment of crackers.

Vera Stevens, Richmond Hill, Georgia

GREEN ONION CHEESE DIP

Yield: 1⅔ cups

12 ounces cream cheese
¼ teaspoon sage
2 tablespoons sweet pickle
   juice
   dash hot pepper sauce,
   to taste

1 teaspoon mayonnaise
3 green onions, including tops,
   chopped

Cream ingredients in blender. Chill before serving.

Linda Harper

SPICY CREAM DIP

Yield: 1½ cups

3 ounces cream cheese, at room
   temperature
1 cup commercial sour cream
1 hard-cooked egg, finely
   chopped
2 tablespoons finely minced
   green pepper
1 tablespoon ketchup
½ teaspoon powdered
   horseradish

1 teaspoon Worcestershire
   sauce
¼ teaspoon hot pepper sauce
1 small clove garlic, minced or
   crushed
½ teaspoon dry mustard
½ teaspoon salt, or to taste

Mash cheese with fork until light. Blend well with remaining ingredients. Cover and refrigerate about two hours to blend flavors.

ORIENTAL DIP

Coriander is known in the Orient as Chinese parsley. Here the ground version spices an unusual cocktail recipe, excellent with bite-sized fresh vegetables, such as sliced mushrooms and cauliflower florets.

Yield: 1½ cups

½ cup minced green onions
¼ teaspoon or more ground
   coriander
1 tablespoon dried or 2
   tablespoons chopped fresh
   parsley

¼ teaspoon ground ginger
1 tablespoon soy sauce
2 tablespoons minced canned
   water chestnuts
1 cup commercial sour cream
2 tablespoons mayonnaise

Blend together all ingredients. Chill and serve. Since the flavors in this recipe are quite delicate, you may wish to experiment with the proportions to suit your taste.

Marilyn Whelpley

MOON RIVER SHRIMP DIP

Yield: 4¼ cups

8 ounces cream cheese	2 tablespoons chopped ripe
1 10¾-ounce can cream of	olives
shrimp soup	1 pound shrimp, cooked and
2 cloves garlic	chopped

Soften cream cheese at room temperature and blend with soup. Put cloves of garlic through a press, and add along with the olives. Mix thoroughly and add shrimp. Chill and serve with corn chips or crisp crackers.

SHRIMP CANAPES

Cut some round slices of bread, about one inch thick, and brown slightly in butter. Peel and chop very fine one quart of shrimp. Stir in one heaping spoonful of butter, one teaspoonful of French mustard; a little salt may be added, but it is not necessary. Spread on rounds of toast, and serve.

Hints From Southern Epicures, *circa 1890*

AUNT MYRL'S LEIDERKRANZ DIP

Yield: 2¼ cups

8 ounces cream cheese	½ teaspoon dill weed
2 ounces Leiderkranz cheese	½ teaspoon Beau Monde
1 cup mayonnaise	seasoning
2 tablespoons minced raw	paprika (optional)
onions or 1 tablespoon dried	dried green onion flakes
onion reconstituted in 1	(optional)
tablespoon water	

Let cheeses stand at room temperature until soft. Mix well with mayonnaise to blend, then with other ingredients, except the last two. Chill. If desired, sprinkle paprika and/or onion flakes on the top before serving. This will keep at least two weeks in the refrigerator, and is even better if made the day before serving. It is especially good with raw vegetables, such as celery, carrot sticks, cauliflower, and broccoli flowerets.

Marilyn Whelpley

BRANDY CHEESE BALL

Yield: about 2½ cups

8 ounces cream cheese	4 ounces blue cheese
1 8-ounce container soft	1 tablespoon brandy
Cheddar cheese	½ teaspoon paprika

17

⅓ cup finely ground or minced
      walnuts or pecans

Let cheeses come to room temperature and blend well. Blend in brandy and paprika. Cover and refrigerate until firm enough to mold into a ball. Roll in nuts. Wrap in plastic and refrigerate until needed. Let stand at room temperature for 15 to 20 minutes before serving. This is good on crackers or accompanied by wedges of tart apples and pears. It is also a marvelous dessert with fruit.

PUFFED MUSHROOMS

Here's a favorite recipe from the personable author of *The Holiday Inn International Cookbook.*

Yield: 2 to 4 servings

1	pound medium-size fresh mushrooms	1	cup milk
1	egg	1	cup bread crumbs, seasoned to taste

Wash mushrooms and let air dry. Beat together egg and milk. Place mushrooms, stems and all, in milk mixture, and then in bread crumbs. Let stand 10 minutes. Fry in deep fat at 350 degrees for 3 to 4 minutes.

Ruth Malone, Little Rock, Arkansas

We are all greatly dependent upon the state of our digestion. Napoleon could not rise superior to an illy-cooked dinner. Hence, his Waterloo. The History of the French Revolution rose and fell with the state of Carlyle's dyspepsia, and many a tragic episode in family life is superinduced by the baleful influence of a tortured stomach. Mighty is the hand that holds the ballot-box, but mightier is the hand that welds to advantage the pepper-box, the salt-spoon, and the sugar shaker.

Breakfast, Dinner, and Supper,
Or, What To Eat and How to Prepare It,
by Maude C. Cooke, 1897

CRAB-STUFFED MUSHROOMS

Yield: about 18

1	pound large, fresh mushrooms vegetable oil	¼	cup commercial sour cream
4	tablespoons butter or margarine	1	egg, slightly beaten
¼	cup minced onion	2	cups soft bread crumbs
1	6-ounce package frozen crab meat, thawed, drained, and flaked	2	tablespoons chopped dill or parsley
		½	teaspoon salt
		¼	teaspoon black pepper

Rinse, pat dry, and remove stems from mushrooms. Chop sufficient stems to make 1 cup, saving any remaining stems for soups, stews, etc. Brush caps with oil; set aside. In a medium skillet, melt 2 tablespoons of the butter or margarine. Add chopped mushrooms and onion. Saute for 4 minutes; cool.

Preheat oven to 350 degrees. In a medium bowl, combine mushrooms and onion mixture with crab, sour cream, egg, 1 cup of bread crumbs, dill, salt, and pepper. Mix lightly. Spoon into mushroom caps, mounding slightly. Melt remaining two tablespoons of butter or margarine. Add remaining cup of bread crumbs; mix lightly and sprinkle over top of each stuffed mushroom. Bake for 15 minutes, or until hot. Serve immediately.

Savannah News-Press

SAUTERNE CLAM PUFFS

Yield: 18 to 20

8	ounces cream cheese		18 to 20 toast rounds
¼	cup Sauterne, other white dinner wine, or dry sherry	5	slices bacon, cooked and chopped
1	7-ounce can minced clams, well drained		

Soften cream cheese. Blend in wine; add clams. Heap on toast rounds; top with bits of bacon. Place on cookie sheet. Broil about 5 minutes, or until bacon is crisp. Serve hot with chilled sherry.

SMOKED OYSTER SPREAD

Yield: 1¼ cups

1	6-ounce can smoked oysters	1	teaspoon lemon juice
6	ounces cream cheese, at room temperature		dried dill weed to taste

19

Drain oysters. Replace 1 teaspoon of the liquid, and chop well. Mix oysters with cream cheese until of a "whipped" consistency. Stir in lemon juice and dill weed. Refrigerate, covered, until needed. When ready to serve, let mixture come to room temperature. Accompany with crackers.

River Road in Thunderbolt, scene of the annual blessing of the fleet. It is on the Wilmington River, part of the Intercoastal Waterway.

Drawing by Pamela Lee

BLUE CHEESE NIBBLES

Yield: 24

1 cup crumbled blue cheese (about 4 ounces) at room temperature
¼ pound (1 stick) butter, at room temperature

1 cup sifted flour
½ cup finely chopped pecans

Preheat oven to 375 degrees. Cream cheese and butter together; work in flour. Roll into balls about 1 inch in diameter. An inch-sized melon baller helps make uniform balls. Roll in pecans. Place on an oiled cookie sheet; flatten slightly. Bake for 14 to 16 minutes. Do not brown.

EMMA LAW'S CHEESE CRISPS

Yield: about 48

¼ pound (1 stick) butter, at room temperature
1 cup shredded sharp cheese (4-ounce package), at room temperature
1 cup sifted flour

¼ teaspoon paprika, or more to taste
$\frac{1}{16}$ teaspoon cayenne pepper, or more to taste
1½ cups Rice Krispies cereal

In a medium bowl, beat together the butter and cheese. Sift the flour, paprika, and cayenne pepper together, and gradually work this into the butter mixture. Mix in the Rice Krispies. Chill if necessary before shaping, to make the dough easier to handle.

Preheat oven to 375 degrees. Roll into small balls, about 1 inch in diameter. (I use the large end of a melon baller.) Place a few inches apart on a lightly buttered cookie sheet. With a small spatula, flatten slightly. Bake about 12 to 14 minutes; do not brown. Remove with a spatula to a wire rack to cool. Store in a tightly-covered tin box in a cool place. If necessary to refrigerate, bring to room temperature again before serving. These freeze well.

SAUERKRAUT DILL DOLLARS

Yield: about 30

2 sticks (11-ounce package) pie crust mix
4 tablespoons (½ stick) butter
1 4½ ounce can pitted ripe olives, drained and chopped
1 cup chopped, drained sauerkraut

1 egg
dill weed or dried tarragon to taste
salt

21

Blend pie crust mix with butter. Crush olives with rolling pin as flat as possible; drain on paper towel. Blend with pie crust mix and sauerkraut. Form into a ball and chill on waxed paper.

Preheat oven to 425 degrees. Roll dough ¼-inch thick on floured board. Cut with 2-inch round cutter. Arrange on baking sheets. Beat egg, and brush tops lightly. Sprinkle with dill weed and salt. Bake 15 minutes, or until golden.

Marilyn Whelpley

BENNE SEED

Benne seed, called sesame seed in the North, is a special Savannah ingredient which was first brought to Georgia by the slaves and planted for good luck around their homes. It was the black cooks who first made benne seed cakes and candy in plantation kitchens and later for sale in the old Savannah market. They also pounded the tiny seed into a paste which was eaten on hominy. The good fortune the seed carried was undoubtedly in its flavor.

TOASTED BENNE SEED

When a Savannah recipe calls for **Toasted Benne Seed**, this means to place the seed in a shallow baking pan in a preheated (350 degrees) oven for about 10 to 15 minutes. Stir several times for uniform coloring. Stir before using.

Cook benne seed to a golden color only; do not brown. Seed need not be browned if it is to be used in a dough which will bake, unless the golden color and more distinctive flavor are desired.

BENNE CHEESE STICKS

Yield: 120 to 140

1 pound sharp Cheddar cheese, grated	2 cups sifted flour
¼ pound (1 stick) butter, at room temperature	½ teaspoon salt
½ cup **Toasted Benne Seed**	¼ teaspoon cayenne pepper, or more (be careful)

Preheat oven to 350 degrees. Cream cheese and butter well. Stir in benne seed. Sift together other ingredients; blend with the first mixture. This will be a very stiff dough. Pinch it off in pieces and roll each to ¾-inch diameter (the length depends on the size of the pinched pieces). Transfer to an oiled cookie sheet, leaving about 1 inch between pieces. Bake 15 to 17 minutes. Do not allow sticks to brown. Remove and cool on racks.

BENNE BITES

Yield: about 36

1 5-ounce jar sharp Cheddar cheese spread	1 cup packaged pancake mix
¼ pound (1 stick) butter, at room temperature	2 teaspoons **Toasted Benne Seed**

Cream cheese and butter together until smooth and a bit fluffy. Add pancake mix and benne seed. Mix until well combined. Roll into small balls, about 5/8-inch in diameter. Place on lightly oiled cookie sheets. Refrigerate several hours. Bake in a preheated (375 degrees) oven about 10 minutes. Do not let get too brown. Serve hot.

THOUSAND ISLAND CRACKERS

These unusual crackers will be a sensation when you entertain.

Yield: about 30

2 tablespoons vegetable oil	2 tablespoons water
2 teaspoons tomato paste	1 tablespoon lemon juice
½ teaspoon Worcestershire sauce	¾ cup sifted flour
¼ teaspoon hot pepper sauce	¼ teaspoon salt
½ teaspoon freeze-dried chives, well-crushed	⅛ teaspoon baking soda
½ teaspoon dried green pepper pieces, well-crushed	¾ teaspoon baking powder

Preheat oven to 425 degrees. Mix first 8 ingredients together; set aside. Sift flour well with salt, soda, and baking powder. Make a "well" in center of flour mixture. Stir first mixture and pour all at once into flour. Stir quickly until dough forms a ball. Turn onto lightly floured cloth and knead quickly, about eight times. Roll very thin. Cut into 2-inch circles. Pierce with fork. Transfer to ungreased cookie sheet. Bake in middle of oven for about 9 minutes.

PRO BALLS

Americans consume over 650 million pounds of peanut butter annually!

Yield: about 48

3 cups crisp butter crackers (such as Ritz), crushed

1⅓ cups crunchy-type peanut butter	½ cup crisp, finely chopped bacon (about 12 slices)
1 8-ounce jar processed cheese spread	4 dozen thin stick pretzels or toothpicks

Crush crackers into fine crumbs, using blender if available. Combine with peanut butter, cheese spread, and bacon. Blend thoroughly. Shape into one-inch balls. Stick one pretzel or toothpick into each ball.

Georgia Peanut Commission

DEVILED ALMONDS

Almond trees are relatives of the peach tree. They were brought first to the American shores by Spanish missionaries, and were treasured for their flowers as well as the fruit of which the almond is the seed.

Yield: 1½ cups

½ pound blanched whole almonds	1 teaspoon celery salt
½ cup vegetable oil	½ teaspoon salt
	¼ teaspoon cayenne pepper

Cook the almonds in the oil over medium heat until they are golden brown. Drain on absorbent paper, and place in a mixing bowl. While still warm, toss with other ingredients.

Take the best fruits of the land in your vessels, and carry down (to) the man a present, a little balm, and a little honey, spices, and myrrh, nuts and almonds.

Genesis, 43:11

DIANA'S CHEESE BALL

Yield: 4¾ cups

6 ounces cream cheese, at room temperature	1 teaspoon Worcestershire sauce
2 5-ounce jars sharp Cheddar cheese spread	2 tablespoons minced onion
6 ounces Roquefort cheese	1 cup finely ground pecans
	1 cup chopped parsley

S.S. Savannah

Drawing courtesy of Frank W. Spencer

Mix all ingredients, reserving ½ cup parsley, and chill. When you are ready to serve, shape mixture into a ball and roll in remaining parsley. Serve with crackers.

Diana Rhinebeck

APPETIZER HAM BALL

Yield: 1½ cups

2 4½-ounce cans deviled ham	3 ounces cream cheese, at room temperature
3 tablespoons chopped stuffed olives	2 teaspoons milk
1 tablespoon prepared mustard hot sauce to taste	

Combine deviled ham, olives, mustard, hot sauce, and a third of the cream cheese; blend until smooth. Shape mixture into a ball. Combine remaining cream cheese and milk; frost ham ball with this mixture. Chill. Remove from refrigerator 15 minutes before serving.

Jean Wickstrom, Food Editor, **Southern Living Magazine**

YOGURT BALL

Yield: 3 cups

3 cups shredded Cheddar cheese	⅓ cup minced ripe olives
⅓ cup crumbled blue cheese	½ cup chopped pecans
½ cup plain yogurt	¼ cup chopped parsley
½ teaspoon Worcestershire sauce	

Mix together the cheeses until smooth. Add yogurt and Worcestershire sauce and beat until creamy. Stir in olives. Cover and chill. Shape into ball and roll in nuts and parsley. Return to refrigerator. Allow to come to room temperature before serving. Serve with crisp, salted crackers.

LOW-CALORIE NIBBLES

Remember the dieters at your party with a few plates of carrot slices, celery sticks, or cauliflowerets (pieces of cauliflower divided into flowerets) which can be offered with dips, or eaten alone. Pieces of raw zucchini make an elegant snack, sliced very thin, and served plain.

Kate Fenner Urquhart

EGGPLANT CHIPS

Peel small eggplant, and cut into very thin slices. Drop slices in hot (375 degrees) fat and fry until golden brown. Drain on paper towels, and serve hot, sprinkled with salt.

SAVANNAH'S FIRST STORE

In early Savannah, the first store of the English colonists stood at 22 Bull Street on Johnson Square, where the Citizens and Southern Bank is now located. The public oven was on the northeast corner of Congress and Whitaker Streets, and the House for Strangers was at 22-24 West Congress Street. The public mill, used for grinding corn, was located on Bryan Street where a parking garage is now situated. Bronze plaques marking these locations were placed around Johnson Square in 1929 by the Bonaventure Chapter of the Daughters of the American Revolution.

Johnson Square, Savannah's earliest square, is now the site of the annual "Night In Old Savannah" celebration, honoring the food, music and dress of its varied ethnic heritage.

WARD McALLISTER

Savannah-born Ward McAllister, a relative of the Telfairs, was the social arbitrator of the late nineteenth century. He coined the phrase "the 400" when he helped Mrs. W. W. Astor plan a dinner party for the elite of New York City. In his memoirs, he recalls Savannah wine parties.

In Savannah and Charleston, from 1800 up to our Civil War, afternoon wine parties were the custom. You were asked to come and taste Madeira at 5 p.m., after your dinner. (The hour of dinner in those cities was then always 3 p.m.) The mahogany table, which reflected your face, was set with finger bowls, with four pipe-stem glasses by each bowl, olives, parched groundnuts (peanuts), and almonds, and half a dozen bottles of Madeira. There you sat, tasted, and commented on these wines for an hour or more.

Society As I Have Found It, 1890

I see that the receipt for Artillery Punch is included.... May Heaven have mercy upon your souls!

Arthur Gordon, **Christ Church Cook Book,** 1956

CHATHAM ARTILLERY PUNCH

One of America's oldest military units, the Chatham Artillery first constructed a battery at what is now Fort Jackson in July 1776. When President George Washington visited Savannah in May 1791, he was honored with a 26-gun salute by the artillery company. He acknowledged it by later sending the unit two bronze field pieces which had been captured at Yorktown. Recently refurbished, they are now on display on Bay Street near City Hall.

The unit is famous not only for its military exploits, but for a lethal concoction which probably started out as an innocent punch served at social gatherings, with various members slipping in a bit of alcoholic beverage when no one was looking!

The Chatham Artillery's Washington Guns on Bay Street by Jean Birnbaum

The tales of its victims are many. It is said that one famous visiting military man imbibed...and then arose to make a speech solemnly nominating himself for the Presidency of the United States. Another had a totally unintelligible address mercifully drowned out by the rousing refrain of Sousa's March, played by a Parris Island Marine Band.

Caution is advised for those attempting the recipe.

Yield: about 10 gallons stock

1	pound green tea	1	gallon rum
2	gallons cold water	1	gallon Hennessey brandy
	juice of 3 dozen oranges	1	gallon rye whisky
	juice of 3 dozen lemons	1	gallon gin
5	pounds light brown sugar	1	pint Benedictine liqueur
2	quarts maraschino cherries		Champagne
3	gallons Catawba or Rhine wine		

Put tea in cold water. Allow to stand overnight. Add fruit juice, and strain. Add sugar, cherries, and liquor. Cover lightly. Allow to ferment for two to six weeks in a large stone or glass crock. Strain off cherries and put liquid in bottles. Chill as needed. Mix 1 gallon of chilled stock with 1 quart of chilled Champagne or chilled charged water at serving time. Pour over ice in a punch bowl, and serve...carefully. Some are said to add "just a pinch" of gunpowder before serving from the punch bowl...You're on your own about that!

To the Constitution of the United States—framed by the wisdom of sages—may our statesmen and posterity regard it as the National Ark of Political Safety, never to be abandoned.

Final toast during the visit of President James Monroe to Savannah in 1819. (It is said that Chatham Artillery Punch was served.)

SUNRISE SPARKLE BREAKFAST

Better for you than the packaged instant breakfast drinks.

Yield: 2 servings

1½ cups cold milk	3 tablespoons wheat germ
½ cup undiluted frozen orange juice concentrate, thawed	2 tablespoons honey
1 egg	nutmeg

Put all ingredients except nutmeg in blender. Cover and blend at high speed about 15 seconds. Pour into glasses and sprinkle with nutmeg.

Martha Sawyer

MACON TOMATO JUICE COCKTAIL

The same flavor as the fancy tomato juice blends.

Yield: 2 quarts

1 46-ounce can tomato juice	1 teaspoon parsley flakes or chopped parsley
1 cup chopped cucumbers	¼ teaspoon salt
1½ cups chopped celery	¼ teaspoon pepper
¼ cup chopped onion	¼ teaspoon garlic salt
1 teaspoon lemon juice	

¼ teaspoon A-1 sauce	¼ teaspoon mustard
¼ teaspoon Worcestershire sauce	2 bay leaves

Put all ingredients except bay leaves in a blender. Mix thoroughly. (You may have to put less than the full can of tomato juice in the blender container, in order to get everything else in, and blend the rest of the tomato juice with the mixture later.) Chill with bay leaves; remove bay leaves before serving.

Mrs. Ronald T. Williams, Macon, Georgia

COFFEE SUBSTITUTES

As substitutes for coffee, some use dry brown bread crusts, and roast them; others soak rye grain in rum, and roast it; others roast peas in the same way as coffee. None of these are very good; and peas so used are considered unhealthy. When there is a large family of apprentices and workmen, and coffee is very dear, it may be worth while to use the substitutes, or to mix them half and half with coffee; but, after all, the best economy is to go without.

The American Frugal Housewife, 1838

MOCHA CHARLOTTE

Yield: 8 5-ounce servings

3 tablespoons sugar	3 cups milk
¼ cup instant coffee powder	whipped cream
1½ cups water	
1 1-ounce square unsweetened chocolate	

Melt chocolate, uncovered, over hot water. Combine sugar, coffee, water, chocolate, and milk. Stir over low heat until hot; do not boil. Remove from heat, and beat quickly with rotary beater until frothy. Pour into cups, and top with cream as desired.

PHOENIX PUNCH

Yield: 2 gallons

1 gallon fudge-ripple ice cream	2 quarts strong coffee, chilled

2   quarts cream soda, chilled

Let ice cream soften slightly outside of freezer. Mash and blend with coffee. Place in a chilled punch bowl, and add cream soda, stirring only until blended. Serve immediately.

You may wish to experiment with other flavors of ice cream, such as coffee or vanilla.

Phoenix Halls of Atlanta

INSTANT COCOA MIX

Yield: 4 pounds

1   pound confectioners' sugar
1   8-quart package powdered
    milk, undiluted
1   16-ounce box unsweetened
    cocoa

1   11-ounce jar powdered coffee
    creamer

Mix ingredients in a large bowl. For hot chocolate, place 2 heaping tablespoons in a large cup and fill with boiling water. Stir, and serve. This is much more economical than the little individual-serving packages!

Kathryn Stewart

HISTORIC DRINK

Tea was a popular drink with the English colonists in Georgia. As everyone knows, it played an important part in the American Revolution when the colonies protested the tax on tea. After tea was banned, a wide variety of herbal and root drinks, such as sassafras tea, were substituted. These were called "Liberty Tea."

Iced tea, now a Southern staple, was first served at the St. Louis World's Fair in 1904. The weather had turned so warm that the displays of fine Far Eastern teas were going untouched. In desperation, the young Englishman at the display began pouring tea over ice to attract a crowd. Iced tea is now so popular that over 24 billion glasses were consumed last year in the United States. The British still consider it a barbaric drink!

Teabags were also developed in 1904, when a tea merchant found them the easiest way to send out samples of his wares. The average cup of tea contains about ¾ grain of caffeine... about half that of a cup of coffee.

The story of tea in Savannah came full circle in 1951 when the Tetley Tea Southern Plant was located here in what had been a World War II ammunition warehouse at the Georgia Ports Authority's Garden City Terminal. The present manager and tea taster is Clive Hale...an Englishman.

CHATHAM ICED TEA

Yield: 1 gallon

2	cups sugar	2	quarts cold water
2	cups water	2	cups orange juice
1	quart hot water	½	cup lemon juice
10	tea bags		

Boil sugar and 2 cups water for 5 minutes in a 2-quart saucepan. Add tea bags as water is removed from the heat, and let steep for 10 minutes, covered. Remove tea bags. Add mixture to two quarts cold water and stir. Add juices and mix well. Serve over ice or store covered in refrigerator until needed. This makes a sweet, fruity drink.

JAMAICA GINGER TEA

(For a cold.)

Make a large cupful of hot lemonade; add a teaspoonful of ground Jamaica ginger, and whisky if liked.

House-Keeping In The Sunny South, 1885

SUN TEA

Yield: 6 6-ounce servings

4	tea bags	1	6-ounce can lemonade
1	quart cold water		concentrate, undiluted

Pour water over tea bags in a glass jar. Cover, and place out in the sun for several hours to steep tea. Mix with lemonade concentrate before serving over ice. This makes a clear, sweet tea, with lemon and sugar already in it!

Kay Lee

CRANBERRY PUNCH

Yield: 11 8-ounce servings

1 quart cranberry juice, chilled
1 quart pineapple juice, chilled

2 12-ounce bottles ginger ale, chilled

Combine juices; add ginger ale. Serve over ice.

Virginia Snedeker

DOLLY'S FRUIT PUNCH

Yield: 50 4-ounce servings

½ gallon cold water
1 12-ounce can frozen orange juice concentrate
2 quarts ginger ale, chilled
1 46-ounce can pineapple juice, chilled

1 pint lemon juice, chilled
2 cups sugar
1 tablespoon vanilla extract
2 tablespoons almond extract

Mix well, and serve in a chilled punch bowl. An ice ring or heart mold of fruit slices frozen in Kool Aid or fruit juice adds to the festivity and flavors the punch.

Mrs. Dolly Lott, Douglas, Georgia

GIRL SCOUT PUNCH

Yield: about 3½ quarts

1 12-ounce can frozen orange juice concentrate, thawed in refrigerator
cold water
2 cups canned pineapple juice, chilled
½ cup lemon juice, chilled

1 cup apricot nectar, chilled
½ cup light corn syrup
3 12-ounce cans ginger ale, chilled
orange, lemon, or lime slices for garnish (optional)

Mix orange juice with three juice cans of cold water. Add other juices and syrup. Pour over block of ice in chilled punch bowl; stir in ginger ale. Garnish with fruit slices if desired.

DOUBLE-DUTY PUNCH

Yield: 9½ cups

1 46-ounce can red fruit punch drink, chilled
1 6-ounce can frozen lemonade concentrate, thawed in refrigerator

1 24-ounce bottle white grape juice, chilled
lemon slices for garnish
gin or rum (optional)

Combine first three ingredients in a very large chilled pitcher. Pour over ice in glasses; garnish with lemon slices. If desired, 1 to 1½ ounces gin or rum may be added to each serving; stir, and serve.

JOHN RYAN, SODA POP PIONEER

Savannah was the site of the Excelsior Bottle Works, operated as early as 1862 by John Ryan for the manufacture of soda pop and other carbonated beverages. Ryan's sodas, in colorful bottles with his name and location, were known throughout Georgia. His operations expanded to Augusta, Columbus, and Atlanta prior to his death in 1885. Today his bottles are collectors' items across the nation.

Drawing by Nancy Mock

SOUTHERN REMEDY

I kept him alive by giving him old Jamaica rum and milk fresh from the cow, taken before his breakfast: an old Southern remedy for consumption.

Ward McAllister, **Society As I Have Found It,** *1890*

PEANUT BUTTER MILK SHAKE

Yield: 1 serving

1	cup milk	2	tablespoons chocolate sauce
2	tablespoons peanut butter		

Blend in blender or mix with beater.

Georgia Peanut Commission

FRENCH COFFEE SHAKE

Yield: 5 4-ounce servings

½	cup vanilla ice cream	1	tablespoon water
⅓	cup creme de cacao	1	teaspoon white creme de
1	tablespoon instant coffee powder		menthe
			6 or 7 ice cubes, crushed

In a blender container, combine all ingredients but ice. Blend at low speed. Add ice, and blend until smooth.

Savannah News-Press

APPLE WINE

A family recipe from the originator of Lane Cake.

To every gallon of fresh sweet cider, put two and a half pounds of granulated sugar. Stir until the sugar dissolves, pour into stone jars, cover with a coarse cloth tied over the top, then put away in a dark place until quite cool weather, so that all fermentation will be over. Strain through a cloth; bottle and cork tightly, and set away for several months, when it will be ready for use, and very fine.

Emma Rylander Lane, **Some Good Things To Eat,** *1898*

MULLED CIDER

Apple cider was the primary drink of colonial Georgians. It is also estimated that the average person in the colonies drank 3¾ gallons of rum per year!

Yield: 8 8-ounce servings

2	quarts apple cider	1	teaspoon whole cloves
¼	cup brown sugar, firmly packed	⅛	teaspoon ground cloves
2	sticks cinnamon	1	unpeeled orange (sliced and seeded if necessary)

Combine ingredients and simmer for 2 to 4 hours.

Linda Wittish

SOLOMON'S PHARMACY AT MADISON SQUARE

Solomon's Pharmacy, a Savannah tradition, was established by Abraham A. Solomon, who came from South Carolina in 1845 to establish what was first called Solomon's Company. The present Solomon's Pharmacy, located in the Scottish Rite Temple, was constructed in 1913. It retains the charm of a lost era with its huge marble soda fountain, mahogany fixtures, Tiffany lamps, stained glass windows, and ceiling fans. And...oh, yes...the pharmacy still has a prescription on file for one Robert E. Lee. The Confederate hero was stationed at Ft. Pulaski early in his army career, visited Savannah to review the coastal defenses during what some still simply call The War, and in 1870 was a guest at what is now the Colonial Dames House.

EGG NOG FOR THE GENERAL

Beat the whites and yolks of five eggs separately, and then together; add a quart of cream or milk, stirring well; then add whisky or brandy and sugar to taste, and grated nutmeg if liked. Never pour the whisky on to the beaten yolks alone. If it is strong, it will curdle them.

General Bolly Lewis,
House-Keeping In The Sunny South, 1885

GENERAL LEE'S BLACKBERRY WINE

Fill a large stone jar with the ripe fruit, and cover it with water. Tie a cloth over the jar and let stand for three or four days to ferment; then mash and press through a cloth. To every gallon of juice, add three pounds of brown sugar. Return the mixture to the jar and cover closely. Skim it every morning for more than a week, until it clears from the second fermentation. When clear, pour it carefully from the sediment into a demijohn. Cork tightly; set in a cool place. When two months old, it will be fit for use.

Mrs. General Robert E. Lee,
Housekeeping In Old Virginia, *1879*

GENERAL LEE'S FOX GRAPE WINE

The fox grape mentioned in this unique recipe was a forerunner of the popular hybrids, the Concord grape and the Muscadine, as well as the famous Scuppernong.

To every bushel of fox grapes, add twenty-two quarts of water. Mash the fruit and let it stand for twenty-four hours. Strain through a linen or fine sieve that will prevent the seed from getting through. To every gallon of juice, add two pounds of brown sugar. Fill the cask not quite full. Let it stand open fourteen days, and then close the bung.

Mrs. General Robert E. Lee,
Housekeeping In Old Virginia, *1879*

GEORGIA'S FIRST BREWERY

Large pieces of tabby on the banks of du Bignon Creek on Jekyll Island are all that remain of the first brewery in Georgia, established to make beer for the soldiers at nearby Frederica on St. Simons Island. Crops of barley, rye, and hops were raised in the fields of Major William Horton of Oglethorpe's Regiment, the first English resident of Jekyll Island. The brewery was destroyed by the Spanish from Florida during a raid after the Battle of Bloody Marsh in 1742.

EXTRA EGGNOG

Left-over egg nog? Make it into a great rice pudding, using egg nog instead of milk!

Marceline A. Newton, **New Life Cookbook**

SOUTHERN SYLLABUB

Related to eggnog, but less potent, because it had no "spirits," **Syllabub** *was known in the South as a ladies' and childrens' drink. One quart of cream, one gill [one pint] of wine, juice of two lemons (or one teaspoonful extract of lemon), whites of six eggs, sugar to taste. Whip to a froth; serve in glasses.*

Mrs. C. R. Upson,
House-Keeping In The Sunny South, 1885

MILK PUNCH FOR INVALIDS

Stir in a glass of new (fresh) milk one tablespoonful of white sugar and the same of brandy; grate nutmeg on the top. One egg, beaten very light, may be added also; the milk must be very fresh, or it will curdle.

Gulf City Cookbook, 1878

STRAWBERRY WINE

One gallon of juice, two and a half pounds of sugar. Mix, and strain several times through a flannel bag. Pour into a jug, and cover with gauze. Let it remain until February.

Miss Mary Davis,
House-Keeping In The Sunny South, 1885

CHAMPAGNE PUNCH

One quart of champagne, one-half pint of brandy, one-half pint of rum, one cup of strong green tea; juice and rind of two lemons. Mix sugar, (to taste), tea, lemon, brandy and rum together, twelve hours before using; add the champagne and a large lump of ice just before using.

Hints From Southern Epicures, 1890

THUNDERBOLT PUNCH

An insidious concoction, well-named:

Yield: about 6 quarts

2 fifths light rum, chilled
1 fifth sauterne, chilled
4 6-ounce cans frozen lemonade, thawed in refrigerator

1 46-ounce can pineapple juice, chilled
2 fifths Champagne, or sparkling water, chilled

Mix all ingredients except Champagne. Keep refrigerated. When ready to serve, place block of ice in a well-chilled punch bowl. Add mixture and Champagne; mix well. Serve in chilled cups.

Caution: A sudden jolt of this has been known to stop a victim's watch, snap his suspenders, and crack his eyeglasses across...all in a single motion!

Helen Kehoe Crolly

To the City of Savannah: May its health and prosperity be commensurate with the urbanity and munificence of its inhabitants.

Major General E. P. Gains, a hero of the War of 1812, at a dinner in Savannah in his honor

MEMORIES OF DAISY
(Juliette Gordon Low)

Mrs. Rosa Lewis, on her side, attributed much of her early success as a London cateress to the Southern recipes and characteristic delicacies she had first encountered when she was with the Lows. In the book she wrote, **Queen of Cooks and Some Kings**, *she had a great deal to say about Willy Low and Daisy, and about General and Mrs. Gordon, her parents, taking pains to impress upon her English readers that "they were your real American aristocracy—from Savannah."*

Willy Low, she said, had brought over the first Virginia hams ever seen in England, and used to give them to her to serve to King Edward and his brother, the Duke of Edinburgh. It was a great thing, in those days, to have a Virginia ham.

Mrs. Lewis used sweet potatoes. . . in a variety of ways, as the piece de resistance at her dinners for royalty; and at charity bazaars made waffles by Nellie Gordon's famous recipe, and served them in their long-handled irons. . . .

Eventually Jackson's in Picadilly began importing Virginia hams, sweet potatoes, terrapin soup, canvas-back ducks and brandied peaches, which Daisy's English friends had enjoyed either at her table or when they visited the Gordons in Savannah. These were in great demand. According to Mrs. Lewis, the growing of sweet corn in England was started as a result of the corn Willie Gordon had sent to Daisy at her home at Wellesbourne.

Lady From Savannah; the Life of Juliette Low, *by Gladys Denny Shultz and Daisy Gordon Lawrence, 1958*

SOUPS

Birthplace of Juliette Gordon Low, (1860-1927) founder of the
Girl Scouts of America in Savannah in 1912. It is now
maintained as a house museum and Girl Scout National
Center.

Drawing by the late Lester Miller, Staunton, Virginia

41

TURTLE SOUP

One of the many treasures of the Girl Scout National Center at Bull and Oglethorpe Streets, birthplace of Girl Scouts of the U.S.A. founder Juliette Gordon Low, is the notebook of Gordon family recipes compiled by her mother, Nellie Kinzie Gordon. It includes this "receipt" for *Turtle Soup:*

Kill turtle by seven o'clock in the morning and let it drip at least three hours. After carefully cleaning it, cut it up and put it on the fire in a pot of water to boil, backs as well as the rest. (Keep your steaks out to make your balls with.) Season with mace, cloves, allspice, onion, thyme, parsley, and black pepper. Thicken with browned flour, rub in the yolks of three hard-boiled eggs, and two heaping teaspoons of butter, and color with a little syrup browned. When ready to serve, slice six hard-boiled eggs and put in a tureen. Make balls as you would force meat balls.

SAVANNAH TERRAPIN SOUP

At the South, terrapin soup, with plenty of eggs in it, was a dish for the gods, and a standard dinner party dish in days when a Charleston or Savannah dinner was an event to live for. But no Frenchman ever made this soup. It requires the native-born culinary genius of the African.

*Ward McAllister, **Society As I Have Found it,** 1890.*

SAVANNAH TOMATO SOUP

One quart canned tomatoes, 1 pint hot water, 1 tablespoonful sugar, 1 teaspoonful salt, 4 cloves, 4 peppercorns (or 1 salt spoonful white pepper), 1 tablespoonful butter, 1 tablespoonful chopped onion, 1 tablespoonful chopped parsley, 1 tablespoonful cornstarch. Put the tomatoes, water, sugar, salt, cloves, and peppercorns on to boil. Put the butter in a small saucepan, and when it bubbles, put in the onion and parsley. Fry five minutes, being careful not to burn it. Add the cornstarch, and when it is well mixed, stir it into the tomatoes. Let it simmer 10 minutes. Add more salt and pepper if needed. Strain, and serve with croutons.

Mrs. L. M. LeHardy,
Favorite Recipes From Savannah Homes, 1904

SAVANNAH'S GREEK COMMUNITY

The Greek Orthodox community of Savannah was founded in the early 1900s with about one hundred persons and was organized under charter in 1907. Since 1941, the center of its activities has been the Lawton Memorial Building at Bull and Anderson Streets. The nearby modern community center was completed in 1950. Now with more than six hundred members, the community also maintains ties with Greece and Savannah's sister city of Patras, the source of this recipe for **Avgolemono Soup.**

AVGOLEMONO SOUP

Yield: 6 to 8 servings

2	quarts strong, strained chicken broth	4	eggs
½	cup raw rice		juice of two lemons

Bring the broth to a boil and add the rice. Cook until rice is tender, about 20 minutes. Remove the broth from the heat. Just before serving, beat the eggs with a rotary beater until they are light and frothy. Slowly beat in the lemon juice and dilute the mixture with 2 cups of the hot soup, beating constantly until well mixed.

Add the diluted egg-lemon mixture to the rest of the soup, beating constantly. Bring almost to a boil, but do not boil, or the soup will curdle. Serve immediately.

Savannah News-Press

SENATORIAL SOUP

Senate Bean Soup has been served in the House of Representatives every day since the humid summer of 1904, when the then-Speaker of the House, Joseph G. Cannon, became incensed at not finding it on the menu. This version was brought to Savannah by an area Congressman.

SENATE BEAN SOUP

Yield: 6 servings

2	pounds white beans, Michigan or White Northern		smoked ham hock, with some meat on it
	salt and pepper to taste	1	medium onion, chopped (optional)
	water		

Cover beans with water and soak overnight. Drain and cover again with water. Add ham hock and simmer slowly for about 4 hours, or until beans are tender. Add seasoning to taste. Remove bone and dice into the soup any meat left on it. Just before serving, mash the beans enough with the back of a spoon or ladle that the soup looks cloudy. Chopped onion may be added during last hour of cooking, if desired.

View of Savannah from the Savannah River, 1855.
Courtesy of Historic Savannah Foundation, Inc.

CHILLED CREAM OF BROCCOLI SOUP

Yield: 6 servings

1 medium onion, sliced	1 teaspoon salt
1 medium carrot, sliced	⅛ teaspoon cayenne
1 stalk celery with leaves	pepper
1 clove garlic	½ cup cooked macaroni
½ cup water	1 cup chicken stock
2 cups cooked broccoli,	¼ cup cream (optional)
coarsely chopped	sour cream (optional)

Simmer onion, carrot, celery, and garlic in one-half cup of water
for 10 minutes. Transfer to a blender; add the chopped, cooked
broccoli, salt, cayenne pepper, and macaroni. Cover and blend at

high speed, then remove cover and with the motor running, add the stock and perhaps the cream. Chill well and serve with sour cream, if cream was not used earlier.

Savannah News-Press

CREAM OF CARROT SOUP

Yield: 6 servings

Stock

2½ cups water	5 stalks celery, thinly sliced
2 chicken-flavored broth	(about 2¼ cups)
packets or cubes	1 small potato, chopped
1 beef-flavored broth packet or	1 small onion, chopped
cube	¼ teaspoon pepper
1 tablespoon chopped parsley	¼ teaspoon salt (or to taste)
5 large carrots, thinly sliced	
(about 4 cups)	

Seasoning

3 tablespoons butter	¼ teaspoon thyme, crumbled
1½ tablespoons cornstarch	¼ teaspoon basil
¼ teaspoon marjoram	½ teaspoon Angostura bitters

Garnish

2 cups milk	
1½ cups commercial sour cream	
sour cream	chopped chives

Cook **Stock** ingredients until very soft, about 30 to 40 minutes. Puree in blender or mash through a sieve. Add the **Seasoning** and mix in blender. Pour mixture back into pan.

Add milk, mix well, and heat over low heat, stirring often, until it thickens, about 5 minutes. Add 1 cup sour cream; mix well. Serve hot with **Garnish** of sour cream and chopped chives.

Jerry Downey

SAVANNAH OKRA SOUP

Yield: 5 quarts (20 servings)

1 large beef bone, with plenty of	1 bay leaf
meat	2 medium onions, chopped
3 quarts water	salt and pepper
3 pounds fresh okra, chopped	8 large tomatoes, chopped, or 2
fine	29-ounce cans stewed
1 piece salt pork or breakfast	tomatoes
bacon	

Cook meat slowly in water for two hours, until well done. Add okra, salt pork or bacon, bay leaf, onion, seasoning, and tomatoes. Let cook another two hours. Add more water if needed.

Hot rice and buttered corn sticks are a tasty accompaniment here. This is a very old recipe. It freezes well, or with shrimp added, becomes a fine gumbo, with rice.

George McDonald, Savannah Beach

HUGUENOT ONION SOUP

The French influence in Savannah dates back to Huguenots, or French Protestants, who settled in South Carolina and then Georgia during the colonial era.

Yield: 8 servings

4	tablespoons (½ stick) butter	4	cups water
7	cups sliced onions (about 2 pounds)	3	tablespoons beef stock base or 12 beef bouillon cubes
2	tablespoons flour	4	cups milk
1	teaspoon salt		

Melt butter in 4-quart saucepan; saute onions until tender, about 15 minutes. Stir in flour and salt. Add water and beef stock base. Bring to a boil; reduce heat, cover and simmer 30 to 40 minutes. Stir in milk. Heat to serving temperature, but do not boil.

Croutes

¼	pound (1 stick) butter	2	cups shredded Swiss cheese
1	small clove garlic, crushed		
8	slices French bread, about 1 inch thick		

To prepare **Croutes**: Preheat oven to 325 degrees; melt butter in a saucepan; stir in garlic. Dip both sides of bread in butter. Place on a flat pan and toast in oven for 10 minutes. Turn and toast an additional 5 minutes, or until lightly browned.

To serve, place soup in ovenproof bowls. Top each with 1 **Croute** and ¼ cup Swiss cheese. Place in oven 5 minutes, or until cheese melts.

Savannah News-Press

PEA SOUP WITH HAMBONE

Georgia hams are famous for their flavor, and make their final appearance in a hearty winter soup.

Yield: 8 servings

1	ham bone with ham on it	½	cup diced celery
2	cups split peas	½	teaspoon freshly ground
6	cups cold water		pepper
2	small onions, each stuck with a clove	⅛	teaspoon dried basil
		1	bay leaf
1¼	teaspoons salt, or to taste	1	teaspoon chopped parsley
½	cup grated carrots	1	teaspoon thyme
1	clove garlic, minced		

Simmer all ingredients with lid slightly tilted 2 to 3 hours, or until peas are cooked. Remove bay leaf; discard ham bone after scraping all meat from it. Dice meat and add to soup. Puree soup through blender, if you have one. Reheat. Serve hot but not boiling.

Savannah News-Press

PRESIDENTIAL PEANUT SOUP

Yield: 8 servings

¼	cup butter	2	quarts chicken stock or broth
1	cup thinly sliced celery	1	cup creamy peanut butter
1	medium onion, chopped fine	1	cup light cream
2	tablespoons flour		

Melt butter in large saucepan over low heat, and add celery and onion. Cook until tender, but not browned. Add flour and stir until mixture is smooth. Gradually add chicken broth and bring to a boil. Blend in peanut butter and simmer about 15 minutes. Stir in cream just before serving.

Georgia Peanut Commission

POTATO SOUP

Boil six large potatoes, after they have been pared and sliced with one small onion. Pass them through a colander and return to the pot, adding salt, cayenne pepper, parsley and one-fourth pound of butter. Boil seven minutes longer. Put soup in a warm tureen, and add one cup of rich cream.

Hints From Southern Epicures, *circa 1890*

HISTORIC BOUILLON

A hot vegetable bouillon was said to have been a favorite pick-me-up of General Robert E. Lee's, with a wine glass of dry sherry stirred in just before serving.

CLAMS MADRILENE

Yield: 6 servings

2	10¾-ounce cans madrilene	2	tablespoons grated onion
2	8-ounce cans minced clams, drained		yogurt to garnish
			lemon wedges
1	cup finely chopped celery		

Pour madrilene into a large bowl and refrigerate until nearly set. Fold in clams, chopped celery, and onions. Refrigerate until firm. Serve in small bowls or soup cups, topped with plain yogurt. Accompany with lemon wedges.

The Oemler home, constructed in the 1880's, is the oldest frame dwelling on Wilmington Island.

Drawing by Pamela Lee

49

BEAUFORT CREAM OF CRAB SOUP

The Low Country has long been noted for its seafood soups. President George Washington was served She-Crab Soup during his visit to South Carolina in 1791, and was so impressed that he spread its fame all the way back to New England!

Yield: 8 servings

1	onion, finely chopped	½	teaspoon mace
1	tablespoon butter	⅛	teaspoon pepper
1	cup chicken stock	½	teaspoon salt, or to taste
1	quart half-and-half		dash red pepper
1	tablespoon finely chopped parsley	1	pound crab meat, free of shells
½	teaspoon celery salt	2	tablespoons flour
		¼	cup dry sherry

In a skillet, saute onion in butter until transparent. Add chicken stock and slowly pour in half-and-half. Stir well. Add seasonings and crab meat. Stir until mixed, then let simmer 15 minutes. Make a thin paste with the flour and a little water, and stir into soup to thicken it slightly. Just before serving, remove from heat and add sherry. Stir once and serve immediately.

AN ANTIDOTE TO SALT

It is not generally known that brown sugar is an antidote to salt. Should you by accident make soup or gravy too salty, add one teaspoonful of brown sugar and the briny taste will disappear.

Milton Arden, **Ye Olde Time Salzburger Cook Book**

FICHYSSOISE

Yield: 4 servings

1	13-ounce can vichyssoise	salt and pepper
1	7¾ ounce can salmon	dill weed
1	cup whipping cream	

Blend vichyssoise and salmon in a blender. Add cream and season to taste. Garnish with dill. Serve chilled.

Marcel Carles, Columbus, Georgia

OYSTER SOUP

One quart of oysters, one quart of milk, one tablespoon of butter, one small tablespoon of flour, cayenne pepper to taste, salt, and celery. Boil the milk with the celery cut up in it. When it comes to a boil, add the flour and butter, which have been rubbed up together, and boil for about 10 minutes, then the pepper and salt, and the oysters, which have not been drained.

Hints From Southern Epicures, circa 1890

MISS EDNA'S SEAFOOD BISQUE

Yield: 6 servings

1 10¾-ounce can green pea soup	½ pound crab meat, cooked
1 10¾-ounce can tomato soup	½ cup dry sherry
3 cups milk	6 lemon peel twists

Blend soups with milk. Heat, and add crab meat and sherry just before serving. Add a twist of lemon peel to each bowl of soup.

H. S. Traub, Jr., **The Pirates' House Cook Book**

BRUNSWICK STEW

Did **Brunswick Stew** originate in Brunswick, Georgia? All we do know is that it is a very old recipe, dating from frontier days when squirrel was the basic meat. As squirrels grew fewer, they were replaced in the stew by chicken.

Stews such as **Brunswick Stew** were popular in early Georgia because they could simmer all day over an open fire... an important consideration at a time when there was no refrigeration except for blocks of ice cut from Northern lakes and shipped in sawdust, which occasionally arrived in coastal towns.

Yield: 6 1-cup servings

1 whole chicken (approximately three pounds)	1¾ cups corn
3 cups water	1 teaspoon sugar
1½ teaspoons salt	½ teaspoon salt, or to taste
1 cup diced potatoes	⅛ teaspoon pepper
1¾ cups lima beans	⅛ teaspoon oregano
1¾ cups tomato sauce	⅛ teaspoon poultry seasoning
⅔ cup chopped onion	few grains cayenne pepper

Simmer chicken in salted water until tender, about 2 to 2½ hours. Drain off broth. Separate the meat from the skin, and discard bones. Cut meat into small pieces.

Skim the fat from the broth. Boil the broth and then simmer for 10 minutes. Add lima beans, tomato sauce, and onions. Cook 20 minutes longer.

Add chicken, corn, and seasonings. Cook 10 to 15 minutes more, until vegetables are tender. If stew is chilled and then reheated, it will be easier to remove all the fat from the surface.

This stew is especially good served with barbecue dishes, or as a main course with cole slaw and fresh homemade bread.

SCOTTISH BREW

The Scottish tradition in Georgia goes back to the hearty highlanders who first settled at Darien in 1736, and fought bravely with James Oglethorpe against the Spanish invasion of the colony from Florida.

Yield: 6 servings

1 left-over cooked lamb leg roast, with meat still on it but visible fat removed	1 tablespoon salt
	1 small bay leaf
2 quarts water	2 stalks celery, diced
1 medium onion, stuck with four cloves	3 carrots, sliced
	2 small turnips, sliced
¼ teaspoon freshly-ground black pepper	¼ cup pearl barley
	½ teaspoon marjoram
	¼ cup Scotch whisky

Place lamb bones in a deep pot. Add enough cool water to cover the meat by 1 inch. Add onion, pepper, salt, and bay leaf. Bring quickly to a boil. Skim fat. Cover the pot and simmer 1½ hours. Cool, and skim off top fat. If you are in a hurry, drop ice cubes into the soup; the fat will collect around them and can easily be removed. Remove bones, chop meat from them and return meat to the soup, discarding bones. Take out onion, discard cloves. Chop onion and return it to soup. Add vegetables, barley, marjoram, and Scotch to broth. Cover and simmer 45 minutes or until vegetables and barley are tender.

WASTE NOT

You ought not to waste fat of any description, or anything else, that may be turned to account: such as marrow-bones, or any other clean bones from which food may be extracted in the way of soup, broth, or stock....Remember, "Wilful waste makes woeful want."

The Guide To Service, 1842

SALADS

Savannah's beloved old City Market in a sketch from *Frank Leslie's Illustrated Newspaper*, 1875. Built in 1870 on the site of an older market, it was demolished in 1953. Savannahians still fondly recall the fruits, vegetables, meats, and other foods they purchased there.

Courtesy of Jack Crolly

SALAD HINTS FROM YESTERDAY'S KITCHEN

Let the ingredients of the salad be well picked, and washed and dried; but do not add the dressing until just before eating, as it is apt to make the salad flabby. The most simple way of dressing a salad is, perhaps, the best; certainly the most wholesome; merely salt, oil, and vinegar to taste; one table-spoonful of the best olive oil to three of vinegar, is a good proportion.... Eggs boiled for salads require 10 to 12 minutes boiling, and should immediately be plunged into cold water.

The Guide To Service, 1842

REGENCY SALAD

Inspired by the tossed-at-your-table salad of Savannah's Regency Room in the Downtowner Motel on Oglethorpe Avenue.

Yield: 6 servings

1	head lettuce	½ cup chopped tomatoes	
½	cup grated carrots	¼ cup sliced green onions	
¼	cup chopped radishes	4 teaspoons Parmesan cheese	
¼	cup diced parsley	4 teaspoons crumbled, cooked	
½	cup chopped celery	bacon or bacon bits	
¼	cup chopped green pepper	½ cup herb-seasoned crutons	
¼	cup chopped stuffed green or salad olives		

Core lettuce and break into cubes, approximately 1-inch. Place all ingredients in a bowl large enough to allow space for tossing. Add a favorite salad dressing, and serve on chilled salad plates. An Italian dressing goes well with this.

Chilled croutons pick up moisture, so it is better to have them at room temperature. Sprinkle them on a salad last, just before adding dressing, so they will be crisp.

EMMA'S APPLE-CHEESE SALAD

Yield: 2 servings

1	cup diced unpeeled red apples	⅓ cup mayonnaise	
¼	cup finely-diced celery	¼ teaspoon dried crushed basil	
⅓	cup finely-chopped pecans	Boston lettuce	
¼	cup dried black currants	2 Cheddar cheese strips	

In a small mixing bowl, mix together all but last two ingredients. Cover and chill. At serving time, mound apple salad on lettuce and garnish with cheese.

SMORGASBORD SALAD

Yield: 12 servings

2	large heads iceburg lettuce	12	cooked asparagus spears
2	cups cooked chicken, turkey, or ham strips, or combination	1	cup drained, chilled pickled beets
1	cup cooked shrimp (optional)	1	cup olives
1	cup carrot strips	1	cup green pepper strips
1	cup chopped celery	1	pint cottage cheese
1	cup sliced cucumber	24	deviled egg halves
1	cup sliced fresh mushrooms		croutons
4	medium tomatoes, sliced, or 1 cup salad tomatoes		

Refrigerate lettuce in plastic bag or crisper until needed. Shortly before serving, cut in bite-size chunks and turn into chilled serving bowl. Arrange other items on a tray and allow guests to make their own salads, with a choice of dressings. This is especially nice for informal buffets, and avoids wasting left-over salad which must be discarded because it has gotten soggy from the dressing!

FAVORITE WALDORF SALAD

The addition of bananas makes this salad unusual.

Yield: 6 servings

2	cups diced unpeeled Delicious apples	1	cup grapes, quartered and seeded
1	cup chopped celery	1	thinly-sliced banana
½	cup chopped nuts		mayonnaise to moisten
½	cup raisins		lettuce

Mix all ingredients but lettuce. Serve on lettuce.

Apple hint: the juice of one-half lemon added to apples will prevent discoloration prior to serving.

SALADE DE PRINTEMPS

Every nationality has a favorite salad, generally to celebrate green, growing things and spring. Here is one from France.

Yield: 6 servings

2	heads romaine lettuce	3	avocados
2	grapefruits		

Wash and cut romaine in quarters. Arrange on salad plates. Wedge grapefruit, and place across romaine. Arrange avocado wedges on side of plate. Serve **Poppy Seed Sauce** on side. Other summer fruits, such as grapes, melon, and bananas may be used.

Poppy Seed Sauce

Yield: 6 servings

1	cup whipping cream	2 tablespoons poppy seeds
½	cup honey	

Combine ingredients. Whip until creamy but not stiff.

Marcel Carles, Columbus, Georgia

DECATUR BEAN SALAD

Yield: 6 servings

1 16-ounce can or 2 cups cooked, red kidney beans, drained	2 tablespoons minced scallions
	1 tablespoon minced parsley
2 11-ounce cans mandarin oranges, drained	¾ cup spicy commercial French dressing

Drain beans and oranges; toss with remaining ingredients. Cover and marinate overnight. Drain and serve with salad greens.

CABBAGE SALAD

Yield: 4 to 6 servings

2 eggs, well beaten	1 teaspoon butter
8 tablespoons cream	½ medium head of cabbage, chopped fine
½ teaspoon salt	salt
6 teaspoons vinegar	

Mix the eggs, 6 tablespoons cream, salt, vinegar, and butter together and cook over low heat, stirring continuously, until thick. Chill. Chop cabbage and sprinkle with salt. When the cooked salad dressing is cold, stir in remaining 2 tablespoons of cream. Pour over cabbage, mix, and serve. This is a recipe of my mother, Mrs. Lillian Woolen England of Dayton, Tennessee, and dates back to at least 1897.

Mrs. Alyne Elizabeth Madden

MRS. BERRIEN'S COTTAGE CHEESE COLE SLAW

Yield: 8 servings

½ cup mayonnaise	1 cup cottage cheese
1 teaspoon prepared yellow mustard	4 cups finely shredded cabbage
seasoned salt or chili powder to taste	1 teaspoon dill seed
dash vinegar or pickle juice (optional)	stuffed olives (optional)
	green pepper rings (optional)

Mix first four ingredients in large mixing bowl. Add cottage cheese and cabbage and toss to coat well. Chill. Sprinkle with dill seed and decorate with a few stuffed olives or green pepper rings, if desired, before serving.

MOULTRIE CORN SALAD

Yield: 4 servings

1	16-ounce can whole kernel corn	1	tablespoon minced parsley
2	tablespoons minced pimiento	⅓	cup vegetable oil
2	tablespoons minced scallions	2	tablespoons white wine vinegar
2	tablespoons minced green pepper	⅛	teaspoon dried basil
½	cup finely diced, peeled cucumber	¼	teaspoon salt (or to taste)

Combine all ingredients and toss well. Cover and refrigerate for several hours, stirring several times. Drain and serve with salad greens, if desired.

TURKISH EGGPLANT SALAD

Yield: 6 to 8 servings

		1	cup diced green pepper
2	medium eggplants (about 1¼ pounds each)	2	cups plain yogurt
			salt and pepper to taste
2	tablespoons olive oil		salad greens
2	tablespoons lemon juice	3	medium tomatoes, cut in wedges
2	tablespoons minced parsley		
1	large clove garlic, minced or crushed	1	small red onion, sliced into thin rings

Preheat oven to 375 degrees. Trim ends from eggplants and cut in half lengthwise. Place, cut side down, on lightly oiled baking sheet. Roast for about 45 minutes, until very soft. Scoop out pulp and mash well. Stir in oil, lemon juice, parsley, garlic, green pepper, yogurt, salt, and pepper. Chill overnight.

If top is quite wet, pour off a little of moisture before serving. Mound on a plate; surround with greens and tomato wedges. Top with onion rings.

CHOP CHOP RICE SALAD

A great use for leftover rice! Also, a bit different from potato and macaroni salads.

Yield: 5 cups

2	cups cooked rice	6	radishes, sliced
1¼	cups mayonnaise	¼	cup chopped green pepper
¾	cup chopped onion	1	tablespoon prepared mustard
1	cup sliced celery	½	teaspoon salt
2	hard-cooked eggs, chopped		

Cook rice according to package directions. Place cooked rice in a bowl. Cover and chill. Add mayonnaise and onion; mix well. Chill one hour. Stir in remaining ingredients; mix well. Chill before serving.

Savannah News-Press

CRANBERRY-GRAPEFRUIT SALAD

Grind fresh or frozen raw cranberries finely in a food chopper. Add half as much ripe, mashed banana, sweetened with honey to taste, and whip until fluffy. Chill for an hour or more, and place in the center of thin slices of ripe grapefruit, peeled and arranged on a salad plate on a bed of romaine lettuce or other chilled greens.

Sally Pearce, Savannah Beach

DEVILED TOMATO SALAD

Yield: 6 servings

6	medium tomatoes (about 1½ pounds)	⅛	teaspoon ground red pepper
¾	teaspoon salt	6	hard-cooked eggs, chopped
¼	cup mayonnaise		mayonnaise
½	cup diced green pepper		chopped chives (optional)
¼	cup minced onion		lettuce

Keep tomatoes at room temperature until fully ripe. Cut out stem and core, and place each, stem end down, on cutting board. Cut into 6 wedges almost, but not quite, to the bottom. Open each up slightly. Sprinkle with ¼ teaspoon salt and set aside. In a medium bowl, mix mayonnaise with green pepper, onion, red pepper, and remaining ½ teaspoon salt. Stir in eggs. Mix. Use about one-third cup of egg mixture to fill each tomato. Top with swirl of mayonnaise and chopped chives, if desired. Serve on bed of fresh lettuce.

Savannah's famous "Gingerbread House" on Bull Street near the Savannah Public Library was built in 1899 for Cord Asendorf, a Savannah grocer, and was owned by that family until recently. It is still a private home.

Drawing by Jean Sanders,
Courtesy of Frame-It-Yourself

BULL STREET BROCCOLI MOLD

Yield: 8 servings

3	ounces cream cheese	1	cup mayonnaise
2	10-ounce packages frozen chopped broccoli	2	hard-cooked eggs, chopped hot pepper sauce
1	10½ ounce can condensed chicken broth		salad greens and radish roses to garnish
1	envelope unflavored gelatin		

Dice cream cheese and soften at room temperature. In a medium saucepan, cook broccoli according to package directions. Drain. Add cream cheese to hot broccoli and stir until it melts.

Pour about half of the chicken broth into a small saucepan. Sprinkle gelatin over it and allow to soften, about 5 minutes. Stir over low heat until gelatin is dissolved. Stir into broccoli. Then, one at a time, stir in mayonnaise, eggs, hot pepper sauce, and remaining cold broth. Refrigerate, stirring often, until chilled and partly thickened. Turn into 6-cup mold and chill until set. To serve, unmold, garnish with greens, and serve with **Sour Cream Dressing.**

Sour Cream Dressing

Yield: 1½ to 2 cups

2 tablespoons minced scallions, including green tops	⅛ teaspoon crushed dried tarragon
1 tablespoon anchovy paste	1 cup commercial sour cream
2 tablespoons lemon juice	½ cup mayonnaise
2 tablespoons white wine vinegar	

Mix together, cover, and chill until needed. Good, too, with other types of salad.

MODENA SAUERKRAUT SALAD

"Gut essen und trinken halt leib und seele zusammen." Old German saying: "Good eating and drinking keep body and soul together."

Yield: 6 servings

1 16-ounce can sauerkraut, drained and chopped	⅓ cup chopped green pepper
1 cup chopped celery	⅓ cup chopped pimiento
½ cup chopped onion	¾ cup sugar (or to taste)

Mix well. Refrigerate 24 hours before serving.

CHATHAM CUCUMBER ASPIC

Yield: 8 servings

2 cucumbers, about 6 inches long	½ cup sugar
1 envelope unflavored gelatin	½ teaspoon salt
¼ cup cold water	6 tablespoons lemon juice
¼ cup white wine	salad greens for garnish
1½ cups boiling water	mayonnaise

If cucumbers were purchased commercially peel the waxed skin; if home-grown leave on the skin. Shred cucumbers coarsely. Sprinkle gelatin over mixture of cold water and wine. Let soften. Dissolve in boiling water. Stir in sugar and salt; let dissolve. Strain in lemon juice and cucumber. Cover and chill in refrigerator until beginning to thicken. Stir well to distribute cucumber, and pour quickly into a lightly oiled (do not use olive oil) 1-quart mold or 8 oiled ½-cup molds. Chill until firm. Unmold on salad greens. Accompany with mayonnaise.

CUCUMBER MOUSSE

Yield: 6 servings

4	medium cucumbers	⅛	teaspoon hot pepper sauce
½	teaspoon dried dill weed	1	cup commercial sour cream
2	envelopes unflavored gelatin		salad greens
1	teaspoon salt		
2	tablespoons lime or lemon juice		

Peel, seed, and dice cucumbers. Place in a blender and whirl smooth. Stop blender; add dill, and whirl in. Strain through a fine sieve into a saucepan, reserving the pulp. Sprinkle gelatin over juice in saucepan, and let soften. Dissolve over hot water or very low heat, stirring constantly. Remove from heat and stir in reserved cucumber pulp, salt, lime juice, and hot pepper sauce, mixing well. Cool completely and blend with sour cream. Pour into a lightly oiled (do not use olive oil) 4-cup mold. Chill until set. Unmold and garnish with salad greens.

CHERRY-OLIVE MOLD

Yield: 4 servings

1	16-ounce can pitted Bing cherries	½	cup sliced stuffed olives, drained
⅓	cup lemon juice		lettuce
1	3-ounce package orange gelatin		sour cream
¾	cup chopped pecans		mayonnaise

Drain cherries. Add water to cherry juice and lemon juice to equal 1¾ cups liquid. Heat, pour over gelatin, and stir until completely dissolved. Chill until partially set. Add cherries, nuts, and olives. Chill. Serve molded on lettuce, with a sour cream dressing made of equal parts sour cream and mayonnaise.

Jerry Downey

YOGURT-GELATIN SALAD

Yield: 4 servings

1	envelope unflavored gelatin	1	tablespoon white wine vinegar
2	tablespoons sugar	2	tablespoons finely chopped scallions
1	cup boiling water	½	teaspoon dill weed
8	ounces plain yogurt		

In a medium bowl, mix gelatin and sugar; add boiling water and stir until gelatin is completely dissolved. Blend in yogurt, vinegar, scallions, and dill. Chill, stirring occasionally, until mixture is consistency of unbeaten egg whites.

Fold in one of the three **Vegetable Combinations** listed below; turn into individual molds or a three-cup mold and chill until firm. Approximately 80 calories per serving.

Vegetable Combinations

1. 1 cup shredded cucumber and ¼ cup shredded radishes
2. ½ cup each chopped cauliflower, green pepper, and tomato
3. ½ cup each chopped tomato, fresh mushrooms, and cooked fresh green beans

Savannah News-Press

SAPELO CRAB SALAD

Yield: 4 servings

8	ounces crab meat	½ teaspoon dried parsley
2	hard-cooked eggs, chopped fine	1 teaspoon Worcestershire sauce
⅓	cup finely chopped celery	salt and pepper to taste
2	tablespoons finely chopped bell pepper	lettuce, olives, tomato slices, and pimiento strips to garnish
½	teaspoon celery seed	

Combine all ingredients except garnish. Serve cold on chilled lettuce with garnish as desired.

LOBSTER SALAD

Take one large or two small lobsters; when well boiled, pull to pieces with fingers instead of cutting; then mix well with Mayonnaise; then place in the lettuce leaves. The dish can be garnished with hard-boiled eggs and the lobster claws.

Hints From Southern Epicures, *circa 1890*

ORIENTAL SHRIMP SALAD

Yield: 8 servings

1	16-ounce can bean sprouts	1 8-ounce can water chestnuts, thinly sliced
1	pound (2 cups) cooked shrimp	¼ cup minced green onions
1	cup chow mein noodles	
¼	cup minced celery	

Rinse bean sprouts in cold water. Drain. Combine all ingredients. Mix **Soy Mayonnaise** and combine with shrimp mixture. May be served on lettuce.

Soy Mayonnaise

¾ cup mayonnaise
1 tablespoon soy sauce
⅜ teaspoon ground ginger

½ teaspoon monosodium
   glutamate
1 tablespoon lemon juice

Donald J. Myers, Savannah News-Press

AVOCADO-SHRIMP MOLD

Yield: 8 servings

2 large or 3 small
   avocados (2 cups pulp)
1 3-ounce package lemon
   gelatin
½ teaspoon salt
1⅓ cups boiling water
2 tablespoons lemon juice
2 teaspoons grated onion
1/16 teaspoon hot pepper sauce

¼ teaspoon Worcestershire
   sauce
1 cup mayonnaise
1 cup minced celery
2 pounds shrimp, cooked,
   cleaned, and chilled
   salad greens
   cucumbers

Prepare pulp by mashing, straining, or putting avocado through food chopper with finest blade. You should have 2 cups.

Dissolve gelatin and salt in boiling water. Chill, stirring occasionally, until consistency of unbeaten egg white. Meanwhile, combine lemon juice, grated onion, hot pepper sauce, Worcestershire sauce, mayonnaise, avocado pulp, and celery. When gelatin is of the consistency described above, fold in avocado mixture, blending well. Pour into lightly oiled ring mold, about 6-cup capacity. Chill until firm. When ready to serve, unmold on platter. Fill center with shrimp. Garnish with salad greens and cucumber slices.

WAYNESBORO CHICKEN SALAD

Chicken salad with a cooked dressing stirred into whipped cream has been a tradition for generations in Waynesboro and vicinity. It is always served at holiday time, in a dressing which is made and chilled well in advance to allow the flavors to blend. Here an old recipe is updated by Emma R. Law.

Yield: 10 servings

4 cups diced cooked chicken
1 cup diced celery (no leaves)

   salad greens
   celery seed (optional)
   paprika (optional)

Toss chicken, celery, and **Cooked Dressing** gently together, mixing well. Store, covered, in refrigerator in glass, stainless steel, or enamelware. When ready to serve, mound on salad greens. Sprinkle lightly with celery seed or paprika.

Cooked Dressing

Yield: about 1 cup

1½	tablespoons sugar	1½	teaspoons flour
1½	teaspoons ground mustard	⅓	cup white wine vinegar
½	teaspoon salt	2	eggs
¹⁄₁₆	teaspoon cayenne or red pepper	½	cup heavy cream

Blend first 5 ingredients together until all lumps are gone, in the top of a double boiler. Gradually add vinegar, stirring until all is smooth. Beat eggs and stir into mixture. Cook over simmering, not boiling, water, stirring constantly until thickened. Remove from heat, cool, cover, and let chill overnight or for 2 days. When ready to use, whip cream until it stands in soft peaks when beater is lifted. Do not overbeat. Fold gently into cooked and chilled dressing.

Chicken may be freshly poached until tender, or use left-overs. Left-over turkey is good, too. Solid white tuna, drained and flaked, may be scalded by having boiling water poured over it in a strainer to remove the fishy taste, and used also.

This is a very rich salad. Not much else is needed with it for lunch except croissants or the traditional Southern bread, **Beaten Biscuits**. A fresh fruit cup is the ideal dessert.

CURRIED CHICKEN SALAD

Curry was first used in America in eastern seaport towns such as Savannah, where it was imported from the West Indies. This unusual chicken salad is a meal in itself.

Yield: 4 to 6 servings

2	cups diced cooked chicken	½ cup mayonnaise
2	6-ounce cans Chinese water chestnuts, drained and diced	lettuce
		flaked coconut
2	teaspoons curry powder (or to taste)	sliced cucumbers
		chutney
2	teaspoons lime or lemon juice	

Mix first five ingredients; chill to mix flavors. When ready to serve, place in lettuce cups. Sprinkle with coconut, garnish with cucumbers, and serve chutney on the side.

TALAHI ISLAND SALAD

Yield: 4 servings

½ pound cooked ham, diced
½ pound cooked chicken, diced
1 banana, sliced
1 orange, in segments, seeded
1 cup sliced white grapes, seeded
1 avocado, peeled and sliced
4 ounces thick cream
4 ounces mayonnaise
1 tablespoon ketchup
1 teaspoon Worcestershire sauce
2 tablespoons lemon juice
2 tablespoons brandy
salt and freshly ground black pepper to taste
lettuce

Combine cooked meat with fruit in mixing bowl. Whip cream; blend in mayonnaise. Add ketchup, Worcestershire sauce, lemon juice, and brandy. Pour over meat and fruit mixture. Season to taste with salt and pepper; mix carefully. Garnish with lettuce.

SALAD DAYS

All greens should be washed and well dried before tossing with any vinegar and oil dressing. If not, dressing will not adhere to greens. Use dressing a bit at a time, until greens are shiny: do not overuse.

SPICY SALAD DRESSINGS

How to spark a salad? Make the dressing robust and garlicky if there's a steak. Stir in tarragon or basil if you're planning a salad to complement chicken. Chili powder is a natural with frankfurters and hamburgers. A dash of ground ginger or a bit more salt works wonders with a too-bland dressing.

Savannah News-Press

CARAWAY DRESSING

Yield: about 1½ cups

1 tablespoon instant or fresh minced onion	2 tablespoons finely chopped parsley or parsley flakes
1 tablespoon water	1 teaspoon sugar
2 teaspoons caraway seed	1 teaspoon salt
¾ cup vegetable oil	¼ teaspoon freshly ground black pepper
½ cup wine vinegar	

Rehydrate instant onion in water for 10 minutes (not necessary for fresh onion). Crush caraway seed with mortar and pestle if desired. In a container with a tight-fitting lid, combine all ingredients. Shake well. Serve over salad greens or sliced tomatoes and cucumbers.

GRANDMA'S COOKED SALAD DRESSING

Yield: 1½ cups

2 tablespoons flour	¼ teaspoon freshly ground black pepper
1 tablespoon sugar	
1 tablespoon onion powder	1 cup milk
¼ teaspoon salt	2 egg yolks, slightly beaten
1 teaspoon powdered mustard	¼ cup lemon juice
½ teaspoon paprika	

In a 1-quart saucepan, combine flour, sugar, and spices. Gradually blend in milk. Cook over medium heat, stirring constantly, until mixture boils and is thickened. Blend a little of the hot milk mixture into the egg yolks. Return all to saucepan and cook gently for 1 minute. Cool slightly. Stir in lemon juice. Chill. Serve over a lettuce and tomato or other vegetable salad.

Savannah News-Press

AMELIA ISLAND SALAD DRESSING

Yield: 1 cup

1 hard-cooked egg, chopped	3 tablespoons vinegar
1 tablespoon chopped chutney	¼ teaspoon salt
¼ teaspoon curry powder	1 teaspoon sugar
½ cup olive oil	few grains freshly grated black pepper
1 tablespoon lemon juice	

Mix well. Chill. Just before serving, beat well with fork to mix ingredients. Serve over greens.

Savannah News-Press

LANIER BLUE CHEESE DRESSING

Yield: 1½ cups

½ cup crumbled blue cheese
1 teaspoon Worcestershire
   sauce
½ teaspoon salt

⅛ teaspoon pepper
¼ teaspoon garlic or onion
   powder
1 cup commercial sour cream

Combine all ingredients except sour cream. Fold in sour cream, cover, and chill.

Savannah News-Press

POPPY SEED DRESSING

Yield: 3½ cups

⅔ cup honey
1 teaspoon salt
⅛ teaspoon white pepper
¾ cup vinegar

6 tablespoons prepared mustard
2 cups vegetable oil
¾ tablespoon poppy seeds
2 tablespoons grated onion

Mix first 6 ingredients. Blend in blender or with electric mixer until thickened, and oil disappears. Add poppy seeds and onion and stir to mix. Good with a fruit salad.

Mrs. A. Illges, Columbus, Georgia

GEORGIA BENNE SEED DRESSING

Yield: 1 cup

1 teaspoon paprika
½ teaspoon ground mustard
½ teaspoon sugar
½ teaspoon salt
¼ cup white vinegar
   dash hot pepper sauce

1 or 2 cloves garlic, minced or
   crushed, to taste
¾ cup peanut oil
4 teaspoons **Toasted Benne
   Seed**

Mix paprika, mustard, sugar and salt well together, rubbing out any lumps. Stir in vinegar, hot pepper sauce, garlic, oil, and seed. Mix well and transfer to a shaker container. Refrigerate until needed. Shake well before using.

AVOCADO DRESSING

Yield: 1 cup

1 ripe avocado
2 tablespoons lemon juice
1 onion slice, about 2 inches
   wide

¼ teaspoon salt
¼ teaspoon garlic salt
¼ cup mayonnaise

Peel and pit avocado. Chop in a few pieces and place in blender with other ingredients. Blend until smooth.

Savannah News-Press

CHILI SAUCE DRESSING

Yield: ½ cup

¼ cup vegetable oil	¼ teaspoon red pepper
¼ teaspoon onion juice	1 teaspoon sugar
2 teaspoons vinegar	2 tablespoons chili sauce
1 teaspoon salt	

Mix all together until smoothly blended.

Mrs. Sophie Meldrim Shonnard

SPRINGFIELD BUTTERMILK DRESSING

Yield: 2 cups

3 slices lean bacon	1 teaspoon dried or 1 tablespoon
1 cup buttermilk	fresh dill weed
2 tablespoons bacon drippings	½ teaspoon salt
⅔ cup commercial sour cream	⅛ teaspoon pepper
⅓ cup sliced green onion	

Cook bacon. Drain, reserving drippings; crumble bacon and set aside. Stir other ingredients together and blend well. Cover and chill. Garnish at serving time with reserved bacon.

GREEN YOGURT DRESSING

Yield: 1¼ cups

1 cup plain yogurt	2 tablespoons chopped parsley
1 teaspoon sugar	½ teaspoon dried tarragon
½ teaspoon salt	

Mix all ingredients in a small bowl. Chill at least an hour before serving to develop flavors.

STRAWBERRY YOGURT DRESSING

Yield: 1½ cups

1 cup plain yogurt	1 tablespoon grated lemon rind
½ cup strawberry preserves or crushed, slightly sweetened, strawberries	

Combine and chill. Serve as a fruit bowl dressing.

Savannah News-Press

TWO-CHEESE DRESSING

Yield: 1¼ cups

¼ cup crumbled blue cheese
¾ cup cream style cottage
    cheese

¼ cup plain yogurt
¼ teaspoon hot pepper sauce
2 tablespoons milk

Blend well and chill before serving.

Savannah News-Press

VERSATILE FRENCH DRESSING

Save money on prepared salad dressings by using the same basic recipe for interesting variations.

Yield: 1½ cups

1 cup corn oil
⅓ to ½ cup vinegar (lemon
    juice may be substituted for
    part or all of the vinegar, if
    desired)

1 to 3 tablespoons sugar, to taste
1½ teaspoons salt
½ teaspoon paprika
½ teaspoon dry mustard
1 clove garlic

Measure ingredients into a bottle or jar with tight lid. Cover and shake well. Chill several hours. Remove garlic. Shake thoroughly before serving.

Zesty French Dressing

Use basic recipe for **Versatile French Dressing**. Add 2 tablespoons ketchup, 1 tablespoon lemon juice, and 1 teaspoon Worcestershire sauce before mixing and chilling.

Mystery Dressing

Yield: 1½ cups

Mix ingredients for **Zesty French Dressing** in a small bowl. Add 1 unbeaten egg white. Beat with rotary beater until thoroughly blended. Store in covered jar in refrigerator to chill. Dressing thickens slightly upon standing. Mix well before serving. This dressing keeps well.

Spicy French Dressing

Heat ½ cup vinegar. Add 1 tablespoon pickling spices, tied in cheesecloth, if desired. Let stand until vinegar is cool. Remove spices. Now follow recipe for **Versatile French Dressing**, using this vinegar.

Lemon Herb Dressing

Follow recipe for **Versatile French Dressing**, using lemon juice for ¾ of the vinegar, reducing sugar to 1½ tablespoons, and substituting ½ teaspoon salad herbs for dry mustard.

Creamy French Dressing

Yield: 2 cups

Follow recipe for **Versatile French Dressing**. Increase sugar to ¼ cup, omit dry mustard and garlic, and add instead ½ cup commercial sour cream and ¼ cup ketchup.

Vinaigrette Dressing

Yield: about 1½ cups

Follow recipe for **Versatile French Dressing**, omitting paprika, dry mustard, and garlic, and adding instead 1 hard-cooked egg, chopped; 1 tablespoon chopped pimiento; 1 tablespoon chopped chives; and 1 tablespoon chopped green pepper.

Diet French Dressing

Follow **Versatile French Dressing** recipe, decreasing vinegar to ¼ cup and using lemon juice instead; add 2 tablespoons water, and decrease sugar and salt to 1 teaspoon each.

Savannah News-Press

LOW-CALORIE YOGURT DRESSING

Most tossed greens are low in calories as well as delicious and healthful. Serve them with diet dressings and enjoy "The Losing Battle."

Yield: ¾ cup

½ cup plain yogurt
1 tablespoon lemon juice
1 tablespoon prepared yellow mustard
½ teaspoon sugar or sugar substitute
½ teaspoon onion salt
½ teaspoon paprika

Stir and chill. Good on either fruit or vegetable salads.

LOW-CALORIE BUTTERMILK DRESSING

Yield: 1 cup

½ cup buttermilk
⅓ cup grated Parmesan cheese
¼ cup low-calorie commercial mayonnaise
1½ tablespoons lemon juice
1 teaspoon chopped parsley
1 teaspoon chopped green onion
⅛ teaspoon salt

Mix all ingredients together in a small jar. Cover and shake well to blend. Chill. Shake well just before serving; only 260 calories a cup.

One of the South's most elegant house museums is the Owens-Thomas House on Oglethorpe Square, designed in English Regency style by William Jay. Three years in the building, it was completed in 1819. Here the Marquis de Lafayette stayed during his visit to Savannah in 1825 and addressed the citizens from the southeast balcony. The house was willed to the Telfair Academy of Arts and Sciences in 1951 by Miss Margaret Thomas, and it is now open to the public. The house includes a wine room, with bottles of early nineteenth century Madeira still intact!

Drawing by the late Christopher Murphy,
Courtesy of Owens-Thomas House

EMMA'S SALAD DRESSING

Yield: 1⅛ cups

1	teaspoon paprika	¼	cup red wine vinegar
1	teaspoon mustard	¾	cup safflower oil
1	tablespoon sugar		salt to taste (optional)

Mix ingredients and chill. Shake well before using. This is especially good on a salad of tossed greens, halved green grapes, and minced scallions.

TELFAIR ORANGE DRESSING

Yield: about ⅔ cup

½	teaspoon grated orange rind, firmly packed	¼	teaspoon onion salt
2	tablespoons orange juice	½	teaspoon dry mustard
2	teaspoons lemon juice	⅛	teaspoon white pepper (optional)
½	teaspoon salt	½	cup vegetable oil (not olive oil)

Beat ingredients together with a fork, or shake together in a small, tightly-covered jar. Use as dressing for sliced avocado or salad greens, along with sections of grapefruit and onion rings.

REGENCY ORANGE-NUT DRESSING

Yield: 1¼ cups

6	ounces cream cheese	2¼	teaspoons lemon juice
2¼	teaspoons sugar	1	tablespoon mayonnaise
⅛	teaspoon salt	3	tablespoons finely minced pecans
⅓	cup frozen orange juice concentrate		

Allow cheese to stand at room temperature until it softens. Cut each package in half for easier blending. Dissolve sugar and salt in juices. Start mashing and creaming cheese. Slowly work in orange juice, and keep working until smooth. Recipe may be doubled. If a thinner dressing is desired, dilute with a little lemon juice.

This dressing is superb over congealed fruit salads. It is also good over orange and grapefruit sections on lettuce, with some very thin sweet onion rings. With the addition of sifted 10-x confectioner's sugar, mixed to spreading consistency, it is also a delicious frosting for cakes and cookies.

A Mouli grater or electric blender is nice to mince the nuts with; they will come out dry and fluffy. Use what you need and refrigerate the rest for later use.

Adapted from a favorite recipe of the Regency Room of the Downtowner Motel on historic Oglethorpe Avenue.

HAM AND HONEY DEW RINGS

Yield: 4 servings

2 cups diced lean ham
¾ cup diced celery
1½ cups sliced fresh or drained
   canned mushrooms
⅓ cup mayonnaise

1 teaspoon dry mustard
1 honey dew melon, chilled
  Boston or Bibb lettuce
  Lemon wedges
  Parsley

Mix ham, celery, and mushrooms; cover and chill. When ready to serve, mix mayonnaise with mustard and combine with ham mixture. Cut four rings, about one inch wide, from center of melon; save ends of melon to eat later in a fresh fruit cup. Discard seeds and peel rings. Place melon rings on lettuce and pile salad in centers. Garnish with lemon wedges and sprigs of parsley.

A sunny afternoon in Savannah is very close to heaven.
Columnist James Kilpatrick

73

206

R.W.Osteen

Wm. Taylor Cotton Warehouse, cir. 1814-1818

BREADS

The William Taylor Cotton Warehouse at 206 West Bay Street, built between 1814 and 1818, was probably the one from which the *S. S. Savannah* left on its famous voyage in 1819, since William Taylor was one of the financial backers of the enterprise. The warehouse, with its great wheel which once helped lift cotton bales, has been renovated as a private home by Dr. and Mrs. C. Lamont Osteen. Mrs. Ann Osteen, an award-winning artist and designer, sketched this picture of her home for this book as well as contributing some family recipes. The house, which has been the subject of articles in several national magazines, is open to the public every year during the Savannah Tour of Homes and Gardens.

WELL-BRED HINTS

- To make holiday bread, criss-cross loaf with white icing.
- For a breakfast treat, sprinkle rolls with cinammon sugar.
- If humidity is high, dough may require up to 1 cup more flour.
- Stale bread? Lightly moisten the top and bottom crusts with a few drops of water. Wrap the loaf tightly in aluminum foil, and heat for 15 minutes in a 400 degrees oven.
- When you are preparing soft bread crumbs, don't throw away the crusts removed from the slices of bread. Dry them and crush fine; store them in a tightly-covered jar in the refrigerator, and you'll find many uses for them, such as in meat loaf and as toppings for casseroles.

EMMA R. LAW'S PEASANT BREAD

Yield: 5 loaves

3½	cups warm water	⅔	cup non-fat dry milk solids
3	packages active dry yeast	⅓	cup vegetable oil
2	tablespoons salt	1	2-pound bag flour
⅓	cup sugar		

Pour warm water over yeast in a large bowl of at least 4-quart capacity. Stir until yeast is dissolved. Add salt, sugar, and dry milk powder. Stir until dissolved. Add oil. Gradually beat in all flour until batter is smooth. Cover bowl loosely and place in a warm place free from drafts; let rise until doubled in bulk. Beat well and divide into 5 oiled round utility pans, each 6 inches by 2 inches. Let rise again until dough almost reaches tops of pans. Preheat oven to 375 degrees. Bake until loaves are golden brown and shrink slightly from pans, about 40 to 45 minutes. Turn out of pans and cool on racks.

TWO-FLOUR BREAD

Yield: 2 loaves

1	package active dry yeast	½	cup evaporated milk
1	teaspoon honey	⅓	cup safflower oil
½	cup warm water	1	egg
1	cup water	¼	cup wheat germ
1	tablespoon salt	⅓	cup corn meal
¼	cup honey	2	cups whole wheat flour
		2	or 3 cups white flour

Dissolve yeast and honey in water. Set aside. Mix water, salt, honey, milk, oil, egg, wheat germ, and corn meal. Add whole wheat flour. Gradually add white flour, one cup at a time. Turn onto lightly floured board and knead 5 minutes. Place in an oiled bowl. Cover and put in a warm place to rise, about 1½ hours. Punch down. Divide in two. Shape into loaves. Place in well-oiled bread pans, 9-by-5-by-2¾ inches. Cover. Let rise until double in bulk, about 1 hour. Preheat oven to 400 degrees; bake loaves for 10 minutes; lower oven temperature to 350 degrees for about 30 to 35 minutes more.

Mary Ellen Kirkland

DUBLIN SODA BREAD

Just right for a Savannah St. Patrick's Day!

Yield: 1 loaf

4	cups unsifted flour	½	cup currants
2	teaspoons baking soda	¼	cup chopped peanuts
2	teaspoons salt	1¼	cups buttermilk
2	teaspoons sugar	1	tablespoon milk
1½	teaspoons caraway seeds		

Preheat oven to 400 degrees. In large bowl, mix together flour, baking soda, salt, sugar, caraway seeds, currants, and chopped peanuts. Make a hole in the dry mixture and pour in buttermilk, mixing from the sides to form a ball of dough. Turn out onto floured board and knead about 5 minutes. Shape into a ball. Place on ungreased baking sheet. With a sharp knife, make a shallow cross-shaped slit across the top of the loaf. Brush with milk. Bake for 50 minutes, or until done.

Aileen Claire, Food Editor, National Editorial Association

MORAVIAN LOVE FEAST

The Moravians, or Brethren, were Protestants who came first from Bohemia and later from Saxony seeking religious freedom as well as an opportunity to be missionaries to the Indians. They were famous for their love feasts, celebrations of breaking bread together in the style of the early Christians. The first of these in North America were held in Savannah from 1735 to 1740. The group later went on to Bethlehem, Pennsylvania, and Salem, North Carolina. Today their descendants carry on the feasts as a musical service, which includes serving coffee and sweet bread to the congregation. The Moravians are said to have originated the tradition of the Easter sunrise service.

CRANBERRY PECAN BREAD

Ideal as a gift at holiday time.

Yield: 1 loaf

2 cups sifted flour	1 tablespoon grated orange rind
1 cup sugar	¾ cup orange juice
1½ teaspoons baking powder	1 well-beaten egg
1 teaspoon salt	1 cup fresh cranberries, coarsely
½ teaspoon baking soda	chopped, or more, to taste
¼ cup vegetable shortening	½ cup chopped pecans

Preheat oven to 350 degrees. Sift together dry ingredients. Cut in shortening. Combine peel, juice, and egg. Add to dry ingredients, mixing just to moisten. Fold in berries and nuts. Turn into oiled 9-by-5-by-3-inch pan. Bake for 60 minutes. Cool. Wrap and store. This is a good party sandwich when sliced thin and spread with butter, or with cream cheese to which some crushed pineapple and chopped nuts have been added.

SWEET GLAZE

A good glaze for a tea loaf or sweet buns may be made by combining a cup of confectioner's sugar with 1 tablespoon melted butter and 2 tablespoons orange juice. If you are freezing the bread, it is better to add the glaze after the bread is thawed again, just before serving.

BARMBRACK

Barmbrack means "speckled bread." It is an Irish Halloween favorite, with a ring, a coin, and a button (denoting single blessedness) sometimes baked in the dough for fortune telling. In Savannah, it would be appropriate before the annual St. Patrick's Day parade.

Yield: 1 round loaf

4 cups flour	2 eggs, well beaten
½ teaspoon ground nutmeg	1½ cups raisins
⅛ teaspoon salt	1 cup currants
2 tablespoons butter	⅓ cup chopped candied fruit peel
1 package active dry yeast	¼ cup milk
2 tablespoons sugar	

Sift flour, nutmeg, and salt together. Rub butter into the flour. Cream the yeast in a cup with a teaspoon of the sugar. Add the rest of the sugar to the flour mixture and mix well. Lightly warm the milk to body temperature. Add to the liquid yeast the milk and most of the well-beaten eggs, reserving a little of the eggs for the glaze. Beat the liquid well into the dry ingredients until the batter is stiff but elastic. Fold in the raisins, currants, and fruit peel. Turn into a buttered 8-inch cake pan, so that the dough only half fills the pan.

Cover with a cloth and leave to rise in a warm place, such as near the stove. (Irish households once had "airing cupboards" for this purpose.) The dough should double in size in about an hour. Preheat oven to 400 degrees. Brush the top of the loaf with the rest of the beaten eggs. Bake for approximately 1 hour, or until a skewer thrust in the cake comes out clean.

Mrs. William J. Doyle

ISLE OF HOPE CINNAMON BREAD

Yield: 2 loaves

6½ to 7½ cups unsifted flour	3 eggs, at room temperature
6 tablespoons sugar	3 tablespoons butter or
1½ teaspoons salt	margarine, melted
2 packages active dry yeast	½ cup sugar
1 cup milk	2 teaspoons ground cinnamon
¾ cup water	1 egg white, slightly beaten
⅓ cup butter or margarine	

In a large bowl, thoroughly mix 2 cups flour, 6 tablespoons sugar, salt, and undissolved yeast. Combine milk, water, and one-third cup butter or margarine in a saucepan. Heat over low heat until liquids are very warm (120 degrees to 130 degrees if you have a thermometer). Butter does not need to melt. Gradually add to the dry ingredients, and beat 2 minutes at medium speed of electric mixer, scraping bowl occasionally.

Add eggs and one-half cup flour. Beat at high speed 2 minutes, scraping bowl occasionally. Stir in enough additional flour to make a stiff dough. Turn out onto lightly floured board; knead until smooth and elastic, about 8 to 10 minutes. Place in oiled bowl, turning to oil top. Cover; let rise in warm place, free from draft, until doubled in bulk, about 35 minutes.

Meanwhile, combine one-half cup sugar and cinnamon. Punch dough down; divide in half. Roll each half to a 14-by-9-inch rectangle. Brush lightly with melted butter or margarine. Sprinkle each with half of cinnamon-sugar mixture. Beginning at a 9-inch end, tightly roll dough as for jelly roll and shape into loaves. Place in 2 oiled 9-by-5-inch loaf pans. Cover; let rise in warm place, free from draft, until doubled in bulk, about 35 minutes.

Preheat oven to 375 degrees. Brush loaves with egg white; sprinkle each with half of **Isle of Hope Crumb Topping**. Loosely top each with an aluminum foil "tent." Bake on lowest rack position for 45 minutes. Remove foil; bake 5 minutes longer, or just until golden brown. Remove from pans and cool on wire racks.

Isle of Hope Crumb Topping

⅓ cup unsifted flour
⅓ cup light brown sugar, firmly packed
1 teaspoon ground cinnamon

3 tablespoons butter or margarine, at room temperature

Mix just until mixture is crumbly.

Good Samaritan Circle, Isle of Hope United Methodist Church

ANADAMA BREAD

It is said that a certain colonial farm woman, Ana, served her husband corn bread and molasses every morning for breakfast until he longed for a change. Finally, in desperation, the farmer said, "Ana, dammit, do it this way!" and proceeded to mix up this bread.

Yield: 2 loaves

7 or 8 cups unsifted flour
1¼ cups yellow corn meal
2½ teaspoons salt
2 packages active dry yeast
⅓ cup butter or margarine, at room temperature

2¼ cups very warm tap water (120° to 130°)
⅔ cup molasses

In a large bowl, thoroughly mix 2½ cups flour, corn meal, salt, and undissolved yeast. Add butter or margarine. Gradually add tap water and molasses to dry ingredients and beat 2 minutes at medium speed of electric mixer, scraping bowl occasionally. Stir in enough additional flour to make a stiff dough. Turn out onto lightly floured board; knead until smooth and elastic, about 8 to 10 minutes. Place in oiled bowl, turning to oil top. Cover; let rise in warm place, free from draft, until doubled in bulk, about 1 hour.

Punch dough down; divide in half. Roll each half to a 14-by-9-inch rectangle. Shape into loaves. Place in 2 oiled 9-by-5-by-3-inch loaf pans. Cover; let rise in a warm place until doubled in bulk, about 45 minutes. Preheat oven to 375 degrees. Bake loaves about 45 minutes, or until done. Remove from pan and cool on wire racks.

Good Samaritan Circle, Isle of Hope United Methodist Church

OLD-FASHIONED CORN MEAL BREAD

Yield: 2 8-inch rounds, or
      2 9-by-5-inch loaves, or
      4 3-by-6-inch loaves

2	cups boiling water	¾	cup molasses or dark corn syrup
2	cups yellow corn meal		
3	tablespoons vegetable shortening	2	packages active dry yeast
		4	tablespoons lukewarm water
2	teaspoons salt	3	or 4 cups sifted flour

Pour water over meal, shortening, and salt. Stir in molasses and cool to lukewarm. Soften yeast in lukewarm water and add to corn meal mixture, stirring well. Add flour gradually, until dough is easily handled. Knead until elastic. Place in lightly oiled bowl, turn to oil top, cover with towel, and let rise until double in bulk, about 1 hour. Punch down, and shape into loaves. Place in oiled pans, oil tops, and let rise until double in bulk, about 30 minutes. Preheat oven to 375 degrees. Bake loaves for 45 minutes to 1 hour.

BUTTERMILK CORN BREAD

Yield: 16 squares

1⅓	cups corn meal	½	teaspoon salt
⅓	cup flour	1	cup buttermilk
1	teaspoon baking powder	1	egg
½	teaspoon baking soda	2	tablespoons melted shortening
1	tablespoon sugar		

Preheat oven to 400 degrees. Sift all dry ingredients together in large bowl. Combine buttermilk and egg; add all at once to dry ingredients. Stir until smooth. Add melted shortening or cooking oil. Bake in an oiled 8-inch square pan for about 25 minutes, or until corn bread is richly browned. Serve hot, with soft butter.

SOUR CREAM CORN BREAD

Yield: 12 servings

1	cup self-rising corn meal	½	cup cream-style corn (optional)
2	eggs, slightly beaten		
½	cup vegetable oil	1	cup commercial sour cream

Preheat oven to 450 degrees. Mix meal, eggs, and oil well, also corn, if desired. Fold in sour cream last, and mix well. Pour into preheated oiled skillet or pan and bake until golden brown, about 20 minutes. Let cool for about 5 minutes, and remove from pan.

Mrs. Eleanor Robinson, Vidalia, Georgia
Savannah News-Press

CORN HOE CAKE

A simple bread which in the early days was baked in hot ashes on a clean hoe.

Mix into a stiff dough, one pint of corn meal with cold water; add a teaspoonful of salt. Dust the gridiron with meal, and lay on in thin cakes.

*Aunt Polly, **House-Keeping In The Sunny South,** 1885*

OLD-FASHIONED CRACKLINGS

Take the fat meat of the hog and either grind or cut it in small pieces. Place it in a large iron pot. Cook over a slow fire. Stir with a wooden paddle while cooking. Cook until grease is removed from fat meat, which will be crisp and a golden brown. Strain through a white cloth into a container. Save the particles in the cloth, known as "Cracklings," to be used in bread or eaten as they are. Store lard in a crock.

Frances Helmly (Mrs. Cecil B.) Gnann
Ye Olde Time Salzburger Cook Book

CRACKLIN' BREAD

Yield: 12 servings

2	cups water-ground corn meal	½	cup water
1	teaspoon salt	1	egg
3	teaspoons baking powder	½	cup finely-chopped cracklings
½	cup milk		

Preheat oven to 400 degrees. Mix and sift dry ingredients. Stir in milk and water and beat until smooth. Drop in egg and beat again. Stir in cracklings and mix lightly. Bake in a lightly oiled iron skillet or 8-inch square pan about 30 minutes. An iron skillet was the traditional cooking utensil for the bread.

SPOON BREAD WITH GRITS

One transplanted Savannahian is still reminded of the time he walked into a Savannah restaurant and innocently ordered: "One grit, please," thinking it was a hominy cake! The word grits means "fragment," and refers to a fine-ground cereal grain which is usually made from corn, but may also be made from other grains, such as rye or rice. Grits ground from corn are known in the South as hominy grits, and are a traditional staple food. In this recipe they are used with another plantation favorite, spoon bread.

Yield: 4 to 6 servings

2	tablespoons butter	1	cup milk
1	cup cooked grits	½	teaspoon salt
2	eggs, well beaten	½	cup sifted white corn meal

Preheat oven to 375 degrees. Stir butter into grits. Mix eggs, milk, and salt. Stir some of the grits into milk mixture; stir it all back into grits. Beat in corn meal until smooth. Pour into a buttered, deep casserole, one which holds about 4 to 5 cups. Bake about 30 minutes. Serve hot.

Helen Kehoe Crolly

PLANTATION SPOON BREAD

Yield: 4 to 6 servings

½	cup yellow corn meal	1	teaspoon baking powder
¼	cup flour	1	egg
1	tablespoon sugar	1½	cups milk
¾	teaspoon salt	2	tablespoons butter

Preheat oven to 375 degrees. Combine and sift corn meal, flour, sugar, salt, and baking powder. Stir in egg and 1 cup milk. Beat well. Melt the butter in the oven in an 8-inch square baking dish. Pour in the batter. Pour over top of this the other half-cup milk. Place in oven. Bake 45 minutes or until good and crusty, but with a soft center. Serve with syrup and bacon. This is a very old recipe.

Oneita Higham

PIONEER HUSH PUPPIES

As the good smell of the evening meal would arise from the cooking fire of the early settlers, the hunting dogs would begin to get restless with hunger. It was easy to quiet them with these.

Yield: about 3 dozen

1	cup corn meal	½	cup finely chopped onion
½	cup flour	1	egg
2	teaspoons baking powder	⅔	cup milk
1	teaspoon salt	2	teaspoons melted shortening
1	tablespoon sugar		deep fat for frying

Sift together dry ingredients. Stir in onion, egg, milk, and shortening. Drop by teaspoons into deep hot fat. Fry until golden brown.

If serving with fish, they have a "fishier" taste when fried in the hot fat immediately after the fish is fried. Keep fish warm while making hush puppies. If there are any left, freeze and use as part of the bread mixture the next time you make dressing. To make them easier to drop, dip teaspoon in a cup of water often.

This is also a good recipe for corn dogs, omitting onion. Mix the batter. Dry weiners on paper towel before dipping in batter. Then fry in hot deep fat. Keeps humans quiet, too....

Ann Smith, Milledgeville, Georgia

SOUTHERN SWEET POTATO BREAD

This delightfully moist loaf is even better with **Orange Cream Spread.**

Yield: 1 loaf

4	tablespoons (½ stick) butter	3	tablespoons milk
		1	teaspoon grated orange rind
½	cup brown sugar, firmly packed	2	cups sifted self-rising flour
		¼	teaspoon nutmeg
2	eggs, beaten	¼	teaspoon allspice
1	cup mashed, cooked sweet potatoes	½	cup chopped pecans

Preheat oven to 350 degrees. Grease a 9-by-5-by-3-inch loaf pan. Cream butter; add brown sugar and beat until light and fluffy. Add eggs, sweet potatoes, milk, and orange rind. Beat with mixer until thoroughly combined. Add flour, nutmeg, allspice, and pecans to sweet potato mixture. Mix thoroughly until smooth. Turn batter into prepared pan and bake for 45 to 50 minutes. Let cool in pan 10 minutes. Remove loaf and cool on rack before slicing.

Orange Cream Spread

Into 3 ounces cream cheese, blend 1 tablespoon orange juice and 1 teaspoon grated orange peel. This is good with other breads, too.

Mrs. Leona B. Henley, Chatham County Extension Agent

ZUCCHINI BREAD

Yield: 2 or 3 loaves

1 cup vegetable oil	1 teaspoon baking soda
3 eggs, slightly beaten	½ teaspoon salt
2 cups sugar	3 teaspoons cinnamon
2 cups grated uncooked zucchini	½ teaspoon nutmeg
	1 cup chopped pecans
3 cups sifted flour	¼ to ½-cup milk
1 teaspoon baking powder	(optional)

Preheat oven to 350 degrees. Combine oil, eggs, sugar and zucchini in a large mixing bowl, blending well. Sift together flour, baking powder, soda, salt, cinnamon and nutmeg. Stir gently into wet ingredients. Fold in pecans. If mixture seems too stiff, gently stir in a little milk. Spoon batter into 2 oiled 9-by-5-by-2¾-inch, or 3 8-by-4-by-2¼-inch loaf pans. Bake for about an hour, or until loaves are golden brown and shrink from the sides of the pan, or when tops spring back when gently pressed with the finger tips. Remove from pans. Cool on racks and store in air-tight containers.

Sandra Osteen Robinson

COCONUT CORN BREAD

Yield: 1 square loaf

1¼ cups white corn meal	¾ cup flaked coconut
1 cup sifted flour	1 egg
⅓ cup sugar	1 cup buttermilk or 1 cup milk
1 teaspoon bakng soda	plus 1 tablespoon white wine
½ teaspoon salt	vinegar
½ teaspoon ground cardamom	3 tablespoons vegetable oil
⅓ cup light brown sugar, firmly packed	

Preheat oven to 425 degrees. Sift meal, flour, sugar, soda, salt, and cardamom together in a large bowl. Stir in brown sugar and coconut. Beat egg in another bowl and blend in buttermilk and oil. Add this to dry ingredients all at once, stirring only until blended. Pour into oiled 9-inch square pan. Bake for about 25 minutes, or until golden brown. While still in the pan, cut into squares of desired size. Serve immediately with soft butter. Good with coffee or tea! Left-overs may be split, buttered, and toasted.

BEER MUFFINS

Yield: 15 to 18

1	12-ounce can beer, at room temperature	3	tablespoons sugar
		3	cups packaged biscuit mix

Pour beer into large bowl. Add sugar and beat until sugar dissolves. (It will be foamy.) Add biscuit mix and stir just until mix is moistened well. Oil muffin tins; allow 1½ tablespoons batter to each muffin. Preheat oven to 425 degrees. Let muffins rise in pans 20 minutes. Bake for 15 minutes, or until lightly browned.

Alphia Hughes, White Bluff, Georgia

DIXIE CORN MUFFINS OR STICKS

Yield: 12

1	cup less 2 tablespoons sifted yellow corn meal	1	egg, beaten
2	tablespoons flour	1	teaspoon sugar
½	teaspoon salt	2	tablespoons vegetable oil
2	teaspoons baking powder	½	cup milk

Preheat oven to 425 degrees. Sift corn meal, flour, salt, and baking powder together. Beat egg, sugar, oil, and milk together. Pour, all at once, into dry ingredients. Stir quickly until all is mixed. Do not overmix. Divide into 12 2½-inch muffin cups, oiled on bottoms only. If preferred, use 12 5-inch corn stick molds, oiled about half way up. Bake for 15 to 17 minutes, or until sides are shrinking from the pans. Remove from pans and serve immediately.

HOMINY MUFFINS

Two cups of fine hominy; boiled and cold; beat it briskly, and stir in three cups of sour milk, half a cup of melted butter, two teaspoons of salt and two tablespoons of white sugar. Then add three eggs, well beaten, one teaspoon of soda dissolved in hot water, and a large cup of flour; bake quickly.

Hints From Southern Epicures, *circa 1890*

SHORTENIN' BREAD
Mama's little baby loves. . . .
Yield: about 40 pieces

4 cups sifted flour	1 pound butter, at room
1 cup light brown sugar, firmly	temperature (but not too
packed	soft)

Preheat oven to 350 degrees. Sift flour and sugar together into large bowl. Rub butter into mixture with back of spoon or rubber spatula until well blended. Roll gently on a floured board or a floured pastry cloth with a floured rolling pin. Cut into desired shapes and sizes. Bake on ungreased cookie sheets for about 25 minutes. Remove from sheets and cool on racks. Store in air-tight container in a cool place. This is a very old Savannah recipe.

Helen Kehoe Crolly

BEATEN BISCUITS

In the Virginia of the olden time no breakfast or tea-table was thought to be properly furnished without a plate of these indispensable biscuits. . . . Let one spend the night at some gentleman farmer's home, and the first sound heard in the morning, after the crowing of the cock, was the heavy, regular fall of the cook's axe, as she beat and beat her biscuit dough. . . . Nowadays beaten biscuits are a rarity, found here and there, but soda and modern institutions have caused them to be sadly out of vogue.

Mary Stuart Smith, **Virginia Cookery-Book,** *1885.*

Constructed in 1821 by Samuel Bryan, this handsome Federal townhouse once stood at the southern boundary of the city. It has been restored by Southern Bell Telephone and Telegraph Company as their business office in Savannah.

Drawing courtesy of Southern Bell
Telephone and Telegraph Company

TRADITIONAL BEATEN BISCUITS

Emma Law recalls that when her mother was a child on a plantation near Waynesboro, the first sound she heard every morning was the cook's little boy, beating the biscuit dough with a clean ball bat which was kept only for that purpose. This he did before the family had breakfast. Few homemakers today would be willing to prepare dough which called for "300 to 500 licks" unless it could be done by machine!

While you are working with the dough, re-roll all scraps from cuttings, so all dough is used. If you are lucky enough to own a beaten biscuit machine, no beating is necessary. Just roll dough through and through rollers, folding each time, until blisters appear. This machine looks rather like an old clothes ringer with steel rollers. The older models had rollers of hardwood, and the dough was worked on marble slabs.

The following recipe has been updated by Emma from her Grandmother Lane's famous *Some Good Things To Eat*. To prepare it is to truly have a taste of the past. . . .

Yield: 50 to 60

4	cups sifted flour	1	cup cold water
1	cup vegetable shortening	4	tablespoons (½ stick) butter,
1	teaspoon salt		melted

Rub flour and shortening together well. (I like a rubber spatula for this.) Dissolve salt in water and add gradually to mixture, mixing well until a stiff, but still sticky, dough is obtained. Flour a board or a pastry cloth, and turn dough onto it. Roll with floured pin or a pin covered with a pastry sock, also floured. Beat the dough with the pin until dough is about a quarter of an inch thick. Flour top, fold over, flour again, and turn over, and flour other side. Flour pin as needed. Continue beating, folding, and flouring until mixture begins to blister, and is pliable and tender. (It's okay to stop and rest if you get tired. Hand beating is not easy!)

Preheat oven to 350 degrees. Roll dough to about half-inch thickness. Dip a 1½-to 2-inch round cutter in flour. Cut, closely together, and place on very lightly buttered or non-stick cookie sheets. Prick tops deeply with four-tined fork three times, making a square design on top. Bake about 35 minutes, or until a pale golden color. Do not brown. When done and still hot, use a bit of cheese cloth or a pastry brush to glaze tops with melted butter. Cool on racks. Store in air-tight container in a cool place.

ANGEL BISCUITS

(Self-Rising)

Yield: about 40 biscuits

5 cups sifted self-rising flour	2 packages active dry yeast
⅓ cup sugar	dissolved in ½ cup warm
1 teaspoon baking soda	water
1 cup vegetable shortening	2 cups buttermilk

Preheat oven to 450 degrees. Combine dry ingredients. Cut in shortening; then stir in dissolved yeast and buttermilk. Roll out on a floured surface and cut as desired. Bake on ungreased cookie sheets until golden brown, about 10 to 12 minutes.

(Regular Flour)

Yield: about 40 biscuits

1 package active dry yeast	3 teaspoons baking powder
2 tablespoons lukewarm water	1½ teaspoons salt
5 cups flour	1 cup vegetable shortening
1 teaspoon baking soda	2 cups buttermilk

Preheat oven to 400 degrees. Dissolve yeast in warm water. Sift all dry ingredients into large bowl. Cut in shortening with pastry blender. Add buttermilk, then yeast mixture. Stir until thoroughly moistened. Turn onto floured board and knead a minute or two. Roll out to desired thickness, and cut into rounds. Brush with melted butter, and bake on ungreased baking sheet for 12 to 15 minutes, or until thoroughly browned.

These baked biscuits freeze beautifully; reheat in aluminum foil in a preheated 450 degree oven.

For soft-sided biscuits, place close together. For crusty sides, place about an inch apart.

After mixing, dough may be refrigerated in plastic bag or covered bowl until ready to use. It keeps well for several days. If using plastic bag, leave a little room for biscuit dough to expand.

These may also be readied for baking the day before and kept refrigerated until an hour before baking, allowing them to attain room temperature.

Brush biscuits with melted butter or margarine before baking for extra golden color and flavor.

Mrs. C. J. Stephens, Savannah News-Press

IT AIN'T PEANUTS!

Peanuts were known in South America over two thousand years ago and are believed to be native to Brazil. The ancient pre-Incan tribes buried their dead with peanuts to give them strength on their long voyage through eternity. These tribes also depicted the peanut on their pottery. The Spanish later took peanuts to Europe, and thence they spread to Asia and Africa. Early Virginians fed them to their hogs, producing particularly delicious pork products. Peanuts became an important agricultural crop in the South after The War Between the States.

Peanuts are one of the most important cash crops in Georgia. The state leads the nation in the production of peanuts, of which the largest share goes into the production of peanut butter.

PEANUT BUTTER BISCUITS

Yield: 9

⅔ cup milk
¼ cup peanut butter
2 cups packaged biscuit mix

3 slices bacon, cooked and crumbled

Preheat oven to 400 degrees. Place milk and peanut butter in a deep bowl or blender container. Beat at high speed until smooth and well blended. Combine biscuit mix and bacon. Stir lightly. Add milk and peanut butter mixture all at once and stir with fork until dough clings together. Turn out on a lightly floured board and knead gently a few times. Pat out to about ¾-inch thickness with floured hands. Cut into 2-inch rounds. Bake on an ungreased cookie sheet for 10 to 12 minutes, or until lightly browned.

Georgia Peanut Commission

APPLESAUCE-CHEESE BISCUITS

Yield: about 21

2 cups flour
2 teaspoons baking powder
¼ teaspoon baking soda
1 teaspoon salt

4 tablespoons shortening
¾ cup applesauce
¾ cup grated Cheddar cheese
milk (optional)

Preheat oven to 400 degrees. Sift dry ingredients, cut in shortening. Add applesauce and cheese. Roll out and cut biscuits or add enough milk to make a slightly thinner batter, and have drop biscuits. Bake for 8 to 10 minutes.

Mrs. Wilkes' Boarding House on West Jones Street is sheltered by live oaks.

Drawing copyright© by Pamela Lee

MRS. WILKES' BOARDING HOUSE CHEESE BISCUITS

Yield: about 16

2 cups self-rising flour
½ teaspoon baking powder
1 tablespoon vegetable shortening
2 tablespoons butter or margarine

1 cup grated Cheddar cheese
⅓ cup buttermilk
⅓ cup milk

Preheat oven to 450 degrees. Sift flour and baking powder into bowl. Cut in shortening and butter or margarine until mixture resembles coarse corn meal. Stir in grated cheese. Fill measuring cup with buttermilk, whole milk, and enough water to make ¾ cup. Make a well in the center of the flour and pour in the liquid. With hands, mix lightly and quickly to form dough moist enough to leave sides of the bowl. Turn on lightly floured surface. Knead by picking up sides of dough away from you, pressing down with palms of hands, pushing dough away. Repeat 6 or 7 times. Work dough into a large ball while kneading. Keep fingers dry by dipping into dry flour frequently. Pinch off portions of dough for desired size of biscuit. Press lightly to make biscuit appear flat until baked, while placing on a well-greased pan. Bake for 12 to 15 minutes.

Mrs. L. H. Wilkes
Favorite Recipes From Mrs. Wilkes' Boarding House in Historic Savannah

SAVANNAH CREAM BISCUITS

Yield: 16

3 teaspoons baking powder
¾ teaspoon salt

2 cups sifted flour
1 cup heavy cream

Preheat oven to 425 degrees. Sift dry ingredients together or use 2 cups sifted self-rising flour instead of first 3 ingredients. Whip the cream until it is very thick. Fold it into the dry ingredients. Turn dough out onto a lightly floured pastry board and knead for one minute. Roll to thickness of one-quarter-inch. Cut with lightly-floured cutter, and place on lightly-buttered cookie sheet. Bake for 10 to 12 minutes, or until golden brown.

Mary (Mrs. Dorsey) Flanders

RINCON SWEET POTATO BISCUITS

Sweet potatoes, in the South, are sometimes simply called "potatoes," while white potatoes are called "Irish potatoes."

Yield: about 2 dozen

2 cups mashed, cooked sweet potatoes	2½ cups flour
½ cup molasses	¼ teaspoon baking soda
¼ cup shortening	¼ teaspoon salt
	¼ cup buttermilk

Preheat oven to 425 degrees. Mix potatoes, molasses, and shortening in a large mixing bowl. Sift in dry ingredients. Stir in milk, mixing thoroughly. Knead on a floured board until dough can be rolled out about ½-inch thick, and cut biscuits. Bake on a lightly oiled baking sheet about 15 minutes, or until golden brown.

I had a dream the other night, when everything was still;
I thought I saw Susanna, a-comin' up the hill;
A buckwheat cake was in her mouth, a tear was in her eye;
But I'm a-comin' from the South; Susanna, don't you cry.

"Oh! Susanna!" by Stephen Collins Foster, 1848

QUICK BUCKWHEAT CAKES

To a pint of buckwheat flour, add a teaspoonful of salt, a teaspoonful of baking powder, a tablespoonful of brown sugar, and a tablespoonful of lard. Mix it with sweet milk, or use buttermilk and soda to make a batter.

House-Keeping In The Sunny South, 1885

CHEESE PANCAKES

Perfect for a lazy holiday breakfast.

Yield: 6

2 eggs	½ cup creamed small-curd cottage cheese
¾ cup commercial sour cream	
1 teaspoon sugar	½ cup sifted flour
½ teaspoon salt	oil for frying

Beat eggs well, but not frothy. Beat in ½ cup sour cream, sugar, salt, and cottage cheese. Fold in flour. Using a third-cup measure almost full, drop batter onto hot, oiled surface and cook until golden brown; then turn to brown other side. Serve hot, topped with another dollop of sour cream. If you want to be sinful with the calories, accompany with jelly or preserves.

HOMINY FRITTERS

Beat up three eggs with a large spoonful of butter, add to these three spoonfuls of cold hominy, a pint of milk, and a pint of wheat flour. Mix all together, and let it rise three hours.... The whole must be well mixed, dropped with a large spoon into boiling lard, and fried brown. Each spoonful makes a fritter.

House And Home; or, The Carolina Housewife,
By A Lady of Charleston, 1855

CORN MEAL POPOVERS

Yield: 8

1 cup less 2 tablespoons water	¾ cup sifted flour
¼ cup dry milk solids	¼ cup yellow corn meal
2 eggs	¼ teaspoon salt
1 tablespoon vegetable oil	

Preheat oven to 425 degrees. In a mixing bowl, dissolve the dry milk solids in the water. Add eggs and oil; beat well. Sift together the flour, cornmeal, and salt; add all at once to liquid mixture. Beat until smooth and free of lumps, or use a blender. Pour into well-oiled 2¾-inch muffin tins. Bake until brown and firm, about 40 minutes. Serve at once.

If it is necessary to keep popovers for a short while before serving, puncture each with a sharp knife to let out steam, loosen and tip sideways in the tins, and leave in oven with heat turned off and door slightly ajar.

BUTTERMILK SCONES

Yield: 12

2 cups unsifted flour	6 tablespoons shortening
½ teaspoon baking soda	¾ cup currants
½ teaspoon baking powder	¾ cup buttermilk
3 tablespoons sugar	

Preheat oven to 375 degrees. Sift together first 4 ingredients. Cut in shortening until mixture is like coarse crumbs. Add currants. Add buttermilk, and mix with a fork. When dough is of a consistency to handle, press into a rectangle on a greased cookie sheet. Cut into 12 squares, about ½-inch thick. Separate slightly, about an inch apart on the sheet, so scones can brown.

Bake until brown, 20 to 25 minutes. Serve warm with soft butter. Note: some scones bakers score the dough, but leave it all in one piece, and bake it slightly longer. They then serve it in one piece, and break pieces off as it is eaten. Serve hot, with soft butter and jam. This is an old family recipe from England.

O. Kay Jackson, Savannah Beach

THE SELF-RELIANT BAKER

Make your own bread and cake. Some people think it is just as cheap to buy of the baker and confectioner; but it is not half as cheap. True, it is more convenient; and therefore the rich are justifiable in employing them; but those who are under the necessity of being economical, should make convenience a secondary object. In the first place, confectioners make their cake richer than people of moderate income can afford to make it; in the next place, your domestic, or yourself, may just as well employ your own time, as to pay them for theirs.

The American Frugal Housewife, 1838

MAIN DISHES

"Old Salzburger Church" *by John C. LeBey*

GERMANS IN SAVANNAH

The German influence in Savannah began in March 1734, when the ship *Purisburg* sailed up the Savannah River with seventy-eight Austrian Lutherans, religious exiles from Salzburg. Given land twenty-five miles farther up the river at a place which they called Ebenezer, they were later joined by more immigrants. Their thriving community was almost destroyed by British occupation during the Revolutionary War, and the people dispersed to the countryside. However, Jerusalem Church, built in 1769, is still in use as a tribute to their heroism. Nearby is the Salzburger Museum, a replica of the colonial "Orphans And Widows House" and one of the early cottages, which has been restored by the Salzburger Society.

PICKLED BEEF OR SAUERBRATEN

An early Salzburger recipe for **Sauerbraten,** or "sour beef," (beef marinated in vinegar) is reprinted in *Ye Olde Time Salzburger Cook Book* from the collection of Pearl Rahn Gnann:

Wipe with a damp cloth a 3 or 4 pound beef shoulder or rump roast. Rub with salt and pepper and garlic if desired. Place in a large bowl or crock.

Heat but do not boil, equal parts of water and vinegar, about a cup of each, or enough to more than half cover the meat; add ½ cup sliced onions, ¼ cup sugar, 1 teaspoon peppercorns, and 2 bay leaves. Pour over meat and set in refrigerator for a week or 10 days, turning the meat over in the liquid every day.

Remove bay leaves and peppercorns from liquid which is reserved as it is drained from the meat, for use in cooking the meat as you would a pot roast.

Much reverence was given to the meal with Grace before and after eating. The Salzburgers were most thankful for their food, for so many hardships were involved before the food was placed on the table. They were ever mindful of God's goodness to them.

Ye Olde Time Salzburger Cook Book

SAVANNAH SAUERBRATEN

Yield: 10 to 12 servings

1	beef chuck roast, approximately 4 pounds	4	to 6 bay leaves, depending on size
3	cups dry red wine	2	teaspoons salt
2	cups thinly sliced onions	6	tablespoons shortening
¾	cup diced carrots	4	tablespoons flour
1	cup diced celery	1	tablespoon sugar
4	whole cloves	8	to 10 gingersnaps, depending on size, finely crumbled
12	whole peppercorns		

Marinate beef in mixture of next 8 ingredients. Place in a covered container (glass, enamel, or stainless steel). Refrigerate for 5 days, turning at least once daily. Drain meat, strain marinade, and reserve. Dry meat well on paper towels. Brown on all sides in 2 tablespoons shortening. Add reserved marinade. Cover, bring to a boil, lower heat, and simmer for about 3 hours.

Melt remaining shortening in large frying pan. Stir in flour and sugar; blend well and let brown. Pour in about half the marinade, stirring until smooth. Return to simmering pot and cook until meat is fork-tender. Remove meat to large, deep, warmed platter. Thicken marinade with ginger snap crumbs. Pour some of marinade around the meat. Serve remaining marinade in a sauce boat with the meat.

EARLY GEORGIA

The planters mostly slaughter oxon and pigs in the autumn and at the beginning of winter when they are fat, and the meat keeps well. This they salt away and smoke it for use in their house in the time ahead. They keep food for an emergency, and whoever has time and skill goes deer hunting, or shoots wild chickens, wild ducks, etc....

I picture the life of the noblemen in Germany to be similar in some respects to the life of our plantation owners, namely that they preserve their own salted and smoked meat, at times slaughter something themselves, are satisfied with flour and milk dishes, bake their own bread. . . .

Johann Martin Bolzius, pastor to the Salzburgers writing back to Europe about 1750

"Octoberfest" by C. C. Powers, Savannah News-Press

GERMAN-STYLE SHORT RIBS

Yield: 6 servings

3 pounds lean beef short ribs	½ cup water
water	3 tablespoons vinegar
instant meat tenderizer	1 teaspoon prepared
⅓ cup flour	horseradish
½ teaspoon salt	1 bay leaf
⅛ teaspoon pepper, or to taste	¼ teaspoon ground allspice
4 tablespoons vegetable oil	¼ teaspoon ground cloves
½ cup thinly sliced onion	
1 10-ounce can condensed beef	
consomme	

Brush meat with water, sprinkle with meat tenderizer. Pierce meat with fork at half-inch intervals. Turn and repeat on all sides of meat. Mix flour, salt, pepper; coat meat with mixture. Heat 2 tablespoons of oil in skillet. Brown meat well on all sides with moderate heat. Place in a 2½ quart casserole.

Preheat oven to 350 degrees. Add the remaining 2 tablespoons of oil to the skillet and cook onion until tender. Stir in consomme, water, vinegar, horseradish, bay leaf, allspice, and cloves. Pour over meat. Cover and bake 1¾ hours to 2 hours, or until meat is fork tender.

Diana Rhinebeck

Old Salzburger House at Ebenezer, now restored, from an 1830 drawing.

Georgia Salzburger Society

GERMAN STEW

Yield: 4 servings

¼ cup corn oil	⅛ teaspoon pepper
1 pound rump or round beef, cut in 1-inch cubes	1 bay leaf
1½ cups diced onions	1 large carrot, pared and cut in strips
2 beef bouillon cubes	½ cup dry red wine or tomato juice
2 cups boiling water	2 tablespoons cornstarch
¾ teaspoon salt	2 tablespoons water
½ teaspoon crushed thyme leaves	

Heat oil in a large skillet. Add beef and onions. Cook over medium heat, turning as needed, until beef is browned on all sides. Dissolve bouillon cubes in boiling water and pour over meat mixture. Add salt, thyme, pepper, and bay leaf. Cover and simmer 35 minutes. Add carrot. Cover and simmer 35 minutes more, or until meat and vegetables are tender. Pour in wine. Mix cornstarch and water until smooth and gradually stir into stew. Bring to a boil and boil 1 minute, stirring constantly, or until juices are thickened. Serve over hot cooked noodles or mashed potatoes.

DIANE'S WEST AFRICAN BEEF CURRY

Yield: 6 servings

2 pounds lean beef, such as round steak, in 1-inch cubes	2 tablespoons curry powder
¼ cup shortening	1 tablespoon flour
salt and pepper to taste	1 cup water
1 large onion, chopped	1 29-ounce can tomatoes

Season meat with salt and pepper and brown in melted shortening in large skillet. Add chopped onion, pepper to taste, and curry powder. Simmer, covered, 5 minutes.

In a separate skillet, brown flour with a little grease from the meat. Add water. Stir until smooth to make a gravy, add to meat mixture, and then add tomatoes. Simmer until meat is tender. Serve over wild or white rice. Suggested condiments: chopped eggs, tomatoes, roasted peanuts, onions, papaya, and crushed pineapple.

Diane Harvey Johnson

TO BROIL A STEAK

Have steaks about three-quarters or half-of-an-inch thick. Place the grid-iron over a clear fire, and rub the bars with suet to prevent the meat from adhering to them. Place the steaks on it, and broil them, turning them frequently with a fork. Prick the fork through the fat; if the steak itself is pierced, the gravy will run out, and it will harden. Have ready a hot dish, on which you have placed a lump of butter the size of a walnut, a tablespoon of mushroom catsup, and a little salt and pepper. Lay the steaks on the dish and serve as quickly as possible.

Hints From Southern Epicures, *circa 1890*

CARPET BAG STEAK

Yield: 6 servings

    3   24-ounce strip steaks
   24   small oysters
        salt and pepper

Slice steaks horizontally with a very sharp knife to within 1 inch of the fat side. Stuff with raw oysters and season. Secure with wooden picks. Broil 8 minutes on each side. Slice slantwise, and serve with **Maitre D'Hotel Butter.**

Maitre D'Hotel Butter

    ¼ pound (1 stick) butter, melted   2   tablespoons chopped parsley
       over very low heat   salt and pepper
       juice of one lemon (about 2
       tablespoons)

Blend ingredients and serve warm over steak.

Marcel Carles, Columbus, Georgia

BROILED STEAK WITH MUSHROOM-WINE SAUCE

Yield: 6 servings

    2   tablespoons butter or   2   teaspoons flour
        margarine   ¼   teaspoon salt
    ¼   pound fresh mushrooms,   ⅛   teaspoon pepper
        thinly sliced   2   tablespoons tomato paste
    2   tablespoons finely chopped   ½   cup dry red wine
        onion   ¼   cup water
    1   clove garlic, crushed   2   pounds boneless sirloin steak

In saucepan, melt butter or margarine over medium heat. Add mushrooms, onion, and garlic; saute until onion is transparent, stirring frequently. Remove from heat. Stir in flour, salt, pepper, and tomato paste. Blend in wine and water. Bring to a boil, stirring frequently. Cover, reduce heat, and simmer 20 minutes. Meanwhile, broil steak to desired doneness. Serve with wine sauce.

Savannah News-Press

GEORGIAN SHISH KEBAB

The word "shish kebab" is derived from the Turkish words for roast meat on a skewer. Nomadic peoples roasted meat in this way over the campfire; the warriors of another Georgia, in Southern Russia, cooked the meat on their swords. This recipe features a **Peanut Butter Sauce.**

Yield: 6 servings

2 pounds sirloin steak	1 teaspoon salt
1 teaspoon ground caraway	¼ teaspoon freshly ground or
1 teaspoon ground coriander	crushed black pepper
1 teaspoon garlic powder or 1	2 tablespoons soy sauce
clove garlic, crushed	1 tablespoon lemon juice
1 tablespoon brown sugar	

Cut steak into ¾-inch cubes, discarding any visible fat. Marinate cubes in refrigerator in mixture of remaining ingredients for at least an hour. Drain and thread on skewers. Grill over charcoal fire or under broiler, turning several times, for about 10 minutes, or to desired degree of doneness. Serve hot with **Peanut Butter Sauce.**

Peanut Butter Sauce

2 tablespoons instant onion	2 teaspoons crushed hot
flakes	red pepper
1 tablespoon vegetable oil	¼ teaspoon salt
1 cup water	2 tablespoons lemon juice
¼ cup peanut butter	

Brown onion flakes in oil over moderate heat until crisp and golden brown. Do not burn! Drain on a paper towel and set aside. Blend remaining ingredients together and bring to a boil. Lower heat and simmer 5 minutes. Serve over **Georgian Shish Kebab** with onion flakes sprinkled on top.

DINNER GIFTS

Now, it must be remembered that this habit of giving ladies presents at dinners did not originate in New York. Before my day, the wealthy William Gaston, a bachelor, gave superb dinners in Savannah, and there, always placed at each lady's plate a beautiful Spanish fan of such value that they are preserved by the grandchildren of those ladies, and are proudly exhibited to this day.

Ward McAllister, **Society As I Have Found It,** *1890*

BURT'S BEEF STEW

Georgia-born actor Burt Reynolds has been a frequent guest in Savannah in recent years, both acting and directing such films as *Gator.*

Yield: 6 servings

3	slices bacon, cut into small pieces	½	cup fresh mushrooms, quartered
	salt and pepper to taste	1	cup dry California Burgundy
2	pounds lean beef, cut into 1-inch cubes and trimmed of fat	1	bay leaf (optional)
	flour to coat meat		few dashes monosodium glutamate
	vegetable oil (optional)	⅛	teaspoon thyme
1	tablespoon sugar	2	medium carrots, coarsely chopped
1	medium onion, chopped	2	large stalks celery, coarsely chopped
1	clove garlic, crushed or minced	2	large potatoes, quartered
1	6-ounce can tomato sauce		
1	cup beef broth, tomato juice, or water		

Cook bacon in heavy pot. Remove and save the bacon for crumbling in a salad. Salt and pepper beef and dip in flour. Brown in the bacon fat, turning often (add a little oil if needed). Sprinkle with sugar. Add onion and garlic and brown them slightly. Add tomato sauce, water or broth, wine, and seasonings. Cover and simmer gently for about 1½ hours. Add vegetables. Cook until meat and vegetables are tender.

Burt Reynolds

FRANK'S MEAT LOAF

Yield: 6 servings

2 eggs, beaten lightly
½ cup chili sauce
1 1¼-ounce package dry onion
   soup mix
¼ cup Burgundy
⅓ cup water

⅛ teaspoon nutmeg
⅛ teaspoon black pepper
½ cup finely chopped green
   pepper
2 pounds lean ground beef

Mix ingredients and shape into loaf. Bake at 350 degrees for 1½ hours.

Frank Penfold Brown

TONY'S PASTA MEAT PIE

Yield: 8 servings

1¼ pounds lean ground beef
2 eggs, well beaten
¼ cup bread crumbs
½ cup finely grated Romano
   cheese

¼ cup minced parsley
½ teaspoon salt
½ teaspoon pepper

Filling

1 cup Stelline or other small
   pasta
1 cup tomato sauce
1 8-ounce can mushroom stems
   and pieces, drained

½ pound pork sausage, cooked,
   drained of fat, and chopped
   finely
8 ounces shredded Mozzarella
   cheese

Preheat oven to 350 degrees. Mix first 7 ingredients into large meat ball. Oil a 15-inch pizza pan. Place meat ball in center of pan and press flat until meat covers bottom of pan evenly. Boil pasta 10 minutes and drain. Add 2 tablespoons of tomato sauce and mushrooms to pasta, and spread evenly over meat. Pour over rest of sauce to cover surface. Sprinkle sausage over this. Sprinkle Mozzarella evenly over all. Bake 20 minutes. Cut into pie-shaped slices with a pizza slicer.

A. C. (Tony) Mathews, Jr.
Savannah News-Press

SCOTTISH MEAT BALLS

Yield: 4 servings

1	pound lean ground beef	3	tablespoons minced onion
1	egg, slightly beaten	3	tablespoons vegetable oil
3	tablespoons flour	⅓	cup chicken broth
½	teaspoon salt	1	8-ounce can crushed
¼	teaspoon freshly ground black pepper		pineapple, drained

Combine first six ingredients. Gently shape into balls about 1 inch in diameter. (If you have a melon baller, it helps standardize size of balls.) Brown all over in oil in 10-inch frying pan. Remove from pan and drain on paper towels. Drain pan, retaining about 1 tablespoon oil. Add broth and drained pineapple. Simmer for 5 minutes. Meanwhile, make the following **Scottish Sauce.**

Scottish Sauce

1½	tablespoons cornstarch	2	tablespoons water
¼	cup sugar	¼	cup Scotch whisky
3	tablespoons soy sauce	⅓	cup chicken broth
3	tablespoons plain red wine vinegar	½	cup diced green pepper

Combine all ingredients except green pepper and mix until smooth. Stir into skillet with pineapple mixture and cook until sauce has thickened. Add meat balls and green pepper. Cook gently about 10 minutes more. Serve with rice.

You might serve these on December 31 to mark Hogmanay, the Scottish celebration of New Year's Eve.

DeBOLT SPAGHETTI SAUCE

Yield: 4 servings

1	pound lean ground chuck	1	teaspoon Worcestershire sauce
1	medium onion, finely chopped		
¼	cup finely chopped green pepper	1	teaspoon commercial barbecue sauce (optional)
½	cup finely chopped celery	1	teaspoon dried oregano, or to taste
1	garlic clove, finely chopped		
1	tablespoon vegetable oil if needed		dash hot pepper sauce
1	6-ounce can tomato paste	⅓	teaspoon chili powder, or to taste
1	8-ounce can tomato sauce		
1	cup tomato juice	½	pound thin spaghetti, uncooked
1	4½-ounce can mushroom bits and pieces with liquid		grated Parmesan cheese

Brown meat, onion, green pepper, celery, and garlic in a large skillet, using oil if needed. Drain fat. Add all ingredients except cheese and simmer, covered, at least 1 hour. Add more tomato juice if mixture becomes too thick. This sauce may be made ahead of time and reheated. Serve over hot, cooked, drained spaghetti. Top with grated Parmesan cheese. Recipe may be doubled.

Serve with hot, crusty French rolls, a hearty tossed salad, and a chilled fruit cup for dessert. Accompaniment: a light rose wine.

SUMMER SPAGHETTI

Yield: 4 servings

⅓ cup butter
⅓ cup olive oil
3 cloves garlic, minced
1 pound mushrooms, sliced
½ teaspoon salt
¼ teaspoon dried oregano
¼ cup minced parsley

⅓ cup dry red wine
½ pound thin spaghetti, uncooked
grated Parmesan cheese
crushed dried red pepper (optional)

In a 10-inch skillet, over moderate heat, cook the butter, olive oil, and garlic for about 1 minute. Do not brown the garlic. Add mushrooms and cook, turning often, until softened...about 5 minutes. Sprinkle with salt, oregano, and parsley. Pour in wine. Stir well to heat wine; cover and keep warm off heat.

Meanwhile, break spaghetti strands in half and cook according to package directions. Drain well. Add mushroom sauce to cooked thin spaghetti, and toss well. Serve on warmed plates. Accompany with Parmesan and red peppers for those who want to sprinkle this over the top.

CALF'S LIVER WITH WINE SAUCE

Yield: 4 servings

⅓ cup (⅔ stick) butter
½ pound mushrooms, thinly sliced
1¼ pounds thinly sliced calf's liver
⅓ cup dry cooking wine
2 tablespoons lemon juice (about 1 lemon)

¾ teaspoon salt
freshly ground black pepper to taste
¼ teaspoon dried basil, rubbed smooth

In preparing any type of liver, remember to remove membrane from outer edge, and cut out any veins present. Melt about 3 tablespoons of the butter in a 12-inch frying pan. Add the mushrooms and cook gently about 3 minutes. With a slotted spoon, remove mushrooms. Add the remaining butter and heat. Add liver and brown lightly, turning once. Add remaining ingredients. Cover and cook gently for about 5 minutes. Return mushrooms to pan and cook, stirring, until heated.

This is a nice change from liver and onions. Delicious with fluffy rice, buttered green peas, tossed green salad, and fresh fruit for dessert.

PARSLEYED HAM MOLD

Yield: 6 to 8 servings

2 pounds cooked ham	⅓ cup chopped fresh
2 cups well-flavored chicken or veal stock or bouillon	parsley
½ cup dry white wine	2 tablespoons unflavored gelatin
freshly ground black pepper	1 or 2 tablespoons tarragon
nutmeg	vinegar

Dice ham. Simmer gently for 5 minutes in chicken or veal stock and white wine, adding freshly ground pepper and nutmeg to taste. Drain, reserving stock, and place diced ham in a wet glass bowl or mold which has been dusted lightly with a little finely-chopped parsley.

Soften gelatin in a little water, according to directions on the package. Stir into hot stock; add remaining parsley and the vinegar. Allow to cool until syrupy and pour over the diced ham. Cover. Refrigerate for 12 hours before unmolding.

Savannah News-Press

SALT PORK AND APPLES

Fried salt pork and apples is a favorite dish in the country; but it is seldom seen in the city. After the pork is fried, some of the fat should be taken out, lest the apples should be oily. Acid apples should be chosen, because they cook more easily; they should be cut in slices, across the whole apple, about twice or three times as thick as a new dollar. Fried till tender and brown on both sides, laid around the pork. If you have cold potatoes, slice them and brown them in the same way.

The American Frugal Housewife, 1838

EVERYDAY DINNER

Some features of the everyday Southern dinner were pilau; i.e.; boiled chickens on a bed of rice, with a large piece of bacon between the chickens; "Hoppin' John," that is, cowpeas with bacon; okra soup, a staple dish; shrimp and prawn pie; crab salad; pompey head, (a stuffed filet of veal;) roast quail and snipe; and during the winter, shad daily, boiled, broiled, or baked.

Ward McAllister, **Society As I Have Found It,** 1890

HOPPIN' JOHN

There is a tradition in the South that **Hoppin' John**, eaten on New Year's Day, will bring good fortune during the coming year. It is said to have been created during the plantation era by a lame black cook who hopped on one leg while preparing and serving it. Leftovers, if any (and they are good, too), are sometimes jokingly called "Skippin' Jenny."

The creator of this recipe says he learned it from his father's cook. Franklin Dugger has been making it for over twenty years, and has even made it for Savannahians to pack in dry ice and take to New York and England during the holidays, to be ready for the New Year!

In some households, the children get in the spirit of the occasion by hopping once around the table before they sit down to eat.

Yield: 12 servings

1½ cups dried cow peas	½ cup finely chopped green pepper
1 cup finely chopped celery	
1½ cups finely chopped onion	1 cup Uncle Ben's Converted Rice (not the 5-minute variety)
¾ pound finely chopped hog jowl or smoked ham	

Soak peas in water overnight and drain well. Combine peas, celery, onion, meat, and pepper in a stainless steel Dutch oven or heavy kettle. Add enough water to cover and simmer gently, covered, about 2 to 3 hours. Drain and measure 2 cups of the liquid. (If necessary, add water to make this amount.) Pour back into peas. Stir in rice. Cook gently, covered, until rice is done but not mushy. If any liquid is left, it is good in soup. **Hoppin' John** also freezes well. Let thaw in refrigerator and then reheat, rather than trying to cook from a frozen state.

Salt is not used in this recipe because the hog jowl is salty; however, a bit of salt may be added to dish if desired.

Franklin Dugger

DIXIE PORK CHOPS

Yield: 4 servings

8	lean pork chops	⅔	cup water
1	cup ketchup	2	bay leaves
1	teaspoon salt	½	teaspoon Worcestershire sauce
1	teaspoon celery seed		
½	teaspoon nutmeg	¼	cup hickory-flavored barbecue sauce (optional)
⅓	cup vinegar		

Trim all visible fat and brown chops in hot fat. Drain. Place in large baking dish. Preheat oven to 325 degrees. Combine rest of ingredients and pour over chops. Cover and bake 90 minutes.

This is good with rice and **Corn Bread Sticks**. Any left-over chops may be removed from the bone, cut up, and served the next day on buns as pork barbecue. This dish may also be prepared ahead of time, chilled, fat skimmed from top, and then reheated, as it gets even better the longer the sauce cooks.

SAVANNAH'S CHINESE

Savannah's Chinese community began in 1889 with the arrival of a nineteen-year-old revolutionary, Robert Chung Chan. He had been involved in an uprising against the corrupt Manchu Dynasty, and was forced to flee China to save his life. Tradition says that upon arriving in the city, he saw the steeple of Independent Presbyterian Church in flame in the terrible Hogan's fire which destroyed much of the downtown area. He took it as a sign from heaven that he should join that church, which he did! He was later followed by two clansmen from Kwantung Province, Jung Home Kigue and Jung Charles Fore, and all raised families in Savannah. **Famous Fried Rice** is from a descendant of Chan.

FAMOUS FRIED RICE

Yield: 6 to 8 servings

½ cup chopped, tender green onions
cooking oil
3 cups cooked rice
2 eggs
1 16-ounce can bean sprouts

1 8-ounce can water chestnuts, drained
1 teaspoon salt
2 or less tablespoons soy sauce
2 cups minced cooked ham, chicken, shrimp, or pork

Saute the onion in a little oil in a wok. Mix in rice. Pile rice along the sides of wok, forming a little space at the bottom. Beat eggs and scramble them in a little space in a bit of oil. Mix into rice. Add bean sprouts, water chestnuts, salt, soy sauce, and meat. With a pancake turner or other flat spoon, turn all ingredients several times until well mixed. Cover for a few minutes to heat thoroughly. Serve. Many people like to add bell pepper with vegetables and meat.

Actually, **Famous Fried Rice** isn't fried at all! It is only wonderfully seasoned, turned over and over in a wok, and covered for no more time than it takes everything to heat to a delicious temperature.

Gerald Chan Seig

SPICY BROILED LAMB CHOPS

Yield: 4 servings

4 loin lamb chops, about ¾-inch thick
⅓ cup minced onion
1 clove garlic, minced or crushed
⅓ cup creamy peanut butter

2 tablespoons lemon juice
1 tablespoon light brown sugar
1 tablespoon soy sauce
dash hot pepper sauce
⅔ cup tomato juice

Cut excess fat from chops and slash at intervals through remaining fat to prevent curling of meat under broiler. Place in a shallow dish. Mix remaining ingredients together and pour over chops, lifting chops with tongs so that the marinade is under as well as over them. Cover lightly and refrigerate for several hours or overnight. Let come to room temperature. Lift chops from marinade and broil under moderate heat to desired doneness, turning as necessary. Meanwhile, heat marinade and serve as a sauce along with the chops.

SOUFFLE AU FROMAGE

Many Savannahians have enjoyed the "Cooking In The French Manner" classes of Sally Haas, a graduate of the Cordon Bleu cooking school in Paris. Some of her recipes are printed here for the first time.

Yield: 4 to 6 servings

4	tablespoons (½ stick) butter	3	egg yolks, beaten
1	teaspoon flour	½	cup grated Swiss cheese
1	cup milk, scalded	4	egg whites
¼	teaspoon nutmeg or to taste		
	salt and pepper to taste		

Grease souffle dish with a little of the butter. Melt rest of butter, and stir in flour. Add milk and seasonings to taste. Remove from heat and add egg yolks and cheese. Return to stove and stir and cook until very thick. Remove from heat and let stand 30 minutes.

Preheat oven to 450 degrees. Beat egg whites and fold in very gently. Fill dish to brim. Bake 10 to 12 minutes and serve immediately.

Sally Haas

MEXICAN CASSEROLE

Savannah's modern cuisine is enriched by recipes which service families, such as those stationed at Hunter Field and Fort Stewart, have brought back from other locales. The following was first served by an Air Force family when living in the Southwest.

Yield: 4 to 6 servings

1	9-ounce bag corn chips	1	cup finely chopped onion
1	12-ounce package grated Cheddar cheese		salt and pepper to taste
4	4-ounce cans whole roasted mild green chili peppers	1	12-ounce package Montery Jack cheese, grated
1	16-ounce can tomatoes, drained, or 2 cups fresh tomatoes		

Preheat oven to 350 degrees. Spray a large baking pan with a non-stick treatment. (My pan is 18-by-12-by-2-inches.) Crush corn chips and line bottom of pan with the crumbs. Over this, spread the grated Cheddar cheese. Split open the whole roasted chili peppers and rinse well under running water, removing seeds. Drain a minute. Place peppers over a layer of cheese. Now, place the drained tomatoes, chopped into coarse pieces, over the peppers. Place chopped onion in the next layer over the

113

tomatoes. Sprinkle lightly with salt and pepper. (Remember there is salt in the chips.) Sprinkle grated Monterey Jack over this and bake until hot and bubbly, about 25 to 30 minutes. Serve hot.

With this, we like a lettuce and avocado salad sprinkled with lemon juice, and a simple dessert—a plate of small pecan pralines and coffee.

Marilyn Whelpley

WAYNESBORO MACARONI AND CHEESE

This recipe is adapted from an old plantation recipe, and makes more of a custard sauce than the usual macaroni casserole.

Yield: 4 to 6 servings

1¾ cups milk	3 eggs, beaten
1 cup grated Cheddar cheese	1 cup ground or minced lean cooked ham
¼ teaspoon salt	
¼ teaspoon paprika	1 cup elbow macaroni, cooked and drained
1 teaspoon grated onion	
⅛ teaspoon hot pepper sauce	

Preheat oven to 350 degrees. Scald milk in two-quart casserole. Remove from heat. Add cheese and let melt very slowly over low heat. Stir in seasonings. Beat cheese mixture slowly into the eggs, which you have beaten in a separate bowl. Stir in ham and cooked macaroni. Pour back into first casserole. Bake for about 35 minutes, or until the mixture is set. Cover to keep warm until served if not served immediately.

Saphronia Dukes Vaughn

WELSH RAREBIT

The First Family of the Confederacy visited Savannah several times. Here is Varina Davis' recipe for **Welsh Rarebit**, reprinted from *House-Keeping In The Sunny South*, published in Atlanta in 1885.

One-half pound of fat, crumbly cheese; one ounce of prime butter; one gill [4 ounces] of milk, or if preferred, of old ale. Cut the cheese into small pieces, and melt over the fire in a shallow pan. Stir constantly, until the cheese is entirely amalgamated; pour over thick toast, slightly moistened with boiled milk; garnish with two poached eggs, celery tops and parsley.

BONAVENTURE BARBECUE SAUCE

The South has always been famous for its long-simmered barbecued meats. This updated version of an old recipe is good with chicken, pork, or beef, and gets better during the cooking process.

Yield: 3½ cups

2 cups water	¼ cup vinegar
1 cup ketchup	1 teaspoon chili powder
¼ cup Worcestershire sauce	1 teaspoon celery seed
¼ cup brown sugar, firmly packed	1 teaspoon salt
	few drops hot pepper sauce

Combine all ingredients in a pan and bring to a boil.

Savannah News-Press.

KEHOE MEAT SAUCE

Whip one pint of heavy cream until it stands in good peaks. (Take care not to overbeat; you will get butter particles.) Stir in prepared horseradish and tart applesauce to taste. Elegant with smoked turkey, ham, roast pork, or other meats! A very old recipe.

Helen Kehoe Crolly

HORSERADISH SAUCE

Yield: 1¼ cups

1 cup commercial sour cream	½ teaspoon prepared mustard
1 tablespoon instant minced onion	½ teaspoon salt
2 tablespoons prepared horseradish	⅛ teaspoon white pepper
	1 tablespoon chopped parsley

Combine and serve with roast beef.

Savannah News-Press

MUSTARD SAUCE

Stir made [prepared] mustard into melted butter in the proportion of two tablespoonsful of mustard to one-half cup of the latter. This is a useful sauce for boiled tripe, herrings, and hot lobsters.

House-Keeping In The Sunny South, 1885

EMMA'S HOT MUSTARD

Yield: 1 cup

1 egg
⅓ cup dry mustard
1 teaspoon salt
½ teaspoon powdered
    horseradish

3 tablespoons cider vinegar or
    white wine
¼ cup heavy cream
¼ cup milk
1 tablespoon butter

Beat egg in top of double boiler. Add mustard, salt, and horseradish, stirring away any lumps. Stir in vinegar or wine, cream, and milk. Drop in butter. Cook over hot water, stirring constantly, until mixture has thickened and coats a metal spoon. Remove from heat. Cool, stirring occasionally. Refrigerate, covered, until needed. (Blender version: dump all ingredients into blender and mix. Pour into top of double boiler over hot water, then cool as directed above.)

MUSHROOM PAN GRAVY

Yield: 1½ cups

½ cup fresh or canned sliced
    mushrooms
2 tablespoons melted butter or
    margarine
2 tablespoons flour

1 cup beef bouillon
    salt and pepper to taste
    dash Worcestershire sauce
    dash nutmeg (optional)

Drain the mushrooms; reserve the liquid. Saute mushrooms in butter for 5 minutes. Stir in flour. Gradually add the mushroom liquid and bouillon. Cook slowly until thickened and smooth. Season as desired. Serve with hamburger, meat loaf, steak, or pasta.

Savannah News-Press

SWEET AND SOUR SAUCE

Yield: 1¼ cups

1 6-ounce can tomato paste
⅔ cup water
2 tablespoons vinegar
2 tablespoons brown sugar

1 teaspoon minced onion
½ teaspoon garlic powder
1 teaspoon Worcestershire
    sauce

Combine ingredients and simmer. Serve with meat as desired.

TOMATO SAUCE

1 quart tomatoes, small slice of onion, 8 cloves, 2 tablespoons butter, 2 tablespoons flour, salt, and pepper. Cook the tomato, onion and cloves 10 minutes, and strain. Heat butter in a frying pan, and add the flour. Stir over fire until smooth and brown, and then stir in the tomatoes. Cook 2 minutes. Season to taste. This sauce is nice with fish, meat, or macaroni.

Favorite Recipes From Savannah Homes, *1904*

SAVANNAH IN THE THIRTIES

One thing I do remember, around 1930 perhaps, was a particular and loved smell of those days, a kind of acquired love, as some have for the marshes. . . . It was partly the smell of humus when the oaks had shed and were beginning to become something more tangible, coupled with the smell of the river, and that particular essence of Rourke's and Kehoe's Iron Works giving off a special ingredient, as curry does to certain foods.

The main meal of the day was soon after 2 p.m., and we children rushed home from school for that meal. My grandfather and one of my uncles always put on their alpaca jackets for this meal, and took a short rest afterwards before returning to their offices. It was a more leisured time, that has gone, now, with a few hurricanes, a time out of mind. . . .

Jack Crolly, Savannah, Georgia

THE PIRATES' HOUSE

Legend has it that this historic frame house by the site of Trustees' Garden and Revolutionary Fort Wayne was once a seamen's tavern. It is said that unfortunate revelers sometimes awoke to find themselves shanghaied for China. Here Captain Flint of Treasure Island fame is supposed to have expired calling, "Darby, bring 'aft the rum!" inspiring the famous novel. Allegedly haunted at night by Flint's restless ghost, the Pirates' House is now a famous restaurant. Perhaps the mysterious "Country Captain" of the spice trade once dined there also!

Drawing by Charley Bland,
Copyright© 1975 by Charley Bland

POULTRY

COUNTRY CAPTAIN

It is said that this famous dish originated when a mysterious old sea captain drifted into Savannah with the spice trade and entrusted his favorite recipe to a friend in repayment for hospitality.

Yield: 4 servings

2½ pound chicken (approximately)	1 clove garlic, minced or crushed
¼ cup flour	1½ teaspoons curry powder
1 teaspoon salt	½ teaspoon dried thyme
¼ teaspoon pepper	1 16-ounce can tomatoes
4 to 5 tablespoons butter	3 tablespoons dried currants
⅓ cup chopped onion	blanched, toasted almonds
⅓ cup chopped green pepper	chutney

Cut chicken into serving pieces. Mix together flour, salt, and pepper, and coat chicken well. Heat butter in large, heavy skillet until very hot but not brown. Add chicken and brown well on all sides. If all fat is absorbed before chicken is browned, add more butter.

Remove chicken and set aside. Add onion, green pepper, garlic, curry powder, and thyme to skillet and cook over low heat a few minutes, stirring in all the brown particles. Then, add the tomatoes. Put the chicken, skin side up, back into the skillet. Cover; cook slowly for 20 to 30 minutes, or until tender when pierced with a fork. Last of all, stir in the currants, heat, and serve with blanched, toasted almonds and chutney on the side.

REAL CHICKEN PIE

No Southern recipe is more beloved than chicken pie. Rhett Butler and Scarlett O'Hara feasted on pie and champagne on their wedding night. General Robert E. Lee was served it at Appomattox. However, the real recipe, chicken and gravy in a rich pastry, has little in common with some of the "chicken stew in a crust" with potatoes and even English peas, served in other parts of the country and even distributed in frozen form.

The following authentic recipe is from Kathryn Tucker Windham, author of *Treasured Georgia Recipes* and other cookbooks as well as several collections of ghost stories, such as *13 Georgia Ghosts* and *Jeffrey*. It's what you'd expect from an author of Southern folklore and history.

Yield: 4 servings

1	hen, 4 to 5 pounds (save giblets for other use)	¼	teaspoon freshly ground pepper
2	ribs celery	2	cups chicken broth
2	sprigs parsley	1	cup milk
¼	cup sliced onion		pastry to line and cover an
6	tablespoons melted chicken fat		8-by-8-by-2 inch glass baking dish (2-quart
6	tablespoons flour		capacity)
½	teaspoon salt		

Disjoint hen and simmer in enough lightly salted water to cover, with celery, parsley, and onion. When drumsticks are tender, remove chicken from broth, discard vegetables, strain broth, and pour back over chicken. Cool, cover, and refrigerate overnight.

Next day, remove layer of fat and measure 6 tablespoons. Place in a 10-inch frying pan and set aside. Bone chicken, discard skin, and cut into large pieces. There should be about 2½ cups. Set aside.

Preheat oven to 425 degrees. Melt chicken fat over moderate heat, sprinkle with flour, and stir until smooth and slightly brown. Sprinkle with salt and pepper. Gradually stir in broth and milk; stir and cook over moderate heat until thickened. Stir in chicken pieces. Remove from heat. Prepare pastry. Line bottom and sides of baking dish with about two-thirds of the pastry, thinly rolled. Gently pour in chicken mixture. Cover with remaining pastry. Pinch edges firmly together. Turn edge upright and pinch into a border. Cut top crust through in several places, making a nice design, to allow escape of steam. Bake for about 35 minutes, or until crust is golden brown.

Leftover broth can be frozen for later use in soups or gravies. Leftover fat may be used for sauteeing chicken for braising, and such. Nice "Go Withs": thick slices of ripe tomatoes, dribbled with melted butter and a bit of curry; mixed green salad with your favorite oil and vinegar dressing; and a fresh fruit dessert.

Kathryn Tucker Windham, Selma, Alabama

SOUTHERN FRIED CHICKEN AND GRAVY

Prepare the chicken as for boiling, and after having salted it, keep in a cool place. When ready to cook, cut up with a very sharp knife, and dry the pieces on a soft towel. Then roll them in flour, and place in boiling lard (placing chickens in cold lard, or slightly warm, is the cause of their being greasy or sodden). Do not cook too fast. You can never make good gravy if the lard is burnt at the bottom of the skillet!

After removing the chicken, add to the gravy a half-cupful of water and the same of milk mixed with a teaspoonful of flour stirred in; or some prefer to add the flour to the gravy and when it looks smooth, to add the milk and the water. (You can use milk alone to make the gravy.) The gravy will generally require more salt. Do not pour it over the chicken, but take it to the table in a gravy boat or small bowl.

Mrs. William Barnes,
House-Keeping In The Sunny South, *1885*

RICH CHICKEN GRAVY

When frying chicken, save what is left of the batter in which the chicken was dipped before frying, to make your rich chicken gravy.

Favorite Recipes From Savannah Homes, *1904*

SOUTHERN BUTTERMILK CHICKEN

Buttermilk has been a staple of Southern cooking since the days when it was difficult to keep milk fresh in warm weather, and many recipes were developed using sour milk. This is an adaptation of an old specialty.

Yield: 4 servings

⅔ cup commercial buttermilk	1 cup sifted flour
½ teaspoon hot pepper sauce	1 2½-pound broiler-fryer, cut up
1 teaspoon salt, or to taste	vegetable oil

121

Combine buttermilk, hot pepper sauce, and salt in a shallow dish. Roll chicken pieces in the mixture. Drain a bit and roll in flour until coated. Let stand on a rack until flour "sets." Heat ½-inch oil in a 12-inch frying pan and brown chicken on all sides. Cover pan and lower heat. Cook until chicken is tender, about 30 to 40 minutes.

PICNIC LOAVES

For an unusual and compact patio or picnic dinner, purchase or bake as many small, crusty French loaves as there are guests. Slice the top third off each loaf, and scoop out the center (save crumbs for bread crumbs, etc.). Butter, and heat in a moderate oven. Fill each loaf with 2 or 3 pieces of hot, crispy, fried chicken. Garnish with small green onions, cherry tomatoes, cucumber slices, carrots and celery, and other finger foods, as well as potato chips or corn chips if desired. Wrap each loaf in aluminum foil. Serve in small wicker baskets with a napkin in the bottom; offer with a chilled drink and a large plate of home-made cookies or fresh melon for dessert.

This may also be done with fried oysters, garnished with lemon slices and dill pickles. This recipe is said to have originated in the Vieux Carre, or French Quarter, of New Orleans.

Adapted from a World War II recipe
in **Mrs. Rasmussen's Book of One-Arm Cookery**
by Mary Lasswell

BARBECUE & BREW CHICKEN

Yield: 4 servings

1	broiler-fryer (about 3 pounds)	½	teaspoon salt
1	12-ounce can beer	1	teaspoon caraway seed
½	cup light brown sugar	2	tablespoons lemon juice
1	teaspoon dry mustard	½	cup ketchup
½	teaspoon onion salt		

Disjoint chicken and place in deep bowl reserving giblets for other use. Mix remaining ingredients and pour over chicken. Cover and marinate in refrigerator overnight.

Preheat oven to 350 degrees. Place chicken on heavy foil. Bring up sides, and brush pieces well with marinade. Close foil tightly and bake on shallow pan for 40 minutes. Open foil and allow chicken to brown for about 20 or 25 minutes, brushing with rest of marinade.

HOW TO CARVE

Carving is really an art, and should be cultivated as one, for much of the success of a good dinner depends upon it. . . . Practice has much to do with it, and a good knife much more. The carving knife should be very sharp, and kept for this use alone. . . . The dish upon which the meat or fowl is served should be of sufficient size to allow room for the carved slices before serving. If this is not the case, another dish should be provided. . . .

Gravies or sauces should be sent to the table very hot. Plates should also be thoroughly heated, as otherwise the eatables will soon get cold, and dinner will be spoiled. When serving gravies, be careful to place it by the side of, and not over, the meat. Then the guest can use as much, or little, as preferred. . . .

In serving any fowl or meat that is accompanied by stuffing or dressing, guests should be asked if a portion is desired, as there are some to whom the flavor is disagreeable. Do not heap plates too full, and keep each article separate, thus insuring a good appearance.

Breakfast, Dinner, and Supper;
Or, What To Eat and How To Prepare It
by Maude C. Cooke, 1897

TAYLOR STREET CHICKEN IN BOURBON SAUCE

Yield: 4 servings

1	broiler-fryer (about 3 pounds), cut up	1	teaspoon ground mustard
3	or less tablespoons vegetable oil	1	teaspoon instant or 1 cube chicken bouillon
3	tablespoons minced onion	½	cup water
2	tablespoons white vinegar	½	cup bourbon whisky
3	tablespoons light brown sugar	½	cup minced celery
	juice of one lemon (about two tablespoons)		freshly ground pepper to taste
¾	cup chili sauce	⅛	teaspoon chili powder
3	tablespoons Worcestershire sauce	1	teaspoon well-rubbed dry tarragon

Discard wing tips and giblets and save for other use. Skin chicken if desired. Brown chicken pieces in oil over moderate heat. Remove chicken; drain grease, if any. Saute onion lightly in same pan. Add remaining ingredients and mix well. Put chicken back into sauce in pan. Cover and simmer over low heat until tender, about 45 minutes. Taste; add salt if needed. Serve with saffron rice.

COFFEE-BARBECUED CHICKEN

Yield: 4 servings

1 cup extra strong black coffee	2 teaspoons salt
1 cup ketchup	1 teaspoon cayenne
1½ cups Worcestershire sauce, or to taste	pepper, or to taste (be careful!)
¼ pound (1 stick) butter	1 2- to 3-pound broiler-fryer, cut up
¼ cup lemon juice	
2 tablespoons brown sugar	2 tablespoons butter

Combine in a saucepan all ingredients except chicken and butter. Simmer for 30 minutes. Broil chicken, turning often and basting with butter for 8 minutes. Then continue broiling, turning and basting with sauce for 15 to 20 minutes, or until done.

Savannah News-Press

GEORGIA CHICKEN CASSEROLE

Yield: 4 servings

½ cup flour	2 tablespoons flour
1 teaspoon salt	¾ cup dry white wine
¼ teaspoon pepper	1 teaspoon lemon juice
1 frying chicken (2½- to 3-pounds), cut up	8 medium stuffed olives, sliced
3 tablespoons olive oil	1 tablespoon minced parsley
2 tablespoons butter	salt and pepper to taste
½ pound fresh mushrooms, sliced, or 3-ounce can, drained	

Preheat oven to 375 degrees. Mix ½ cup flour, salt, and pepper together. Dip pieces of chicken into this, coating well. Heat oil in large skillet over moderate heat. Add coated chicken and brown on all sides. Remove to 1½-quart casserole. Add butter to skillet. Add mushrooms and saute over moderate heat for about 10 minutes. Blend 2 tablespoons flour into wine until free of lumps. Stir in lemon juice. Pour wine-flour mixture into mushrooms and cook, stirring constantly, until sauce is thickened and satiny. Stir in olives and parsley. Add more salt and pepper if desired. Pour sauce over chicken pieces in casserole; cover and bake for 40 minutes.

Chicken may be prepared for casserole ahead of time, refrigerated, and heated just before serving, allowing an extra 10 minutes cooking time. Serve with rice or noodles; green noodle are especially colorful.

EMMA LAW'S COCA-COLA CHICKEN

Coca-Cola, a Georgia drink, was first originated in Atlanta in 1886 by a druggist, Dr. John Styth Pemberton. He later sold his rights to the product for $1,750. Dr. Pemberton is buried in Columbus, Georgia, where he once worked as a pharmacist.

Yield: 4 servings

1	chicken (2½- to 3-pounds), cut up	¾	cup Coca-Cola
	vegetable oil	¾	cup ketchup
2	tablespoons finely minced onions or scallions	1	tablespoon Dijon-type mustard
			minced parsley to taste

Brown chicken in 10-inch skillet and remove from pan. Pour off excess oil. Add onion and cook gently until limp, but not brown. Mix remaining ingredients; stir well in pan, scraping up all sticking particles. Return chicken to the sauce. Cover and simmer gently until tender, about 35 to 45 minutes.

This chicken is even better if prepared the day before and reheated gently before serving. Store covered in the refrigerator in a stainless steel, enamel, or plastic container. The sauce is also good with other meats!

YOGURT-MARINATED CHICKEN

Yield: 4 servings

2	tablespoons lemon juice	¼	teaspoon freshly ground pepper
2	whole chicken breasts, about 12 ounces each, halved and boned, skinned if desired	1	tablespoon chopped fresh mint or 1 teaspoon dried mint, crumbled
2	cloves garlic, crushed		
1	teaspoon salt	1	cup plain yogurt

Sprinkle lemon juice over chicken in a glass or ceramic baking dish. Let stand for 10 minutes, turning once. Chop garlic with salt, then crush to a paste. Combine with pepper, mint, and yogurt in a small bowl, mixing well. Spread mixture over chicken, spooning any excess lemon juice over chicken as well. Allow to marinate for one hour at room temperature.

Arrange chicken on rack of broiler pan about 7 inches from heat. Broil 8 to 10 minutes on each side. Any leftover marinade can be heated in a small saucepan and served with the chicken. Only 241 calories per serving.

125

This is a nice change from heavy barbecue marinades. The lemon juice and yogurt have a tenderizing effect on the meat. The marinade also makes a wonderful cold sauce for chilled sliced meats or vegetables, such as cucumbers, tomatoes, or celery.

Savannah News-Press

PEANUTTY CHICKEN

Yield: 6 servings

6 chicken thighs, skinned	5 or 6 turns of the pepper mill or
3 chicken breasts, boned,	¼ teaspoon ground pepper
skinned, and halved	2½ cups chicken broth
¼ cup lemon juice	⅓ cup crunchy peanut butter
¼ cup vegetable oil	minced scallions, as desired
1 teaspoon salt, or to taste	minced parsley, as desired

Sprinkle chicken with lemon juice. Cover and let stand one hour. Heat oil in 12-inch frying pan. Saute chicken, half at a time, until golden brown. Remove from pan and sprinkle with salt and pepper. Drain pan of oil and stir in broth and peanut butter. Bring to a boil and add chicken. Cover and simmer gently about 35 to 40 minutes, or until tender. Serve with rice. Sprinkle all with scallions and parsley.

It is always more economical to buy and cut up as many chickens as you need, saving pieces not called for in a specific recipe to be cooked in other ways, rather than buying packages of specific parts.

CHICKEN BREASTS ROSE

Yield: 6 servings

¾ cup rose wine	1 teaspoon ginger
¼ cup soy sauce	¼ teaspoon oregano
¼ cup vegetable oil	1 tablespoon light brown sugar
2 tablespoons water	3 chicken breasts, skinned and
1 clove garlic, minced or	halved
crushed	

Preheat oven to 350 degrees. Combine all ingredients but chicken. Arrange chicken breasts in buttered baking dish. Pour wine mixture over them. Cover and bake 45 minutes to one hour, testing chicken for doneness with fork before removing from oven. Serve over rice or buttered noodles.

ESCALLOPED CHICKEN

Wonderful for covered dish dinners!

Yield: 8 servings

1	large chicken (about 3½ pounds) cooked and boned	1½	teaspoons salt, or to taste
			black pepper to taste
2	cups cooked white rice	1	teaspoon poultry seasoning
2	cups fresh bread crumbs	5	cups chicken broth
1	2-ounce jar chopped pimientos	4	hard-cooked eggs, chopped
		½	cup chopped almonds

Preheat oven to 325 degrees. Cut chicken into bite-sized pieces. Mix with other ingredients. Place in large, buttered pan or casserole. Bake for 1 hour. If desired, accompany with **Easy Mushroom Sauce.**

Mrs. Lehman Lanier, Alma, Georgia
Savannah News-Press

EASY MUSHROOM SAUCE

Yield: almost 2 cups

1	10¾-ounce can cream of mushroom soup	½	soup can milk or dry white wine

Combine and heat to steaming but do not boil. Serve hot.

Shrimp Sauce

Substitute a can of condensed cream of shrimp soup; add wine and a sprinkling of dried dill weed.

Tomato Sauce

Use tomato soup and cream or wine, with a dash of Worcestershire sauce.

Celery Cream Sauce

Use cream of celery soup for a bland sauce which goes well with many dishes.

GOLD COAST CHICKEN LIVERS

Yield: 4 servings

6	slices bacon	½	cup sifted flour
1	pound chicken livers	½	cup dry white wine
½	teaspoon salt		finely chopped parsley
⅛	teaspoon pepper		

Fry bacon crisp; drain on paper towels. Measure drippings, returning ¼ cup to the skillet. Dredge chicken livers in seasoned flour and brown lightly in hot bacon fat. Turn heat low, add wine. Cover and steam 5 minutes, or until livers are cooked. Crumble bacon and sprinkle with parsley over livers. Serve on crisp toast or over hot rice or noodles.

Savannah News-Press

CLASSIC HUNTERS SAUCE FOR WILD DUCK
(Or Any Fowl)

Yield: 1 cup

½ cup red currant jelly
¼ cup port wine
¼ cup ketchup
½ teaspoon Worcestershire
sauce

2 tablespoons butter or
margarine

Combine and melt over low heat. Serve warm.

Savannah News-Press

STUFFING HINT

Savory stuffing for roast turkey or chicken is even better when moistened with a dry white dinner wine, such as Rhine, chablis, or sauterne. Follow directions on the stuffing mix package, substituting wine for water. Serve the same wine with the meal. For another variation, add a few chopped, drained, canned Chinese water chestnuts, or a few dried black Chinese mushrooms, rehydrated in dry white wine.

DRESSING REHEARSAL

When making dressing for your holiday turkey, make about three times as much as you need. Freeze the unused dressing in divided portions. Pop it out as you need it to serve with fowl. It's a real time saver, and your family will love it.

*Marceline A. Newton, **New Life Cookbook***

CHICKEN-PLUCKIN' CAPERS

In 1927 a man named Ray Capers started to work for Johnny Harris' Restaurant, which was then located at the corner of Bee Road and Victory Drive in Savannah. His fame in processing chickens for the restaurant grew until he was featured in the popular column, "Believe It Or Not," as the world's champion chicken plucker... *cleaning 1,700 chickens in eight hours!*

TO STUFF A GOOSE

Two ounces onion, 1 ounce green sage; chop very fine, and add 4 ounces stale bread crumbs, a bit of butter about as big as a walnut, and very little pepper and salt. Some cooks add half the liver, chopped, parboiling it first, and the yolk of an egg or two. Incorporating the whole together, stuff the goose, but do not quite fill it. Leave a little room for the stuffing to swell. Send up gravy and apple sauce with it when it is roasted.

The Guide to Service, 1842

FIRST THANKSGIVING

The first Thanksgiving celebration of the thirteenth colony was held in Beaufort, South Carolina, on January 28, 1733, as the English settlers gave thanks for their voyage across the Atlantic to the new country. Two weeks later, they were in Savannah after their brief stop in South Carolina.

Part of the historic Tybee Lighthouse dates back to 1733, though it has been damaged several times by storms and warfare, and then rebuilt.

Drawing by Pamela Lee

SEAFOOD

SAVANNAH DEVILED CRABS

Prepare the crabs, then add a tablespoonful of butter, salt, pepper, a little vinegar, mustard, and two well-beaten eggs. Place in backs (shells) and sprinkle lightly with cracker crumbs. Bake lightly.

Hints From Southern Epicures, *circa 1890*

SAVANNAH'S ITALIAN HERITAGE

When the good ship *Ann* left England for the new colony which was to become Georgia in 1732, one of the skilled artisans aboard was Paul Amatis, an Italian proficient in the making of silk. He represented England's hope for a flourishing silk industry in the New World. Amatis was placed in charge of Savannah's famous Trustee's Garden, where he cultivated white mulberry tree seedlings he had earlier started in Charleston. Other Italian families, such as the Camusis, were also involved in the making of silk. One was responsible for the erection of a public filature, or silk house, in Reynold's Square. Silk was later replaced by cotton in the colonial economy. Many of Savannah's modern Italian families are involved with the seafood industry. They are also noted for their expert cuisine, as they serve local products with an Italian touch.

INDIVIDUAL DEVILED CRAB CASSEROLES

Yield: 4 servings

1½ cups fresh bread crumbs
¼ teaspoon salt
⅛ teaspoon pepper
1 teaspoon dry mustard
½ cup butter or margarine
½ cup minced celery
½ cup minced green pepper
⅛ teaspoon hot pepper sauce
⅛ teaspoon Worcestershire sauce
1 tablespoon cider vinegar
2 tablespoons lemon juice
2 6½-ounce cans flaked crab meat
2 eggs, lightly beaten

Preheat oven to 400 degrees. Mix crumbs with salt, pepper, and mustard and set aside. Melt butter over moderate heat. Add celery and green pepper. Saute until slightly tender but not brown. Remove from heat. Stir in hot pepper and Worcestershire sauces, vinegar, lemon juice, and crumb mixture. Blend in crab meat and eggs. Place in four lightly buttered 8-ounce shallow baking dishes or shells. Bake for 17 minutes or until brown. This recipe was inspired by the Pirates' House Deviled Crab.

IMPERIAL CRAB PARMESAN

Yield: 4 servings

4 tablespoons (½ stick) butter, at room temperature
1 egg
2 tablespoons mayonnaise
2 tablespoons Worcestershire sauce
½ teaspoon salt
¼ teaspoon white pepper
¼ cup finely chopped green pepper
¼ cup finely chopped pimiento
2 tablespoons capers
¼ teaspoon hot pepper sauce
1 pound fresh lump crab meat
Parmesan cheese

Preheat oven to 375 degrees. Brush four 8-ounce casserole dishes with butter. In a deep bowl, beat egg lightly. Add all other ingredients except crab meat and cheese. Mix well. Add the crab and mix gently but well. Spoon mixture into casseroles evenly and mound centers. Sprinkle each lightly with cheese. Bake for 10 minutes until hot clear through. If desired, brown under broiler until top is crisp. Be careful not to burn.

David Schneider, Jekyll Island, Georgia
Savannah News-Press

CRAB-STUFFED POTATOES

Yield: 6 servings

6	medium Idaho baking potatoes (about 4 inches long)	1	teaspoon salt
1	8-ounce can crab meat	½	teaspoon cayenne pepper
¼	pound (1 stick) butter	5	teaspoons grated onion
½	cup light cream	1	cup grated sharp cheese
		½	teaspoon paprika

Bake potatoes in 350 degree oven about 1 hour, or until done. Turn oven up to 450 degrees. Drain and pick over crab meat. Cut potatoes in half lengthwise. Scoop out inside and whip in a bowl along with the butter, cream, salt, cayenne, onion, and cheese, using an electric mixer if you have one. Mix in crab meat with a fork and refill potato shells. Sprinkle each with paprika. Reheat in oven about 15 minutes. These potatoes may be frozen, in which case reheat them in a preheated 450 degree oven for 30 minutes.

Betty W. (Mrs. John J.) Rauers

CLASSIC CRAB NEWBURG

The following recipe is from the Blue Channel Company of Port Royal, South Carolina, founded in 1938 and pioneers in the successful canning of the meat of the Atlantic blue crab. It is the largest processor-canner of crab meat in the United States, annually processing twelve million pounds of the crustacean.

Yield: 4 servings

4	tablespoons (½ stick) butter		dash white pepper
2	egg yolks	2	6½-ounce cans white crab meat
½	cup heavy cream		
3	tablespoons sherry (optional)		optional seasonings (see below)
¼	teaspoon salt		

Melt butter over low heat. Beat egg yolks into cream, and then stir into butter. Add sherry if desired. Cook over low heat, stirring constantly, until mixture thickens.

Take from heat. Stir in salt, pepper, and crab meat. Other seasonings are optional, such as cayenne pepper, nutmeg, Angostura bitters, or a few drops of Worcestershire sauce. Reheat for a minute or two over low heat. Serve on hot buttered toast triangles.

Blue Channel Company

TO BAKE A SHAD

Take a large shad, clean it. Then take the crumbs of stale bread, some onions and parsley (chopped), pepper, and salt. With this seasoning, stuff the fish; put it into a baking pan, season with pepper and salt, and sprinkle bread crumbs over the fish. Put small lumps of butter all over the fish, pour in water to a depth of two inches, sprinkle over it a little flour, put the pan into a well-heated oven, and bake an hour and a half. While baking, it must be occasionally basted with the gravy, that it may not become too dry. Any large fish may be dressed in the same manner.

House and Home; or, The Carolina Housewife
by A Lady of Charleston, 1855

BARBECUED FISH WITH SOY SAUCE

In the Low Country, fish is still served as it was in Colonial times, with "1 whole fish" including the head....

Yield: 4 to 6 servings

1	whole white fish (red snapper, trout, bass, etc.) about 2½ pounds, dressed and drawn	2	tablespoons lemon juice
		1	tablespoon crushed hot red pepper
¼	pound (1 stick) butter, melted	½	teaspoon salt
		¼	teaspoon freshly ground black pepper
2	tablespoons soy sauce		

Preheat oven to 350 degrees. Wash cleaned fish and pat dry with paper towels. Make several diagonal slashes on each side, and place in an ovenproof dish. Mix remaining ingredients and pour over fish. Bake uncovered about 30 minutes, basting several times, or until fish is done and flakes easily with a fork. Serve with hot fluffy rice.

WILMINGTON ISLAND BAKED FISH

Yield: 6 to 8 servings

1	dressed and drawn whole bass, 3½ to 4 pounds	1	cup cubed fresh tomatoes
½	cup flour	¾	cup finely chopped onion
¼	cup half-and-half or canned milk, more if desired	⅓	cup melted butter
			salt and freshly ground pepper, to taste
¼	pound (1 stick) butter, melted	½	cup chopped celery, including leaves
4	cups bread crumbs	1½	cups milk
½	cup cubed cucumber		

Prepare fish. Make sure it is very dry, so the coating will stick. Mix a coating of the flour, half-and-half, and butter, and stir until creamy. Set aside. Preheat oven to 400 degrees. Make a stuffing of the bread crumbs, cucumber, tomatoes, onion, butter, and celery. Salt and pepper inside of fish well, and stuff with crumb mixture. Wipe fish again, and cover both sides with the coating mixture.

Place in a large, uncovered roaster, and pour milk around fish. Bake about 45 minutes, or according to the size of fish, basting it every 15 minutes with the milk in the pan. Remove when it's a light brown. Place on a warm platter; cut in 2-inch slices.

We like hot French bread, wrapped in foil and warmed in the oven, along with the fish, and a tossed salad.

Pat Donaldson

GROUPER PARMESAN

Yield: 6 servings

2	pounds grouper fillets	1	tablespoon grated onion
	butter	½	teaspoon salt
1	cup commercial sour cream		dash hot pepper sauce
¼	cup grated Parmesan cheese		paprika to taste
1	tablespoon lemon juice		chopped parsley

Preheat oven to 350 degrees. Skin fillets and cut into serving-sized portions. Place in a single layer in a well-buttered baking dish. Combine remaining ingredients except for paprika and parsley. Spread sour cream mixture over fish. Sprinkle with paprika. Bake for 25 to 30 minutes, or until fish flakes easily with fork. Garnish with parsley.

Dr. Frank Johnston
Savannah News-Press

MULLET IN CORAL SAUCE

Yield: 6 servings

2	pounds mullet fillets	1	teaspoon grated onion
4	tablespoons (½ stick) butter or margarine, melted	1	teaspoon paprika
		1	teaspoon salt
2	tablespoons lemon juice		dash pepper

Preheat oven to 350 degrees. If using frozen fillets, thaw. Place in a single layer, skin side down, in a well-oiled baking dish, 12-by-8-by-2-inches. Combine remaining ingredients and mix well. Pour sauce over fillets. Bake for 20 to 25 minutes, or until fillets flake easily.

Savannah News-Press

FARGO FILLETS

Soak fillets in salted milk (½ teaspoon salt to ½ cup milk for each pound of fish). Then, dip the fish in flour. Pan-fry quickly in a generous amount (about ¼ inch) of hot, but not smoking, butter or oil, or half butter and half oil.

Savannah News-Press

GORDONSTON FILLETS

Place fish fillets in a greased broiler pan. Spread top of each with mayonnaise. Broil until lightly browned. No further seasoning necessary: mayonnaise seasons the fish. If fillets are thin, they may be broiled on only one side. Thicker fillets should be turned and also spread with mayonnaise, and cooked until fish flakes when tested with tines of a fork.

Alice (Mrs. Clyde) Blank

EMMA'S LOBSTER QUICHE

Yield: 6 to 12 servings

1	9-ounce package South African lobster tails	3	egg yolks
1	uncooked 9-inch pastry shell	2	eggs
9	ounces cream cheese, at room temperature	½	teaspoon salt
¾	cup heavy cream	⅛	teaspoon white pepper
		1	tablespoon grated onion
		½	teaspoon dried dill weed

Parboil lobster by dropping into boiling salted water. When water re-boils, remove from heat, drain, and cover with cold water to cool quickly. Remove shell and membrane from lobster and cut meat into small pieces.

If desired, take about 2 teaspoons of unbeaten egg white from one of the eggs at this point and brush around inside of pie shell. This will keep the bottom of the crust tender, and yet crisper.

Preheat oven to 400 degrees. Sprinkle lobster evenly over bottom of pie shell, and set aside. Blend cheese with cream until smooth. Beat eggs. Combine cream mixture, eggs, and rest of ingredients and pour over diced lobster. Bake for about 30 minutes, or until firm, puffy, and golden. Cool on a rack for at least 10 minutes before cutting.

Yields 12 wedges for appetizers, or 6 for a luncheon dish with a tossed green salad. Shrimp or crab may be used in place of lobster.

Emma R. Law

EARLY OYSTER ROASTS

When the first settlers arrived in Savannah in 1733, they were frequently guests at oyster roasts on the bank of the Savannah River at low tide, with their host being the Indian mica, Chief Tomachichi of the Creek Indians. Oyster shells were so plentiful in early Georgia that they were frequently used for roads, or in a building material called tabby.

SAVANNAH OYSTER ROAST

Probably Savannah's most picturesque and popular form of outdoor entertaining is the oyster roast. The city is sixteen miles from the sea, on the edge of the great tidal marshes. Through these green and amber prairies wind countless rivers and creeks, and on the bluffs overlooking these streams, country homes have been built in settings of staggering beauty. The great oak trees dripping moss, the camellias glowing in their glossy foliage, the play of light on marsh and water and sky. . . these are things to be remembered.

On a soft winter evening, when bushels of the small, sweet Georgia oysters are steamed open on sheets of iron laid across pits full of glowing coals, then eaten from wooden tables set up under the placid moon, the results are messy and marvelous.

Arthur Gordon, **Christ Church Cookbook**

BAKED OYSTERS

Here's another favorite Savannah way with the bivalves.

Yield: 6 to 8 servings

3 pints oysters, drained
2 cups commercial herb
   seasoned stuffing mix
½ cup finely chopped parsley

½ cup finely chopped celery
salt and pepper
6 tablespoons (¾ stick) butter,
   melted

Preheat oven to 350 degrees. Place a layer of oysters in an oiled 3-quart baking dish. Combine other ingredients, except for butter, and layer stuffing crumbs and oysters in the dish, ending with crumbs. Pour melted butter over all. Bake 30 minutes.

Mrs. Merritt Dixon, Jr., **Christ Church Cookbook**

He was a bold man who first ate an oyster.

Jonathan Swift, 1745

OLD LINE BROILED OYSTERS

Yield: 2 to 4 servings

1 dozen large oysters, in shell
Worcestershire sauce
hot pepper sauce

1 strip bacon, finely chopped
paprika

Open oysters, letting oyster remain in deep half of shell. Discard other half. Arrange oysters in a single layer in shallow baking pan. On each oyster, put 1 to 2 drops Worcestershire sauce, hot pepper sauce, 3 to 4 bits of bacon, and a sprinkle of paprika.

    Broil, about 4 inches from source of heat, until edges of oyster curl and bacon is done, 3 to 4 minutes.

Buck Briscoe, Annual Oyster Festival,
St. Mary's County, Maryland

OYSTERS ROCKEFELLER

Oysters Rockefeller is said to have originated on Jekyll Island in the carefree days before World War II, when it was the playground of New York millionaires. It is now a state park, with some of the palatial "cottages" open to the public.

Yield: 6 servings

3	dozen large oysters	1	cup minced, well-washed raw
4	tablespoons (½ stick) butter		spinach, or ¾ cup canned
½	cup bread crumbs, from		or frozen, well-drained
	firm white bread	¼	cup minced onion
3	tablespoons sherry	¼	teaspoon rock salt
1	teaspoon Worcestershire	½	cup grated Parmesan cheese
	sauce	6	lemon wedges
1	teaspoon seasoning salt	6	parsley sprigs

Shuck oysters and rinse thoroughly. Discard flute shell, leaving curved shell to hold oyster. Preheat oven to 400 degrees. Melt butter, but do not brown. Combine with bread crumbs and sherry. In a separate bowl, combine Worcestershire sauce and seasoning salt with spinach and onion. Arrange rock salt in a baking dish, and place oysters on this. Pour spinach mixture on oysters, and top with cheese. Sprinkle with bread crumbs. Bake for 10 minutes or until golden brown. Serve hot. Garnish with parsley and lemon wedges. Bon Appetit!

David Schneider, Jekyll Island

OYSTER OMELET

Have 1 quart of oysters par-boiled and drained very dry and chopped very fine. Season with a little salt, and celery and parsley, chopped very fine. Beat 8 eggs separately. Add black and red pepper to taste. Mix well together, and fry on a hot skillet as an omelet.

Mrs. Sophie Meldrim Shonnard

SCALLOPED CORN AND OYSTERS

Barbara and Carter Olive are the proprietors of The Soup Bowl, a home-style daytime restaurant on Drayton Street which is a favorite downtown spot for coffee breaks and lunch. Here is one of Carter's favorite "at home" recipes.

Yield: 6 servings

¼	cup finely chopped celery	1	beaten egg
1	10½-ounce can oyster stew	¼	teaspoon salt
1	16-ounce can cream style corn		dash pepper
1½	cups medium-coarse cracker	2	tablespoons butter, melted
	crumbs	½	cup cracker crumbs
1	cup milk		

Preheat oven to 350 degrees. Combine first eight ingredients. Pour into greased 1½ quart casserole. Mix butter with cracker crumbs. Spoon this over top of mixture. Bake for one hour, or until knife inserted in center comes out clean.

Carter Olive

SAVANNAH SHRIMP

Shrimp, like other seafood, has long been a mainstay of Low Country cooking. During the Federal blockade of the War between the States, Savannahians even ate shrimp for breakfast. Colorful vendors no longer carry their catch through the streets of Savannah on their heads, but good shrimp recipes abound. The following suggestions are offered for storing the fragile seafood:

Cook and refrigerate fresh shrimp if they are to be kept more than twenty-four hours before being served.

When you take fresh shrimp home, unless they are to be used right away, the best method of storage is freezing. Plastic quart containers are the best for the job because they stack easily, and have tight lids. Fill the containers about three-quarters full of shrimp, and then fill with water almost to the top. However, leave some room for the water to expand when it is frozen.

Savannah News-Press

SHRIMP AND OYSTER PILAF

Mayor John P. Rousakis, an active member of Savannah's Greek community, is known for his interest in cooking. Here's his favorite recipe, which he even prepared in one of Savannah's squares with the assistance of Mike Douglas and Burt Reynolds while a guest on the Mike Douglas Show!

Shrimp vessel at Thunderbolt by Pamela Lee

Yield: 8 to 10 servings

2 cups chopped onion	2½ cups Uncle Ben's Converted Rice (not instant variety)
½ pound (2 sticks) butter	
1 15-ounce can tomato sauce	1 pound raw shrimp, peeled and deveined (if large, cut in bite-sized pieces)
1 15-ounce can whole tomatoes	
5 cups chicken broth	
salt and pepper	1 quart raw oysters, drained

Place onion in a 4-quart pot and brown slightly in one of the sticks of butter. Add tomato sauce and whole tomatoes, mashed thoroughly. Let simmer for about 30 minutes. Add chicken broth, salt and pepper to taste, and let simmer for another 30 minutes. Bring to a boil, and add rice, shrimp, and oysters. Reduce heat immediately to very low. Cover pot and cook, without removing lid, for 20 minutes.

While this is cooking, place 1 stick butter in a skillet and burn until black. (Author's note: the faint of heart might try just browning it well the first time.) Take pilaf pot off the fire, remove top, and stir well. Pour hot burnt butter into pilaf pot. Stir again, and serve.

Mayor John P. Rousakis

141

SHRIMPER'S CASSEROLE

Yield: 6 to 8 servings

2 pounds large fresh shrimp,
    peeled and deveined
1 tablespoon lemon juice
3 tablespoons salad oil
¼ cup minced green pepper
¼ cup minced onion
2 tablespoons butter
¾ cup long-grain rice, uncooked
1 teaspoon salt

⅛ teaspoon pepper
⅛ teaspoon mace
    dash cayenne
1 10¾-ounce can tomato soup
1 cup heavy cream
½ cup dry white wine
½ cup slivered almonds
    paprika

Preheat oven to 350 degrees. Boil shrimp five minutes. Drain, place in a two-quart casserole, and sprinkle with lemon juice and oil. Saute pepper and onions in butter, and add with rice and all other ingredients except ¼ cup of the almonds and the paprika, to the shrimp mixture. Top with remaining almonds and the paprika. Bake 55 minutes.

Mike Cessaroni, Jr.

CREOLE GUMBO SAVANNAH

An original recipe from a popular Savannah hostess, Mrs. Carver Byrd.

Broth

Yield: 4 to 6 servings

2 pounds fresh small shrimp or
    1 24-ounce package frozen,
    peeled and deveined shrimp
1 quart water
2 bay leaves
1 tablespoon salt
½ lemon, sliced
¾ pound fresh okra, sliced, or
    10-ounce package sliced
    frozen okra

⅛ cup Worcestershire sauce,
    or to taste
1 teaspoon dried parsley
½ teaspoon dried basil
    several dashes hot pepper
    sauce

Make the **Broth** by bringing the shrimp to a boil in a heavy 4-quart saucepan with the water, bay leaves, salt, and lemon. Remove shrimp immediately, discard lemon, and refrigerate shrimp. Add the remaining ingredients to the **Broth**, and let simmer gently uncovered, while preparing **Roux.**

Roux

2	medium onions
1	medium bell pepper
2	cloves garlic
1	cup water
½	cup vegetable oil or bacon drippings

¾ cup flour
1 16-ounce can tomatoes and liquid

Put first 4 ingredients in the blender and chop until fine. Drain, and add seasoned water to **Broth** mixture. In a black iron skillet, heat oil, add flour, and stir constantly on medium-high heat until dark brown. Add the reserved chopped vegetables to **Roux,** stirring constantly until well blended. Blend tomatoes in blender on low speed or put through a sieve until liquified. Add slowly to **Roux** mixture, stirring constantly. Let cook gently on medium heat about 10 minutes, stirring frequently. Stir **Roux** mixture into **Broth**. Simmer one hour, uncovered.

Seafood

2 cups cooked crab meat (add several small claws if available)

12 ounces oysters, drained (check for small pieces of shell)

Add **Seafood** with reserved shrimp to **Broth**, bring back to simmer until oysters curl, and turn down to warm until ready to serve with **Rice.**

Rice

2 cups water
1 teaspoon salt

1 cup uncooked rice

Bring salted water to a boil. Add rice. Stir, and cover tightly. Cook on low heat for 15 minutes. Remove lid, stir with a fork, and let stand 5 minutes, keeping warm, to dry out.

Serve **Gumbo** in soup bowls with a scoop of cooked **Rice** on top.

Mrs. Carver Byrd

ANDREW JACKSON'S SHRIMP AND BEER

The globe-trotting Harmans, authors of *Fielding's Guide to the Caribbean Plus the Bahamas* and several other travel books, say this is a favorite at-home recipe.

Yield: 2 to 3 servings

1 cup sifted flour
1 teaspoon baking powder
¼ teaspoon salt
¼ teaspoon sugar
nutmeg and pepper to taste

1 beaten egg
1 cup beer
1 pound uncooked shrimp, peeled and deveined
hot fat for frying

143

Combine dry ingredients. Beat egg and beer together. Stir in flour mixture. Drop shrimp in batter, then fry until golden brown. Drain and serve while hot. More beer is good with this!

Jeanne and Harry Harman III, Valdosta, Georgia

CURRIED SHRIMP

Yield: 6 to 8 servings

2 tablespoons minced onion	salt and freshly ground pepper
2 tablespoons butter	to taste
2 tablespoons flour	4 cups (about 2 pounds) cooked,
2 tablespoons curry powder	peeled, deveined shrimp
(more if desired)	½ cup dry sherry
2 cups milk, chicken stock, or	
half-and-half	

Saute onion in butter in a 12-inch frying pan until tender but not too brown. Push to sides of pan, and slowly sprinkle in flour. Stir until smooth. Stir in curry powder. Slowly add milk or stock, stirring until mixture begins to thicken. Season with salt and pepper. Add shrimp and stir in sauce mixture. Let heat slowly, about 5 minutes. Stir in sherry; let heat a minute or so. Do not let boil. Serve over rice, accompanied with chutney.

Depending on the size of the shrimp, you may want to halve them lengthwise. Large shrimp are less trouble to clean, but are more expensive to buy. Do not overcook shrimp; it makes it tough and stringy. If desired, dish may be accompanied with other curry toppings, such as chopped hard-cooked egg, minced green peppers and green onions, or chopped peanuts.

Dorothy Clemmens Googe

LE CREVETTE ST. JOHN

Yield: 4 servings

¾ cup peeled, diced tomatoes	4 shallots or green onions,
¾ cup diced onion	minced
10 large mushrooms, sliced	½ cup dry white wine
1 clove garlic, chopped or	1 teaspoon tarragon leaves
crushed	½ teaspoon salt
3 to 4 tablespoons butter (more	¼ teaspoon pepper
if needed)	⅓ teaspoon oregano, or to taste
1 pound peeled, deveined	½ cup bread crumbs
shrimp	½ cup grated Parmesan cheese

Saute first 4 ingredients in butter in a hot skillet. Remove, and set aside. Saute shrimp in same hot skillet with butter, then add shallots. When shallots or onions are clear, add white wine, tarragon leaves, and tomato mixture. Cook for 5 minutes, and season to taste. Place in 4 ceramic dishes. Top each with a mixture of bread crumbs and cheese. Place under the broiler for a minute or two, watching carefully so they don't burn. Serve as appetizer or entree.

Ted Kleisner, General Manager, DeSoto Hilton Hotel

SHRIMP DEJONGHE

Lena E. Sturges, popular former food editor of *Southern Living* magazine, says that her favorite Georgia recipe was inspired by a trip to scenic Jekyll Island.

Yield: 4 to 6 servings

¼ pound (1 stick) butter, at room temperature	⅓ cup dry sherry
1 teaspoon salt	⅛ teaspoon cayenne pepper
1 clove garlic, minced	2 pounds shrimp, cooked, peeled and deveined
⅔ cup fine dry bread crumbs	
2 tablespoons finely chopped parsley	

Preheat oven to 375 degrees. Combine softened butter, salt, garlic, crumbs, parsley, sherry, and cayenne. Arrange shrimp in a shallow 3- or 4-quart casserole and top with crumb mixture, spreading it so it covers all the shrimp. Bake 20 to 25 minutes, or until topping melts over shrimp and becomes slightly brown. Do not overcook.

Lena E. Sturges

SHRIMP VERMOUTH

Yield: 4 servings

1¼ pounds shrimp, peeled and deveined	1½ tablespoons butter
¼ cup dry Vermouth	2 tablespoons plain white wine vinegar
1 tablespoon lemon juice	
salt and freshly ground pepper to taste	

Place shrimp in a 10-inch stainless steel frying pan. Pour Vermouth over and let marinate for about an hour. Add lemon juice, and, if necessary, enough water to barely cover shrimp. Sprinkle in salt and pepper. Add butter. Simmer 5 minutes; add vinegar and simmer another 5 minutes. Serve over **Saffron Rice** and sprinkle with parsley.

SAFFRON RICE

Cook 1½ cups of rice as directed on package, adding saffron along with the other seasonings.

SHRIMP WITH DILL SAUCE

Yield: 4 servings

5 tablespoons butter	¾ cup dry white wine
1 tablespoon chopped shallot or onion	3 tablespoons flour
	1½ cups milk
1 pound shrimp, peeled and deveined	1½ teaspoons chopped fresh dill or ¾ teaspoon dried dill

In a saucepan, melt 2 tablespoons of the butter. Add the shallot or onion, shrimp, and wine, and cook 5 minutes. In a separate saucepan, melt the remaining butter. Add flour and stir with a wire whisk until well blended. Gradually add the milk, stirring until the sauce is thickened and smooth. Add the sauce and dill to the shrimp mixture, and cook slowly 5 minutes longer. Serve immediately with hot rice.

Savannah News-Press

EGGPLANT AND SHRIMP CASSEROLE

Yield: 6 servings

3 large eggplants (about ¾ pound each)	1 cup bread crumbs
1½ pounds medium shrimp, peeled and deveined	2 tablespoons butter or margarine, melted
2 tablespoons butter or margarine	salt and pepper to taste
¾ cup finely chopped onion	2 tablespoons butter or margarine for dotting casserole
3 large cloves garlic, crushed or minced	

Peel eggplant. Cut into large pieces and boil about 25 minutes. Preheat oven to 350 degrees. Cut up shrimp in small pieces and fry in butter or margarine until soft. Add chopped onion; fry until soft. Drain and mash eggplant; add to shrimp and onion. Add garlic and ¾ cup bread crumbs; add melted butter or margarine to keep it soft. Pour into casserole. Top with rest of bread crumbs. Dot with pieces of butter or margarine. Bake 30 minutes.

Antonio Aliffi, Sr.

CURRIED SHRIMP WITH ORANGE RICE

Yield: 4 servings

⅓ cup butter or margarine
3 tablespoons flour
1 tablespoon curry powder, or to
    taste
½ teaspoon salt
¼ teaspoon paprika
¼ teaspoon ground nutmeg
2 cups half-and-half
2 cups cooked, peeled, and
    deveined shrimp

1 tablespoon finely chopped
    candied ginger
1 tablespoon onion or lemon
    juice
1 teaspoon dry sherry
1 teaspoon lemon juice
    dash Worcestershire sauce
    salt to taste

Melt butter. Blend in flour, curry powder, salt, paprika, and nutmeg. Gradually stir in cream; cook until mixture thickens, stirring constantly. Add remaining ingredients; heat through. Serve with **Orange Rice.**

Orange Rice

1 cup rice
½ cup orange juice

1 teaspoon orange rind

Cook rice according to package directions. Add orange juice and orange rind. Serve hot.

Ronald Pierce
Savannah News-Press

WALNUT SHRIMP

Shrimp with an oriental flavor...

Yield: 4 servings

1 pound shrimp, peeled and
    deveined and cut into thirds
1½ teaspoons light soy sauce
2 teaspoons dry sherry
¼ teaspoon white pepper
1 teaspoon cornstarch
4½ tablespoons vegetable oil
½ cup diced bamboo shoots
½ cup walnut halves

1 slice ginger, ¼-inch wide
2 green onions with stems,
    diagonally sliced into
    1-inch strips
1 teaspoon salt
¼ teaspoon monosodium
    glutamate
½ teaspoon sesame oil

Put the cut-up shrimp in a bowl and sprinkle with the soy sauce, wine, pepper, cornstarch, and 1 tablespoon oil. In a preheated wok, heat 1½ tablespoons oil. Quick-fry the bamboo shoots and walnuts for 1 minute and set aside in a bowl.

Add 2 tablespoons oil to the wok. When hot, swirl the ginger slice around the sides and bottom, and then discard. Add onions and shrimp and quick-fry for 2 minutes. Add bamboo

147

shoots and walnuts and stir well. Then add salt, monosodium glutamate, and sesame oil, and stir evenly.

Luke Chan
Savannah News-Press

BLUFFTON BOIL

One of Savannah's favorite informal outdoor get-togethers is the Low Country seafood boil. A large canning pot or other utensil is filled approximately two-thirds full of water, which is salted and brought to a boil. Into the pot go large raw potatoes, in the skins and cut in half, and whole Vidalia sweet onions. Boil 20 minutes. Add 10 pounds shrimp, in the shell; 3 whole buds (not the individual cloves) of garlic; commercially packaged seafood boil in amount sufficient to flavor amount of seafood used (if it is not in a boiling bag, which is easiest, tie the spices in cheesecloth); 4 to 6 lemons, cut in half; 1 cup vinegar; crabs, with the backs removed; and desired amount of corn on the cob.

Cook 10 minutes, and allow to cool in the pot 10 minutes. Drain carefully, and dump on a newspaper-covered picnic table or in the largest bowl you can find. Furnish soft butter, cocktail sauce for the shrimp, salt and pepper, and plenty of napkins and cold beer, and allow guests to help themselves. A large, chilled watermelon is the perfect dessert.

Allow plenty of food per serving! There is something about the outdoor air and the company which makes people consume tremendous quantities at such times!

Dolores (Mrs. H. A.) Highland

SAVANNAH'S SALMON MOUSSE

From the popular co-author of the classic guidebook, *Sojourn In Savannah.*

Yield: 4 servings

1	envelope unflavored gelatin	½ teaspoon paprika
2	tablespoons lemon juice	1 teaspoon dried dill
1	small onion slice	1 16-ounce can salmon, drained
½	cup boiling water	1 cup heavy cream
½	cup mayonnaise	

Empty the gelatin into the container of an electric blender. Add the lemon juice, onion, and boiling water. Blend for forty seconds. Turn motor off. Add mayonnaise, paprika, dill, and salmon. Cover and blend briefly at high speed. Remove cover and add the cream, one third at a time, blending a few seconds after each addition. Blend thirty seconds longer. Pour into 4 one-cup molds and chill.

Betty W. (Mrs. John J.) Rauers

SHRIMP CROQUETTES WITH RICE

Peel and chop fine two quarts of shrimp. Put one ounce of butter and one of flour together in a sauce pan, and stir until they begin to bubble, then add one-half pint of milk and a gill (4 ounces) of rich cream. Stir and cook until it forms a rich creamy sauce, then add 1 cup dry boiled rice. Stir in the shrimp. Add a little pepper and salt to taste. Put on ice until firm, then mould and fry like other croquettes.

Hints From Southern Epicures, *circa 1890*

CAPTAIN SAM'S TUG BOAT MULL

Yield: 10 servings

2	pounds medium size headed shrimp	½	cup finely chopped green pepper
1	quart medium oysters	½	cup finely chopped celery
1	15-ounce can crab soup	1	pound red snapper fillet
8	cups raw minute rice		bread crumbs
½	pound lean bacon		salt and pepper to taste
1	cup finely chopped onion		paprika and parsley to garnish

Peel, devein, and wash shrimp. Boil 5 minutes in 1½ cups water. Season to taste. Drain, saving the stock. Put the drained shrimp in a saucepan. Clean and wash the oysters, letting them drain into a colander. Save the natural juice of the oysters to add to the cooking water. Cook oysters in enough liquid barely to cover them until the edges curl, about 20 minutes. When done, drain, and save the stock; put oysters in the saucepan with shrimp.

Put the crab soup and a soup can of water into a pan. Add stock from shrimp and oysters. Bring to a slow boil. Take off the stove, and measure by cupfuls into a 1-gallon cooker. Add enough water to bring amount of liquid in cooker to 8 cups. Season this to taste and bring to a slow boil. Add rice and stir one time. Cover, remove from heat, and let stand 20 minutes.

Cut bacon in ¼-inch strips cross-wise. Place with onion, celery, and green pepper in fry pan and cook until bacon is done, but not crisp. Drain and place in saucepan with shrimp. Save this bacon grease to grease the baking pan, and start cooking the fish.

Preheat oven to 350 degrees. Cut the fish in strips ½-inch thick, ¾-inch wide, and 3 inches thick. Bread with crumbs and seasoning. Place in baking pan and cook for 15 minutes then take out to cool, leaving oven on. By now the rice should be ready; add the fish and the bacon mixture, and stir well.

Grease a baking pan (9½-by-13½-by-2½) with the bacon grease, and fill the pan ½-inch deep with rice. Cover the rice with the oysters and add one inch more of the rice. Put in layer of shrimp and add one inch more of rice. Place the fingers of red snapper on the rice and press lightly. Pour two cups of stock over rice, and bake for 10 minutes. Sprinkle lightly with paprika and place parsley around sides of pan. Serve hot.

TYBEE SEAFOOD GUMBO

Yield: 4 to 6 servings

6	strips lean bacon	1	6½-ounce can or 1 cup fresh
2	large onions, chopped		crab meat, cartilage removed
1	green pepper, chopped	1	cup corn kernels
2	8-ounce cans tomato sauce	1	cup baby lima beans
1	cup water		salt and pepper to taste
2	pounds cut okra		
1	pound shrimp, peeled and deveined		

In a large, deep pot, over medium heat, fry the bacon. Remove, drain, and save for later use. Saute onions and pepper in the bacon drippings until tender. Add tomato sauce to the pot, with ½ cup water swished around in each can to get what remains of the tomato sauce. Cook over medium heat about 10 to 15 minutes, stirring constantly. Add okra to ingredients in pot. Cook about 15 minutes, then add bacon and remaining ingredients. Cover pot and cook another 15 minutes, stirring to prevent sticking. Add more water only if necessary. Serve over hot cooked rice.

Delores Hill

SAUCE FOR FISH

Take the yolks of two hard cooked eggs; pulverize them well; add mixed mustard, pepper, salt, three tablespoonsful of salad oil; three of vinegar; one tablespoonful of tomato catsup.

House-Keeping In The Sunny South, 1885

COCKTAIL SAUCE FOR SHRIMP

Yield: 4 cups

½ cup sugar
1 teaspoon salt
1 teaspoon ground ginger
½ teaspoon dry mustard
½ cup ketchup

¼ cup lemon juice
¼ cup vinegar
2 cups vegetable oil
   dash Worcestershire sauce
½ cup finely chopped onion

Mix dry ingredients, then add liquids and onion. This is sufficient dip for 2 pounds of shrimp.

Mrs. Carston Tiedeman

FISH SAUCERY

(1) For a good basting sauce for trout or other fish, mix equal parts melted butter, a dry white dinner wine, and lemon juice. Heat, but do not boil. Baste fish with hot sauce while cooking; serve remaining sauce, if any, with fish.
(2) Skillet-brown fish for 5 minutes, then add ¼ cup white dinner wine, more if desired. Cover and simmer over low heat until tender.

FLORIDA ORANGE SAUCE

Yield: 1 cup

¼ pound (1 stick) butter
½ cup orange juice

½ teaspoon finely grated orange
   rind

Melt butter in a small saucepan. Stir in juice and rind. Heat and use to baste fish several times while broiling. Serve remaining sauce with fish.

MRS. WILKES' TARTAR SAUCE

Yield: 1¾ cups

1 cup mayonnaise
¼ cup finely chopped onion

½ cup pickle relish

Combine ingredients. Stir until thoroughly mixed. Cover and chill before serving.

Mrs. L. H. Wilkes, **Famous Recipes**
From Mrs. Wilkes Boarding House in Historic Savannah

RALPH'S REMOULADE SAUCE

Yield: about 1½ cups

1 cup mayonnaise
⅓ cup ketchup
1 tablespoon prepared
   horseradish
1 tablespoon minced, drained
   capers

1 tablespoon safflower or other
   vegetable oil except olive oil
¾ teaspoon paprika
   dash hot pepper sauce

Mix ingredients and chill, covered. Use with seafood salads or cooked shrimp.

VEGETABLES

Main gate of Bethesda Home For Boys, the oldest American orphanage in continuous existence. With the help of the boys themselves, the gateway was completed on the two hundredth anniversary of the founding of the home and school by the Reverend George Whitefield in 1740. Bethesda is on the National Register for Historic Places.

Art by Chris Fredeman,
Courtesy of Bethesda Alumni Association

EMMA'S VEGETABLE WITCHERY

Mash a pimiento into small bits with a table fork, and add a little melted butter and lemon juice to taste, to perk fresh or frozen cooked asparagus.

A few crushed dried basil leaves, added to melted butter or margarine along with salt and pepper, makes a sprightly sauce for cooked asparagus.

Poppy seed or **Toasted Benne (Sesame) Seed**, mixed with melted butter, makes a good dressing for green beans or stewed celery.

Top commercial sour cream with fresh chopped, frozen, or freeze-dried chives as a zippy dressing for green beans or baked potatoes.

Green beans will also profit from a dash of dill mixed with the soft butter with which they are seasoned just before serving.

SAVANNAH RED RICE

"How are Savannahians like the ancient Chinese?" goes an old joke. "Because, they eat rice, and worship their ancestors."

One of the city's most famous rice dishes is **Savannah Red Rice**, a savory mixture of pork, seasonings, and tomatoes. One of its most noted cooks is Cyrus McKiver, the popular chef at Bethesda Home For Boys since 1939. No occasion at the 238-year-old school would be complete without Cyrus and the **Red Rice**, especially the spring alumni picnic. One year, rather than disappoint his "Bethesda Boys," Cyrus even came back from sick leave on crutches to prepare his specialty! He says his secret is lining the skillet lid with heavy brown cooking paper to prevent moisture in the lid from condensing back on the rice. He stirs it, if necessary, with a fork rather than a spoon!

Yield: 6 to 8 servings

¾ cup diced onion	½ teaspoon salt
⅓ to ½ cup diced green pepper vegetable oil	2 tablespoons sugar
1½ pounds cooked ham, finely chopped	2 cups Uncle Ben's Converted Rice (not the instant variety)
2 8-ounce cans tomato sauce	
2 8-ounce cans water (swish water around in can to get all the sauce)	

Saute onion and pepper in a little oil until slightly tender. Add ham, and mix it all together well. Continue to cook a few minutes, until onion and pepper are limp but not brown.

Add tomato sauce, water, salt, and sugar, and mix well. When mixture boils, add rice and stir well. Bring to a full boil, then cover and let simmer over low heat for about 15 minutes. Take lid off skillet, and stir rice with a *fork*. Lay a large piece of brown kitchen paper over the skillet, so moisture will not condense on skillet lid and drip back on rice. Cover skillet again, with the lid over the paper. Continue to cook on the lowest possible heat for about 15 to 20 more minutes, or until all moisture is absorbed. Add more salt, or pepper, to taste if desired.

Cyrus McKiver, Bethesda Home For Boys

ARTICHOKE CASSEROLE

Yield: 6 servings

1 cup Italian-seasoned bread crumbs
¾ cup grated Romano or Parmesan cheese
3 cloves garlic, crushed or finely minced
½ cup olive oil
1 tablespoon dried parsley flakes
1 14-ounce can artichoke hearts, drained
½ of one can of juice from artichokes

Preheat oven to 350 degrees. Mix all items except artichokes and juice. Sprinkle a layer of the crumb mixture in a buttered casserole. Add a layer of drained artichokes; repeat with bread crumbs, sprinkling some of the artichoke juice on each row of crumbs to keep it moist. Add another row of artichokes. Top with bread-crumb mixture. Bake for 30 minutes.

Antonio Aliffi, Sr.

ARTICHOKE SQUARES

Yield: 6 3-inch squares

2 6-ounce jars marinated artichoke hearts
1 small onion, finely chopped
1 clove garlic, minced
4 eggs
¼ cup dry bread crumbs
¼ teaspoon salt
⅛ teaspoon pepper
⅛ teaspoon oregano
⅛ teaspoon hot pepper sauce
½ pound Cheddar cheese, shredded
2 tablespoons minced parsley

Preheat oven to 350 degrees. Drain the juice from one jar of artichoke hearts into a frying pan. Drain juice from second jar and reserve for use in salad marinade. Chop artichokes; set aside. Cook the onion and garlic in the artichoke liquid until the onion is transparent. Beat eggs in a small bowl until frothy.

155

Add bread crumbs, seasoning, cheese, parsley, chopped artichokes, and onion mixture. Turn into a buttered 7-by-11-inch baking pan and bake for 30 minutes. Let cool in the pan, then cut into three-inch squares. May be served cold, or reheated in 325 degree oven for 10 to 12 minutes just before serving.

Savannah News-Press

EMMA'S CRANBERRY BEAN BAKE

Yield: 12 servings

4 tablespoons vegetable oil	4 16-ounce cans pork and beans
½ cup chopped onions	½ cup ketchup
½ cup chopped green pepper	¼ cup brown sugar
2 pounds ground chuck	2 teaspoons dry mustard
salt, pepper, and garlic salt to taste	3 cups fresh cranberries

Preheat oven to 375 degrees. Heat oil in large skillet. Saute onions and green pepper until tender but not browned. Season ground chuck to taste with salt, pepper, and garlic salt. Shape into small meat balls. Add meat balls to the skillet and continue cooking until meat balls are lightly browned on all sides. Drain off excess fat. Transfer balls to 3-quart shallow casserole and add remaining ingredients. Mix well. Bake about 30 minutes, or until meat balls and cranberries are cooked.

You may wish to reserve some of the meat balls as you mix ingredients in the casserole, to arrange in an attractive manner on top of the beans.

GREEN BEANS AND ONIONS IN SOUR CREAM

Yield: 6 servings

2 pounds green beans, prepared for cooking	2 tablespoons butter or margarine
1 1⅜-ounce package dry onion soup mix	½ cup commercial sour cream
1½ cups boiling water	⅛ teaspoon pepper

Place beans in a large saucepan with onion soup mix and water; cover and boil gently 20 to 25 minutes, or until tender and most of the liquid has evaporated. Mix in butter and sour cream; serve.

.·· *Savannah News-Press*

BEETS WITH DOUBLE FLAVOR

Yield: 4 servings

1	medium onion, sliced	¼	cup sugar
3	tablespoons vinegar	2	tablespoons butter, at room
⅛	teaspoon ground cloves		temperature
½	teaspoon salt	2½	cups cooked sliced beets

Place first 6 ingredients and ½ cup beets in blender. Blend on high speed for 10 seconds. Pour over remaining beets in saucepan and bring to a boil, then simmer 10 minutes, stirring occasionally.

If you have been throwing away beet tops, you really should try washing them well and cooking them in a small amount of salted water, with a bit of bacon or ham added for flavor, until tender. Just like greens, that old Dixie favorite.

Carter Olive

FRANKLY SAVORY CABBAGE

Yield: 6 to 8 servings

4	tablespoons (½ stick) butter	1½	teaspoons salt
1	teaspoon caraway seeds	¼	cup flour
2	cups onion rings	2	cups milk
8	cups coarsely shredded	3	tablespoons prepared mustard
	cabbage (approximately 1½	1	pound frankfurters
	pounds)		

Melt butter in Dutch oven or deep skillet. Add caraway seed and onion. Saute onion until tender. Add cabbage. Cover and simmer 3 minutes. Sprinkle salt and flour over cabbage. Stir to blend well. Mix mustard into milk and gradually add to cabbage. Heat to boiling, stirring constantly. Boil and stir 1 minute.

Cut franks into 1-inch pieces. Add to cabbage and simmer about 5 minutes, stirring occasionally, until franks are heated through. Or, turn into a 2-quart baking dish and bake in a preheated 350 degree oven 25 minutes.

Savannah News-Press

CARROTS IN MUSTARD SAUCE

When you bring carrots home from the store, cut the green stem part off as quickly as possible if it is still attached to the carrot. The stem takes the "life" from the carrots, so they store better if it is removed.

Yield: 4 servings

1	pound carrots	2	tablespoons butter, melted
3	tablespoons light brown sugar		
1	tablespoon Dijon-type mustard		

Peel carrots and cut them about ⅛-inch thick on a slant, to give longer pieces. Cook, covered, over moderate heat in just enough water to barely cover, until carrots are tender but crisp. Thoroughly mix remaining ingredients. When carrots are done, drain and add mustard mixture. Toss well. Heat again if necessary, but do not let burn.

TARRAGON CELERY

A different cooked vegetable dish starring an old salad favorite.

Yield: 6 servings

3	cups celery crescents, diagonally sliced about ⅜-inch thick	1	teaspoon dried tarragon, rubbed fine
1	10½-ounce can chicken broth		4 to 5 turns of the pepper mill
¼	cup pale dry cocktail sherry		butter as desired

Combine all ingredients except butter. Bring to a boil and simmer gently until tender-crisp, about 8 to 10 minutes. (Test with a fork.) Drain and add butter. Cover pan and shake gently to coat celery with butter.

CORN FRITTERS

One dozen ears of corn, grated; half-pint milk; a tablespoonful of self-rising flour; three eggs; a little salt and black pepper; fry in boiling lard; then lay them on a large piece of brown paper to absorb the grease, and serve.

Hints From Southern Epicures, *circa 1890*

GREEN CORN PUDDING

Grate one dozen ears of young corn (three cups). Mix with it one pint of milk, two eggs, one spoonful of butter, black pepper and salt to taste. Bake for 30 to 60 minutes in a moderate (350 degrees) oven. Serves 6 to 8.

Gordon family recipes, courtesy of
Juliette Gordon Low Girl Scout National Center

TYBEE CORN CASSEROLE

A good in-place-of-potatoes dish with a meat loaf or other oven-baked meat.

Yield: 4 to 6 servings

    1   16-ounce can cream-style corn
    2   eggs
    1½ cups milk
    1   tablespoon flour
    1   tablespoon sugar
    1   tablespoon soft or melted
            butter or margarine (you
            might melt it in the casserole
            while preheating the oven,
            and then add the other
            ingredients)

Preheat oven to 350 degrees. Place all ingredients in a greased casserole. Mix well. Bake for about one hour, or until set.

Sally Pearce, Savannah Beach

CUCUMBERS IN ORANGE SAUCE

A really different vegetable that will delight all diners.

Yield: 6 servings

    3   large cucumbers, each about 8   salt and freshly ground pepper
            inches long   to taste
    3   tablespoons butter   1   teaspoon grated orange rind,
    1   tablespoon flour   slightly packed on spoon
    1   cup orange juice

Peel cucumbers and cut in half lengthwise. Remove seeds with a teaspoon or large end of a potato baller. Slice crosswise, on a slant, into ½-inch pieces. Cook in enough boiling, lightly salted water to cover, for about 5 minutes or until crisply tender. Drain and put in a warmed dish. Keep warm. Melt butter in 1-quart saucepan. Stir in flour and barely simmer for about 2 minutes. Do not let get brown. Add juice. Cook over gentle heat, stirring, until smooth and thickened. Stir in rind, mixing well. Pour over cucumbers. Serve warm.

CREAMED CUCUMBERS

Peel and slice cucumbers. Add salt and sour cream to moisten. Let stand for a few minutes. Gradually add a small amount of vinegar to taste.

Matilda Hinely Helmly,
Ye Olde Time Salzburger Cook Book

159

DIXIE BAKED EGGPLANT

Yield: 6 servings

1	large eggplant, about 1½ pounds	2	eggs
½	cup chopped onion		small amount of milk (optional)
4	tablespoons (½ stick) butter or margarine, at room temperature		salt and pepper to taste
			crushed saltine crackers as desired
1	cup soft bread crumbs		extra butter as desired

Peel eggplant and cut into chunks. Place with chopped onion in a saucepan and cover with boiling salted water. Bring quickly to a boil, reduce heat, and simmer until eggplant is tender. Drain in a colander.

Preheat oven to 350 degrees. Place eggplant in mixing bowl. Add butter and bread crumbs and mix until eggplant is mashed and blended with crumbs. Beat eggs slightly and add to mixture. Add enough milk, if needed, to make mixture like a cake batter. Season with salt and pepper. Turn into buttered baking dish. Sprinkle top with crushed saltines and dot with butter or margarine. Bake for 30 or 35 minutes, or until golden brown.

Savannah News-Press

FRIED EGG PLANT

Slice plant, and then lay in salt and cold water for about an hour or two; dredge with corn meal, and fry a light brown.

Hints From Southern Epicures, *circa 1890*

BAKED HOMINY

Boil hominy thoroughly; let cool; then beat in one egg; one cup milk; one tablespoon butter; a little salt. Bake light brown.

Hints From Southern Epicures, *circa 1890*

MUSHROOMS WITH SHALLOTS

Who said vegetable dishes were dull?

Yield: 4 servings

1 pound fresh mushrooms	⅓ cup safflower or other neutral
¼ cup minced shallots, pearl	vegetable oil
onions, or very tender	salt and freshly ground pepper
scallions	to taste
1 tablespoon Dijon-type	minced fresh parsley
mustard	Boston lettuce or watercress
3 tablespoons white wine	
vinegar	

Wash, drain, and dry mushrooms. Cut in thin "umbrella" shaped slices. Place in a bowl. Mix remaining ingredients, except greens, and pour over mushrooms. Marinate in refrigerator at least 2 hours. Drain, if necessary, and serve with greens.

OKRA PILAU

Along with benne seeds, okra was a vegetable brought to the New World on African slave ships. The cooks of the plantation kitchens first became expert in its use as a flavorful vegetable and thickening agent in soups and stews. Savannah, like New Orleans, is noted for its savory okra dishes. The green pods are often used in combination with onion, green pepper, and tomatoes.

Yield: 6 to 8 servings

2 cups thinly sliced okra	1 16-ounce can tomatoes, well
3 slices bacon, diced	drained and chopped, or
½ cup chopped green pepper	3 fresh tomatoes, medium
¾ cup chopped onion	size, peeled and quartered
1 cup uncooked, long grain rice	1 teaspoon salt, or to taste
2 cups chicken broth	

Saute okra and bacon until lightly browned. Add green pepper and onion and continue cooking until vegetables are tender. Add rice, chicken broth, tomatoes, and salt. Bring to a boil. Stir once, cover, reduce heat, and simmer 15 minutes, or until rice is tender. Fluff lightly with a fork and serve.

FRIED OKRA FRITTERS

Boil a quart of okra, pour off the water when the okra is tender, and mash it smooth. Season with butter and salt and pepper. Beat in thoroughly one egg, and add flour to make a stiff batter. Fry in hot fat like a fritter.

Favorite Recipes From Savannah Homes, 1904

SALZBURGER ONION PIE

Some of the sweetest, mildest onions come from Vidalia, Georgia, and are much sought-after for certain dishes.

Yield: 8 servings

1½ cups flour
¾ teaspoon salt
1½ teaspoons caraway seeds
½ cup vegetable shortening
2 to 3 tablespoons cold water

Make a pastry of flour, salt, and caraway seeds. Cut in shortening with pastry blender until mixture resembles coarse corn meal. Stir water in lightly with fork; stir until mixture follows fork around bowl. Turn on flat surface between two large pieces of wax paper; roll to ⅛-inch thickness and peel off one side of wax paper, using the other to position dough in 10-inch pie pan. Then peel off second piece of paper. Or, use floured board and chill dough before rolling out; work quickly for ease of handling. Flute edges of crust. (Or use a frozen prepared crust, or crust from a mix, and press the caraway seeds into frozen dough as it thaws, or add to prepared mix before adding water.) Bake crust in preheated 425 degree oven 10 minutes, or until lightly browned. Add **Onion Filling.**

Onion Filling

3 cups thinly sliced onions, Vidalias preferred
3 tablespoons melted butter
2 eggs, well beaten
½ cup milk
1½ cups commercial sour cream
1 teaspoon salt
3 tablespoons flour
3 bacon slices, crisply cooked

Preheat oven to 325 degrees. Saute onions in butter until limp but not too brown. Spoon into pastry shell. Add to eggs the milk, 1¼ cups sour cream, and salt. Blend flour with remaining ¼-cup sour cream. Combine with egg mixture; pour over onions. Bake 30 minutes, or until firm in the center. Garnish with crisp bacon.

Savannah News-Press

VIDALIA ONIONS IN FOIL

As the perfect accompaniment to an oven meal, remove stems from as many large Vidalia (mild) onions as you wish, allowing one per serving. Place each onion on an individual piece of aluminum foil, season with salt and pepper, and place a bit of butter on top of each. Fold in foil, closing ends tightly, and roast at 350 degrees for approximately an hour, like a baked potato. Excellent!

Ann (Mrs. Ben) Ritzert

VIDALIA ONIONS WITH WINE

Yield: 6 to 8 servings

5	or 6 sweet onions, about 3 inches in diameter	3	whole cloves
3	tablespoons butter	½	teaspoon salt
		1	cup Burgundy wine

Cut off root end of each onion and peel back skin. Use stem end as a handle and cut into ¼-inch slices. Separate slices into rings. Heat butter in Dutch oven, heavy frying pan, or electric skillet. Add onion rings and toss (I prefer a wooden spoon) until they are coated with butter. Add cloves and salt. Cook over low heat until onions just start to brown. Add wine, cover pan, and simmer about 15 minutes. Remove lid and simmer until wine is reduced almost to a glaze. Remove cloves. Serve. These are good with almost any meat. However, use only mild Vidalia onions (sometimes called Spanish onions); other varieties are too strong.

Savannah News-Press

VIDALIA ONIONS WITH RICE

Yield: 8 servings

1	cup long grain rice	4	cups thinly sliced onions
2	quarts boiling water	½	teaspoon salt
1	teaspoon salt	⅛	teaspoon paprika
4	tablespoons (½ stick) butter or margarine	2	tablespoons grated Parmesan cheese

Drop rice into rapidly boiling water with 1 teaspoon salt. Boil uncovered for five minutes. Drain at once. Melt butter in 2-quart casserole in oven; stir in onions. Add ½ teaspoon salt and stir onions in butter until they are yellowed and coated. Then add rice and stir to distribute evenly. Cover and bake in 325 degree oven for 1 hour. Sprinkle with paprika and cheese.

Savannah News-Press

SAVORY STUFFED ONIONS

Yield: 6 servings

6 onions (about 3 inches in diameter)	¾ cup grated Cheddar cheese
1 cup cooked rice	⅛ teaspoon dried thyme or
¼ cup tomato sauce or puree	⅛ teaspoon summer savory
2 tablespoons vegetable oil	1 teaspoon dried basil
	salt

Peel onions and cut slice off stem end of each. Cook uncovered in salted water for about 30 minutes, or until tender but still firm. Drain and cool. Remove the centers of the onions, saving them for use in stuffings or a stew.

Preheat oven to 425 degrees. Arrange the onions in a greased casserole. Mix together the rice, sauce, oil, ½ cup grated cheese, and seasonings to taste. Fill onions with this mixture. Sprinkle with remaining cheese. Bake for 20 minutes. Excellent with beef or other meats.

Savannah News-Press

PEARL BARLEY WITH ONIONS

Try barley, one of humanity's oldest grains, as a change from rice.

Yield: 4 to 6 servings

1 cup pearl barley	¼ cup minced onions
salt and pepper to taste	¾ cup boiling water or
1 tablespoon butter	consomme

Brown barley lightly over moderate heat. Add remaining ingredients. Cover and simmer over low heat for about an hour.

Instant barley may be used. If so, use amount of liquid and timing suggested on package, but you can still brown it and combine it with onions as shown above.

EASY BAKED PEAS

Yield: 4 servings

1 10-ounce package frozen peas	½ cup chopped, canned mushrooms
1 tablespoon butter or margarine	¼ cup mushroom liquid
¼ teaspoon onion salt	1 tablespoon chopped parsley

Preheat oven to 350 degrees. Combine ingredients in a casserole. Cover and bake for about 40 minutes. Uncover and stir gently to mix well before serving. Excellent with an oven-baked meat.

Minnie Hodge

CORNFIELD OR BLACK EYE PEAS

Shell peas early in the morning. Throw into water until an hour before dinner, when put them in boiling water, covering while cooking. Add a little salt just before taking from the fire. Drain and serve with a large spoonful of fresh butter, or put into a pan with a slice of fat meat, and simmer for a few minutes. Dried peas must be soaked overnight and cooked twice as long as fresh. . . . They may be boiled with a piece of ham until tender.

Housekeeping In Old Virginia, 1879

BELL PEPPERS TO BE SERVED WITH BEEF

Take half a dozen sweet bell peppers, and slice as you would a tomato. Boil vinegar with salt and sugar; when cold, pour over peppers.

Hints From Southern Epicures, circa 1890

COLCANNON

Savannah has had an Irish population since the early days of the colony, when Irish prisoners were sent to Georgia to serve as laborers. Others came as indentured servants. Some families recall the Emerald Isle with this traditional dish.

Yield: 6 to 8 servings

1½	pounds potatoes	1	tablespoon butter
	water	1	tablespoon chopped parsley
1½	cups milk		salt and pepper to taste
6	scallions, minced and scalded		
1½	cup boiled greens, such as cabbage or kale		

Peel the potatoes and steep covered in cold water for one hour. Drain. Cover with cold salted water and boil until tender. Drain well and mash. Heat milk to boiling; add to potatoes with the scalded scallions. Beat until fluffy. Toss the cooked greens gently in melted butter. Add to the potatoes, together with the parsley, and fold well. Season with salt and pepper as needed.

Mrs. William J. Doyle

ROQUEFORT POTATOES

Yield: 4 servings

4 Idaho baking potatoes (about ½ pound each)
   vegetable oil
½ to ¾ cup commercial sour cream
¼ cup crumbled Roquefort cheese

salt and freshly ground pepper to taste
4 tender young scallions, minced (using some of the tops)
   paprika

Preheat oven to 425 degrees. Scrub potatoes, dry well, and oil lightly all over to keep the skins soft and pliable. Bake until soft, about 45 to 60 minutes. Aluminum baking nails, horizontally inserted, may speed baking time.

Cut a slice from the top of each potato and scoop out, being careful not to break the shell. Mash potato well and beat with sour cream, cheese, salt and pepper, adding enough sour cream to make a rather fluffy mixture. Stir in scallions. Spoon potato mixture back into shells, molding slightly. Place on baking sheet and dust lightly with paprika. Return to oven until lightly browned.

IRISH POTATOES WITH PEANUT BUTTER

Bake 6 large Irish potatoes. Cut in halves and remove the insides, being careful not to break the skins. Mash and season with one-half teaspoonful of salt, one-half teaspoonful of white pepper, a dash of cayenne, a heaping tablespoonful of butter, one cup of sweet milk, and ½ cup of peanut butter, or to taste. Put back into the skins, and bake potatoes to a light brown.

Gulf City Cookbook, 1878

CHEESE POTATOES

Peel as many potatoes as needed, and cut into julienne strips. These can also be made with frozen shoestring potatoes, but are not as good. Soak potatoes in cold water for several hours. Drain well. Butter as large a baking dish as needed for the potatoes. Put in a layer of potatoes, and sprinkle generously with shredded sharp Cheddar or Switzerland Swiss cheese. Sprinkle each layer lightly with salt, freshly grated pepper, and a dash of red pepper. Alternate layers until dish is almost filled. Dot generously with butter. Bake in a preheated moderate 350 degree oven for 30 minutes. Increase heat to 375 degrees until top becomes crisp.

Helen Kehoe Crolly

MAGGIE'S SWEET SCALLOP

Sweet potatoes are a native American vegetable, since they originated in the tropical part of the continent. The Indians cultivated them long before the coming of the colonists, who grew them in the gardens of the South. They later spread to such places as China, Japan, and Indonesia, where they are very popular. The sweet potato is a member of the morning glory family. Yams, with which they are used interchangeably in recipes, are of a different botanical species. This easy sweet potato recipe is excellent with pork, and a refreshing change from too-sweet dishes.

Yield: 6 servings

6	medium sweet potatoes, peeled and sliced	¼	cup brown sugar
4	medium cooking apples, peeled, cored, and sliced	3	tablespoons butter
		⅓	cup apple cider, apple, or orange juice

Arrange potatoes and apples in a buttered casserole. Sprinkle with sugar and dot with butter. Pour liquid all over. Cover and bake in a 350 degree oven for about an hour, or until tender.

LOW COUNTRY RICE

Rice, that staple of Low Country living, came to these shores by accident. In 1694 a vessel out of Madagascar bound for Liverpool was blown so far off course that she put in at Charleston, South Carolina, for repairs. When Landgrave Thomas Smith, an early South Carolina planter, boarded the ship, he was given a small package of rice seed by the captain. The first crop supplied rice for the entire colony.

BOHEMIAN RICE

Yield: 4 to 6 servings

4	tablespoons (½ stick) butter	½	teaspoon pepper
1	cup uncooked rice	1	10½-ounce can consomme
½	cup minced onions	¾	cup water
¾	teaspoon chili powder	1	3- or 4-ounce can mushroom
½	teaspoon curry powder		bits and pieces or ½ cup
1	tablespoon parsley flakes		chopped fresh mushrooms
1	teaspoon salt		

Brown rice in butter. Add onions and brown a bit more. Combine with all other ingredients and bake for about 1½ hours in a 350 degree oven. This is a good plan-ahead oven dish to serve guests.

Carter Olive

BROWN RICE WITH HERBS AND MUSHROOMS

Ivan Bailey is Savannah's village blacksmith, a talented iron worker whose Bay Street forge is an unforgettable place to visit. Janet Bailey, his wife, is known for her weaving and for healthful recipes.

Yield: 4 to 6 servings

1	tablespoon butter	¼	teaspoon thyme
1	clove garlic, minced or crushed	¼	teaspoon rosemary
½	cup chopped onions	1	cup brown rice
¼	pound mushrooms, chopped	2	cups water
¼	teaspoon sage	1	cube beef or chicken bouillon
			chopped parsley

Melt butter and saute garlic, onions, and mushrooms until tender. Add sage, thyme, and rosemary and cook two minutes. Add rice, water, and bouillon cube and bring to a boil. Lower heat, cover, and simmer 40 to 50 minutes, or until done. About 5 minutes before end of cooking, add parsley.

Janet Bailey

SPINACH

Boil spinach until tender. Then place in flat dish, and pour a little melted butter over it; slice hard-boiled eggs, and place on top. Salt and pepper to taste.

Hints From Southern Epicures, *circa 1890*

CREAMY SPINACH

Save utilities: bake a vegetable along with the oven entree.

Yield: 6 servings

2　10-ounce packages frozen chopped spinach, defrosted and drained

1　cup commercial sour cream
1　1¼-ounce package onion soup mix

Preheat oven to 350 degrees. Combine ingredients and bake in a tightly covered casserole for 30 minutes.

CURRIED SPINACH

Yield: 6 servings

2　10-ounce packages frozen chopped spinach
1　tablespoon butter or margarine
2　tablespoons commercial sour cream

2　tablespoons curry powder
⅛　teaspoon nutmeg
½　teaspoon salt
⅛　teaspoon pepper

Cook spinach according to package directions. Drain well and replace in pan. Cover and keep warm. In a separate small pan, melt butter over low heat. Blend in remaining ingredients. Pour sauce over spinach, toss well to mix, and serve. This has about 80 calories per serving.

Savannah News-Press

HERB-BAKED SUMMER SQUASH

Squash is a truly American food which originated in the Western hemisphere. The term comes from the Indian word "askutasquash," a green thing eaten green.

Yield: 4 servings

1　10½-ounce can condensed chicken bouillon
2　pounds yellow summer squash
2　tablespoons butter or margarine, melted

½　teaspoon salt
1　teaspoon fresh or ½ teaspoon dried rosemary or oregano

Preheat oven to 350 degrees. Heat bouillon with an equal amount of water until very hot. Cut stem ends from squash. Cut squash in half lengthwise. Place halves, cut side down, in a large, shallow baking dish. Pour bouillon around squash. Bake, uncovered, for 20 minutes. Turn squash. Brush sides with butter combined with salt and rosemary. Bake 15 minutes longer, or until squash is tender. Before serving, brush with more butter if desired. This can be baked along with an entree for a complete oven-ready meal.

Savannah News-Press

FLUFFY RUTABAGA

In the North, rutabagas are called yellow turnips. The name itself is Swedish. The easiest way to peel one is to slice it first and then peel around the slices. This recipe is a pleasant change from mashed potatoes.

Yield: 4 servings

1 medium rutabaga, about 1½ pounds salt and freshly ground pepper to taste	2 or 3 tablespoons sugar

Slice rutabaga, peel around the edges of the slices, and cut into small dice. Simmer in just enough water to cover until tender. Drain and save liquid. Mash rutabaga and whip well, adding seasoning. It is better slightly sweet. Use some of the reserved liquid, if necessary, to keep it from being too stiff.

Mary Osteen

BROILED TOMATOES

Broil quickly sufficient tomatoes to fill a chop platter. Pour over them a sauce made of heating together two tablespoons of olive oil, 1 teaspoon of prepared mustard, a dash of cayenne pepper, ½ teaspoon sugar, and 3 tablespoons vinegar. Serve hot.

Favorite Recipes From Savannah Homes, 1904

TOMATOES AND MUSHROOMS SAUTEED

Put a small lump of butter in a chafing dish. When it begins to sizzle, put in peeled mushroom caps. When they have cooked about 3 minutes, add thick slices of raw tomatoes, and as you turn and cook them, add salt and pepper. When the tomatoes have browned on both sides, place them on buttered toast and pile the mushrooms on top. For two servings, you need about ½-pound of mushrooms and two large tomatoes.

From a favorite luncheon dish of Juliette Gordon Low, courtesy of Juliette Gordon Low Girl Scout National Center

MOMMA ALIFFI'S TOMATO PIE

This recipe was originally created by Mrs. Carmelina Rizza Aliffi, an artist and native of Sicily. She passed her interest in cooking along to her family, including her son, Antonio.

Yield: 6 servings

⅓ cup olive oil	½ teaspoon oregano
⅓ cup vegetable oil	¼ teaspoon black pepper
2 pounds Spanish or Bermuda onions	¼ teaspoon garlic salt
	¼ pound Romano cheese, bulk
2 pounds fresh tomatoes, not too ripe	4 cups packaged biscuit mix
	1 cup milk
salt to taste	

Heat olive oil and vegetable oil in large skillet until hot. Put in onions cut in slices. Cook until limp. Add fresh tomatoes cut in chunks. Add seasonings. Cook about 10 minutes. Add cheese cut in small chunks. Leave on low heat. Cover pan. Taste for correct amount of salt and pepper. Add more if needed. Prepare biscuit mix with milk. Blend with spoon until nice dough is formed.

Preheat oven to 450 degrees. Grease large pie pan with vegetable oil. Place dough about size of small ball in center of pan. Take moistened fingers and pat dough to thin layer to cover bottom and ½-inch on sides. Spoon tomato filling over dough. Bake for 15 minutes. Set aside for about 15 minutes. Cut and serve.

Antonio Aliffi, Sr.

CREOLE TOMATOES AND OKRA

Yield: 6 servings

4½ cups fresh okra	3 teaspoons flour
1½ cups chopped green pepper	2 teaspoons salt
1½ cups chopped onion	¾ teaspoon pepper
6 tablespoons bacon drippings	4 fresh quartered or 1 16-ounce can tomatoes
3 tablespoons sugar (less if desired)	

Cut okra into ½-inch slices; cover with water. Boil 10 minutes; drain. Cook pepper and onion in bacon grease until tender but not brown. Add to okra in kettle. Blend dry ingredients and add to okra mixture. Meanwhile, cook peeled quartered tomatoes until tender, or add canned ones to okra mixture. Blend and cook over medium heat until mixture is medium thick, or as thick as desired. Left-overs are good in vegetable soup.

BUFFET VINAIGRETTE

Yield: 5 to 6 servings

½ small head of cauliflower, divided into flowerets	1 3-ounce jar pitted green olives, drained
2 large carrots, pared and cut into 2-inch pieces	¾ cup plain white wine vinegar
2 large ribs celery, cut into ½-inch strips	½ cup vegetable or olive oil
1 green pepper, cut into ½-inch strips	2 tablespoons sugar
	1 teaspoon salt
1 4-ounce jar pimientos, cut into strips	½ teaspoon dried oregano
	¼ teaspoon pepper
	¼ cup water

Combine all ingredients in a large skillet. Bring to a boil, stirring occasionally. Reduce heat and simmer, covered, for 4 or 5 minutes, until all vegetables are tender-crisp. Cool at once. Refrigerate for at least 24 hours. Drain well and serve. A good plan-ahead buffet item. Don't worry about the left-overs. They are wonderful additions to a tossed green salad!

Marilyn Whelpley

LEIGH'S ZUCCHINI CASSEROLE

Yield: 6 servings

5 or 6 zucchini squash	½ cup buttered bread crumbs or wheat germ
3 ounces cream cheese, diced	
⅛ teaspoon garlic salt	⅛ teaspoon paprika
⅛ teaspoon onion salt (or to taste)	Parmesan cheese

Slice squash into 2-inch pieces. Cook in a small amount of boiling water 8 to 10 minutes. Preheat oven to 350 degrees. Drain zucchini well. Mix in cream cheese. Add garlic and onion salt. Put in a buttered casserole and top with bread crumbs. Sprinkle with paprika and cheese. Bake 30 minutes.

Savannah News-Press

FRITTER-FRIED BENNE ZUCCHINI

Yield: 4 to 6 servings

1 cup flour	⅓ cup milk
1½ teaspoons baking powder	2 to 3 tablespoons **Toasted Benne**
½ teaspoon salt, more if	**Seed**
desired	4 medium-large zucchini, about
⅛ teaspoon pepper	1¼ pounds
2 eggs	deep fat for frying

Sift flour, baking powder, and salt. Beat eggs well in a small bowl, and stir in milk. Stir flour mixture into egg mixture and add **Toasted Benne Seed**. Beat until smooth and well blended.

Scrub zucchini in cold water; cut off the ends and discard. Dry, and cut into ½-inch sticks. Blot sticks with paper towel. Dip the sticks in fritter batter, and fry in deep fat (370 to 375 degrees) 2 to 5 minutes, or until brown. Drain and sprinkle with more salt if desired. Serve as an appetizer, or as a vegetable with the main course.

EARLY GARDENS

Before the arrival of the English, Spain colonized the coast of Georgia for more than a century. Beginning in 1568, Jesuit and later Franciscan missionaries labored to Christianize the Indians. In their mission gardens they cultivated figs, peaches, oranges, and other plants introduced from Europe. They were finally driven farther south in 1656 by Indian uprisings, pirate raids, and British depredations. A map of St. Simons Island made in 1739 by Captain John Thomas, engineer in James Oglethorpe's regiment there, located "an Old Spanish garden" on the island, and materials from that period have also been found in the vicinity of Demere Road and Ocean Boulevard.

THE PINK HOUSE

No building in Georgia has aged more beautifully than The Pink House at 23 Abercorn Street, built for James Habersham, Jr., in 1789. The old bricks have turned the covering stucco a unique color. In addition, it is noted for its portico and fine Palladian window. Formerly headquarters of the Bank of the U.S. and later a Federal headquarters during Union occupation, it is now a planters' tavern, fine restaurant, and antique shop. It is noted for its Low Country specialties such as seafood, spiced carrots, and **Savannah Trifle**.

Drawing by Charley Bland
Copyright© 1975 by Charley Bland

DESSERTS

SAVANNAH TRIFLE

Yield: about 12 servings

1½	quarts milk	½	cup sherry
1½	cups sugar	1	pint whipping cream
2	tablespoons cornstarch	1½	pounds sliced pound cake
6	eggs		maraschino cherries (optional)

Heat milk in the top of a double boiler, but do not boil. Beat together sugar, cornstarch, and eggs in mixing bowl until smooth. Add this to warm milk and stir until mixture thickens and coats a metal spoon. Set aside until cool. When cool, add sherry to custard. Whip cream. In a 13-by-9¼-by-2-inch baking pan, put a layer of cake, a layer of custard, and a layer of whipped cream. Repeat until all ingredients are used. Top each serving with a cherry, if desired.

Herschel McCallar, Jr., and Jeffrey Keith, owners, The Pink House

SAVANNAH FLOATING ISLAND

A very old, and favorite recipe, somewhat updated by Emma R. Law.

Yield: 6 servings

Custard

3	egg yolks, beaten	2	cups milk, scalded
¼	cup sugar	½	teaspoon vanilla or almond
¼	teaspoon salt		extract

Make **Custard:** Mix egg yolks, sugar, and salt in top of double boiler. Slowly stir in milk. Cook over hot (not boiling) water, stirring constantly, until mixture coats a metal spoon, about 6 to 8 minutes. Remove from heat. Strain, if desired, in case bits of egg white clung to the egg yolks. Stir in extract, and chill in a shallow float bowl.

Meringue

3 egg whites
¼ teaspoon salt
6 tablespoons sugar

¼ teaspoon spice (cinnamon, allspice or nutmeg), if desired

Make **Meringue**: beat egg whites until stiff but not dry. Beat in salt. Add sugar, very gradually, beating all the while. Drop by heaping tablespoons into boiling water. **Meringue** should be "set" in 2 or 3 minutes. Lift gently on slotted spoon, drain a bit, and place on top of custard. Finish **Meringues**, place on top of custard, and let stand in a cool place until time to serve.

SHERRY CUSTARD

Yield: 6 servings

2 eggs
¼ cup sugar
¼ teaspoon salt
1 cup half-and-half or
    light cream

¾ cup water
¼ cup cream sherry

Preheat oven to 350 degrees. Beat eggs lightly. Stir in sugar, salt, milk, and water, stirring until sugar is dissolved. Blend in sherry. Pour into custard cups. Set in pan of hot water. Bake for 1 hour, or until barely set. Cool before serving.

VARINA DAVIS' ITALIAN CREAM

Take a pint of milk, yolks of eight eggs, and a little powdered (confectioner's) sugar. Make a cooked custard, flavoring it according to taste. When it is quite cold, whip a pint of cream very stiff, and mix the custard and cream together. Pour into a mold and serve cold.

Mrs. Jefferson Davis,
House-Keeping In The Sunny South, 1885

DESSERT DUMPLINGS

Yield: 6 servings

Dumplings

1½ cups flour	4 tablespoons (½ stick) butter
1½ teaspoons baking powder	⅔ cup milk
⅓ cup sugar	½ teaspoon vanilla extract
¼ teaspoon salt	

Sift flour, then measure and sift with baking powder, sugar, and salt. Cut in butter; add milk and vanilla. Mix quickly and drop by teaspoons into boiling **Caramel Sauce.**

Sauce

2 tablespoons butter	¼ teaspoon salt
1½ cups brown sugar, firmly packed	1½ cups boiling water

Mix ingredients and bring to a boil. Drop in **Dessert Dumplings**. Cover the dumplings and sauce and simmer gently for 20 minutes. Do not lift cover during cooking time! Top with whipped cream or ice cream, if desired.

Dennis Rogers
Savannah News-Press

APPLE SNOW

Boil six large apples pared and sliced, in enough water to cover. When soft, press through a sieve and sweeten. (Do not add the sugar while cooking, as it hardens the fruit.) Add half a teaspoon grated nutmeg, half a teaspoonful of cinnamon, half a teaspoonful of mace, and a pinch of ground cloves. Beat all thoroughly, and stir in the frothed (beaten) whites of four eggs. Serve with rich cream.

House-Keeping In The Sunny South, 1885

MIDWAY BAKED APPLES

Yield: 6 servings

6 baking apples, about 3 inches in diameter	½ cup sugar
¼ cup dried black currants	1 teaspoon grated orange peel
¼ cup chopped, slivered, blanched almonds	¼ cup orange juice
1 tablespoon orange marmalade	1 tablespoon butter
	cream

Core apples, leaving a "cup" in middle to hold stuffing. This is easiest with a melon baller. Also, make 6 equidistant slits from top of core down about one-third of the apple and open a bit to absorb extra syrup during baking. Leaving the skin on adds to flavor of apples. Combine currants, almonds, and marmalade; stuff apples with mixture. Combine remaining ingredients in small saucepan; stir over low heat until sugar dissolves. Let simmer 5 minutes.

Preheat oven to 350 degrees. Place apples in a heavy baking pan; pour syrup over and let it run down over apples. Cover; bake for 45 minutes to an hour, basting often with syrup in the pan. When tender, baste again, and put under broiler to glaze. (Watch carefully!) Serve warm with plain or unsweetened whipped cream.

The **Apricot Chutney** recipe in the **Pickles and Relishes** chapter is also excellent as a filling for baked apples. Baste apples during baking with a mixture of equal parts apple juice and honey, or apple juice.

GRANOLA CRISP

Yield: 6 servings

5 medium tart cooking apples, cored and sliced	⅓ cup light brown sugar, firmly packed
⅓ cup sifted flour	1½ cups granola-type cereal
1 teaspoon cinnamon	⅓ cup butter or margarine,
½ teaspoon nutmeg	at room temperature

Preheat oven to 350 degrees. Place apples in buttered 9-inch square baking pan. Combine flour, cinnamon, nutmeg, sugar, and granola. Add soft butter, mixing well. Sprinkle this over fruit. Bake 25 minutes. Serve warm or cold with cream or vanilla ice cream.

GORDONSTON BROWN BETTY

This recipe for a favorite apple dish of the Gordon family was named for their farm near Savannah, now a residential area.

Two cups of chopped tart cooking apples, one cup grated dry bread crumbs, ½ cup light brown sugar, one teaspoon cinnamon, and two tablespoons butter (in small pieces over apples). Butter a covered baking dish well and put in layers of apples and other ingredients, beginning with apples and ending with crumbs and butter. Place in a moderate (350 degrees) oven, covered, for 40 minutes. Remove cover and brown for 15 minutes at 400 degrees. Serve warm with cream or a butter sauce.

Courtesy of Juliette Gordon Low
Girl Scout National Center

OLD FASHIONED BUTTER SAUCE

Take fresh butter just from the churn; salt it lightly, and cream it. To a cupful, add sugar until it is thick. Serve it over cake or pudding, with some orange peel or nutmeg grated over it.

Mrs. E. R. Tennent,
House-Keeping In The Sunny South, *1885*

DIXIE AMBROSIA

Grate one coconut; the white part only. Sweeten to taste, and put part of it in a large glass bowl. Put in alternate layers of orange segments and pineapple chunks. Sprinkle sugar between each layer. Sprinkle more fresh coconut on top.

Mrs. C. R. Upson,
House-Keeping In The Sunny South, *1885*

AVOCADO CREAM

Yield: 4 to 6 servings

2	ripe avocados, about 5 inches long	⅓	cup sugar
2	tablespoons lemon juice	½	cup commercial sour cream
⅛	teaspoon grated nutmeg		slivered almonds

Peel and pit avocados. Mash through a sieve; there should be about 2 cups. Stir in lemon juice and nutmeg mixed with sugar. Stir in sour cream and mix well. Cover and chill for about 2 hours. Beat well and pile in sherbet cups. Garnish tops with slivered almonds.

CRANBERRY CHRISTMAS PUDDING

Baked holiday puddings are part of the Southern heritage from the first English settlers.

Yield: 2 puddings, 1 2-cup and 1
2-quart

½	pound (2 sticks) butter or margarine	1	pound golden raisins
1½	cups sugar	1	cup chopped, pitted dates
6	eggs	2	cups chopped pecans
3	cups flour	1	cup diced citron
2	teaspoons baking powder	1	cup chopped candied cherries
2	teaspoons vanilla extract	1	11-ounce package mixed dried fruit, chopped
½	teaspoon lemon extract	2	cups fresh cranberries
½	teaspoon almond extract		

Preheat oven to 350 degrees. In a large bowl, cream butter until light and fluffy. Beat in sugar. Beat in eggs, one at a time, beating well after each. Stir in flour and baking powder until well blended. Stir in remaining ingredients. Mix well. Spoon and press batter into an oiled and floured 2-quart mold, and an oiled and floured 2-cup mold. Bake for 1 hour and 15 minutes for the small mold, and 2 hours for the large mold. Cover cakes with foil during last 15 minutes of baking time if necessary. Unmold while pudding is still hot.

Cool thoroughly. To store, wrap puddings tightly in foil. Store in a cool, dry place until ready to serve. This pudding tastes best when it is aged about 2 weeks before serving. It keeps well, and mails well at the holiday season.

Savannah News-Press

BRANDIED GRAPES

Yield: 4 to 5 servings

1	teaspoon lemon juice	2½	cups halved seedless grapes
¼	cup honey		commercial sour cream
2	tablespoons brandy		grated nutmeg

Combine juice, honey, and brandy. Add grapes and marinate well, covered, in the refrigerator for at least three hours; overnight is even better. Serve in sherbet cups with a dollop of sour cream and a whisper of grated nutmeg on the cream.

THE COTTAGE SHOP

The beautifully restored Cottage Shop at 2422 Abercorn Street was once a plantation cottage, built about 1798 by John Maupas on land that had been part of his mother's share of the extensive Drouillard Plantation. His grandfather, Andre Drouillard, had come to Savannah from the colony of Santo Domingo as a refugee from the slave insurrection led by Tousant L'Ouverture. Maupas developed a plantation which was known prior to The War Between the States for its production of a high grade of long staple cotton. The little house was badly damaged during the war, as it was in the direct line of fire when Northern troops overran the Southern defenses of the city. Happily, the home which was once called "the bride's house" of the plantation, where newlyweds of the family lived until the new family outgrew it, has now come full circle. Now a gift shop, it is still visited by Savannah brides and their families when a wedding is being planned.

*Drawing by the late Christopher Murphy,
Courtesy of The Cottage Shop*

LEMON CHARLOTTTE

An old, and treasured recipe.

Yield: 8 to 10 servings

1 envelope unflavored gelatin	1½ teaspoons grated lemon peel
½ cup lemon juice	1 teaspoon vanilla extract
4 eggs, separated	2 4-ounce packages (about 16)
1½ cups sugar	plain ladyfingers
⅛ teaspoon salt	2 cups heavy cream
3 tablespoons butter	

Soften gelatin in lemon juice; set aside. Beat egg yolks with 1 cup of sugar and salt until thick. In top of double boiler, combine egg yolk mixture, softened gelatin, and butter. Cook over hot, not boiling, water, stirring constantly, until mixture coats a metal spoon and is thickened, about 10 minutes. Stir in lemon peel and vanilla. Cool.

Meanwhile, line bottom and sides of a 9-inch slip-bottom angel food pan with split ladyfingers. Beat egg whites only until they hold soft peaks. Gradually add other half-cup sugar. Beat until stiff but not dry. Whip cream until it holds soft peaks. Fold whites and 1 cup of whipped cream into lemon mixture. Refrigerate several hours, until set. Remove from pan to serve. Garnish with other cup of whipped cream.

The staff of The Cottage Shop

FRESH PEACH CRISP

Yield: 6 to 8 servings

4 cups sliced peaches	¼ teaspoon grated lemon peel
½ cup flour	¼ teaspoon nutmeg
½ cup light brown sugar,	⅛ teaspoon salt
firmly packed	4 tablespoons (½ stick) butter

Preheat oven to 375 degrees. Arrange peaches in a buttered 9-inch pie plate. Combine dry ingredients; cut in butter until mixture resembles coarse crumbs. Sprinkle flour mixture over peaches. Bake 35 to 40 minutes or until topping is lightly browned. Serve warm, with ice cream, if desired.

CHERRY-POACHED PEARS

Yield: 4 servings

½ cup dry white wine	½ cup light brown sugar,
¼ cup cherry liqueur	firmly packed
¼ cup water	2 large winter pears, ripe but firm

Place wine, liqueur, water, and sugar in an 8-inch frying pan. Let come to a boil. Meanwhile, quarter and core, but do not peel, pears. Add pears to boiling liquid. Cover, lower heat, and poach for about 10 minutes, or until pears are tender but not mushy. Remove from heat and let cool uncovered. Cover and refrigerate until needed. Serve chilled, with juice.

PORTLY PLUMS

Yield: 4 to 5 servings

2 pounds plums, halved and pitted	grated peel from ½ orange
1 cup sugar	6 cloves
2 cups port	1 cinnamon stick

Combine ingredients in heavy saucepan. Bring to a boil and simmer about 10 minutes, or until plums begin to soften. Marinate in port sauce in refrigerator a day or so before serving. At serving time, remove plums and strain liquid to remove the cloves and cinnamon stick. Pour sauce back over plums before serving. Poaching plums is an ideal way to cook them, since it makes them even juicier and leaves the color almost intact.

EMMA'S PERNICIOUS PRUNES

Yield: 6 servings

1 12-ounce can moist pitted prunes	⅓ cup sugar
¾ cup Burgundy	heavy or lightly whipped unsweetened cream
¾ cup water	

Marinate prunes in wine and water, covered, in refrigerator overnight. (The longer, the better.) Add sugar, and simmer very gently for about 15 minutes. With a slotted spoon, remove prunes. Gently boil liquid until the consistency of a thick syrup, being careful not to burn. Pour syrup over prunes and chill. Serve with cream.

EMMA'S POACHED STRAWBERRIES

Yield: 4 servings

1 pint fresh strawberries	1 tablespoon lemon juice
⅓ cup sugar	3 ounces cream cheese
¼ cup orange juice	

Rinse berries and hull. In a quart-sized saucepan, stir together sugar, orange juice, and lemon juice, until sugar is dissolved. Bring to a gentle boil and cook 5 minutes. Add berries; cover and barely simmer 3 minutes. Remove from heat; uncover. Berries should be whole and puffy. With a cheese cutter or sharp knife frequently dipped in hot water, cut cheese into ¼-inch cubes. Divide half of cheese among 4 sherbet glasses. Pour warm berries with syrup over cubes. Cover with rest of cheese. Let cool. Cover with foil or plastic wrap and refrigerate until needed. May be done early in the morning for dinner, or even the day before.

STRAWBERRY-YOGURT DELIGHT

Yield: 6 servings

1	pint strawberries	½	cup light corn syrup
1	pint vanilla yogurt	¼	cup sugar
1	egg white	1	tablespoon lemon juice

Reserve 3 nice berries for garnish. Combine ingredients in a blender or electric mixer until smooth. Freeze until firm in a shallow 1-quart bowl. Scoop into chilled dessert dishes and garnish each serving with a strawberry half.

JELLIED BOURBON

A light, mysterious dessert for a company meal!

Yield: 4 servings

1	tablespoon unflavored gelatin	½	cup orange juice
1	cup water	½	cup bourbon whiskey
⅓	cup sugar		

Sprinkle gelatin over ¼ cup water. Boil remaining water and pour over softened gelatin, stirring until dissolved. Stir in sugar and let dissolve. Stir in orange juice and bourbon. Pour in individual molds and chill until set. Serve garnished with whipped cream topped with a light sprinkle of nutmeg.

SHERRY JELLY

Follow recipe for **Jellied Bourbon**, except use ¾ cup cream sherry, 1 tablespoon lemon juice, and a dash of salt, in place of the bourbon. Garnish with whipped cream and sliced strawberries, if available.

MINCEMEAT GELATIN

For a light dessert after holiday meals, prepare a 3-ounce package of orange gelatin as directed on package. Chill slightly, and then fold in one cup of canned or reconstituted dried mincemeat. Serve in a mold or individual dishes with a bit of whipped cream topping, if desired. This recipe was first developed in a hospital for those whose diets excluded the traditional mince pie; it cuts calories while keeping the mincemeat flavor associated with festive occasions. Yield: 6 4-ounce servings.

MADAME SALLI'S CHOCOLATE SOUFFLE

Yield: 4 servings

4	ounces semi-sweet chocolate	1	tablespoon almond flavoring or
3	egg yolks		2 tablespoons Grand Marnier
4	tablespoons sugar	4	egg whites

Butter and sugar a 1½-quart souffle dish; set aside. Melt chocolate in a double boiler; set aside. Beat egg yolks well. Slowly add sugar and beat until lemon-colored. Add chocolate and desired flavoring, beating constantly.

Preheat oven to 400 degrees. Beat egg whites stiff, but not dry. Fold whites carefully into chocolate mixture and put in prepared dish. Bake 15 minutes and serve immediately. Serve plain, or with a little sweetened whipped cream if desired.

Recipe may be prepared about 1 hour before dinner, up to beating of egg whites and folding in chocolate mixture. If you do this, be sure to stir chocolate mixture well before stirring in egg whites. This is a very simple souffle, made without flour, and is a delightful dinner dessert with a bit of planning.

Sally Haas

EASY CHOCOLATE MOUSSE

An easy blender variation of a rich and famous dessert.

Yield: 8 servings

1	12-ounce package semi-sweet	3	eggs
	chocolate morsels	1	cup milk
¼	cup sugar	2	tablespoons brandy or rum

Combine chocolate morsels, sugar, and eggs in electric blender. Scald milk, and pour into blender. Cover and blend on medium speed until mixture is smooth. Pour into 8 pot de creme or other small containers. Chill at least 1 hour. Top with a garnish of whipped cream if desired. Butterscotch or coconut morsels may be used for variation. Or, vary garnish with a bit of grated sweetened coconut.

COFFEE TORTONI

A light, easy-to-prepare dessert which can be whipped up before guests arrive.

Yield: 8 servings

1	egg white	¼	cup sugar
1	tablespoon dry instant coffee	1	teaspoon vanilla extract
⅛	teaspoon salt	¼	teaspoon almond extract
2	tablespoons sugar	¼	cup finely chopped
1	cup heavy cream		toasted almonds

Beat egg white, adding coffee and salt when partially stiff. Beat mixture until stiff but not dry. Gradually add 2 tablespoons sugar; beat until stiff and satiny.

Whip cream until thickened; gradually add ¼ cup sugar, vanilla, and almond extract as you continue to whip until mixture holds peaks.

Fold with nuts into egg white mixture. Pour into eight 2-ounce souffle cups. Cover and freeze until ready to serve.

Jerry Downey

PEACH-MINCE SUNDAE

Yield: 6 to 10 servings

2	cups peach slices, drained	2	cups chopped pecans
2	cups peach juice (less for a thicker topping)	2	tablespoons brandy, sherry, or rum
1	to 2 cups chopped mincemeat	½	gallon vanilla ice cream

Combine peaches, juice, mincemeat, and nuts. Bring to a simmer; remove from heat. Stir in flavoring. Spoon hot over ice cream, and serve.

PEANUT BUTTER RIPPLE ICE CREAM

Yield: 2 quarts plus 1 cup

½	cup crunchy peanut butter	1	teaspoon orange extract
¾	cup honey	½	gallon vanilla ice cream, slightly softened
½	teaspoon ground nutmeg		

Combine peanut butter, honey, nutmeg, and extract. Layer ice cream and peanut mixture in a metal bowl or other 2-quart freezer container, beginning and ending with ice cream. Freeze until firm.

PEANUT BUTTER PUDDING OR PIE FILLING

Yield: 4 to 6 servings

2½ tablespoons cornstarch	2 egg yolks, beaten
¼ cup sugar	2 egg whites
2 cups milk	¼ teaspoon salt
¼ cup peanut butter	½ teaspoon vanilla extract

Mix cornstarch and sugar. Add milk slowly, stirring until smooth. Cook over boiling water in double boiler until thickened, 10 to 15 minutes, stirring frequently. Blend in peanut butter. Stir a little of the hot mixture into egg yolks. Then add yolks to the rest of the hot mixture, and continue cooking a minute or two longer. Cool slightly, and stir in the vanilla.

If you are making a pie, pour slightly cooled mixture into a baked pie shell, and top with a meringue if desired, or serve with whipped cream. May also be poured in heat-proof pudding dishes for a peanut pudding.

Mrs. G. W. Burke, Garden City, Georgia
Savannah News-Press

BOURBON DESSERT SAUCE

Yield: about 2 cups

¼ pound (1 stick) butter	1 egg, beaten
1 cup sugar	⅓ cup bourbon whiskey

Cook butter and sugar together over very low heat until sugar is dissolved; let butter bubble slightly and remove from heat. Pour in slow but steady stream into egg, whipping all the time. Cool, and stir in bourbon. Good over ice cream, pound or angel food cake. May be varied with rum or cream sherry.

BRANDIED FRUIT SAUCE

An old Southern recipe from the days when brandy was used as a preservative.

Place 1 quart brandy (or rum) in a large stone crock with a lid. As they come in season, add 1 quart each of various fresh fruits...EXCEPT bananas, pears, blackberries, apples, or currants. With each addition of fruit, add as much sugar by weight, and some more brandy or rum. Stir every day until the last of the fruit has been added. Keep fruit always covered with liquid, and air-tight. It takes 6 weeks for each layer of fruit to mature. Keep in a cool place. It will keep indefinitely. Stir well before serving as a sauce with vanilla ice cream, puddings or pound cake, or as a sauce for ham.

Lou Dobbs

FOAMING SAUCE FOR A FRUIT PUDDING

Yield: 12 servings

½ pound (2 sticks) butter, at room temperature
2 cups sifted confectioner's sugar

2 egg whites
½ cup cream sherry
¼ cup boiling water

Beat butter in a large bowl until fluffy. Gradually beat in sugar. Stir in egg whites, one at a time, and beat well. Beat in sherry. Place bowl in a basin of hot water, and stir about 2 minutes, until sauce becomes a foaming froth. Serve warm. A good sauce for gingerbread, pound cake, or ice cream, too!

Helen Kehoe Crolly

PEANUT BUTTERSCOTCH SAUCE

Yield: 2½ cups

¼ pound (1 stick) butter
2 cups light brown sugar, firmly packed
⅔ cup (1 small can) evaporated milk, half and half, or cream

½ cup creamy peanut butter

Melt butter in a saucepan over low heat. Gradually stir in sugar,- then milk. Add peanut butter and cook, stirring constantly, until well mixed. Good over ice cream or pound cake.

Georgia Peanut Commission

GINGERED RAISIN SAUCE

Yield: about 1½ cups

1 cup sugar
¾ cup water
½ cup clear corn syrup
¹⁄₁₆ teaspoon salt
1 cup minced seedless golden raisins

1 tablespoon minced crystallized ginger
2 tablespoons lemon juice
1½ teaspoons grated lemon rind
½ cup chopped pecans

Combine all ingredients except pecans in small saucepan. Stir over moderate heat until sugar is dissolved. Let simmer until mixture has thickened slightly. Remove from heat and stir in nuts. Serve hot or cold. Good over ice cream, plain cake, or bread pudding.

COFFEE CUSTARD

Make a cooked custard from one pint of strong coffee, and one pint of milk, boiled together; six beaten eggs, and one and a half cups of sugar. Serve warm with cake.

Mrs. F. Perry,
House-Keeping In The Sunny South, 1885

WINE SAUCE

1 cup butter, 2 cups powdered (confectioner's) sugar, ½ cupful hot wine. Beat butter to a cream, add the sugar gradually, and when very light, add the wine, a little at a time. Place the bowl in a basin of hot water, and stir for 2 minutes. It should be smooth and foamy.

Favorite Recipes From Savannah Homes, 1904

ENGLISH PLUMBS

Records of the Ann, *the ship in which Oglethorpe and the Georgia colonists came to the New World, indicate that the vessel's menu included beef four times a week, pork two times, and fish once a week. Every five persons were alloted two pounds of flour, "and one half pound plumbs for dessert...."*

Colonial Receipts and Remedies *by Mary H. Freeman*

This 1973 drawing of River Street by Mark Lindsay was done before the recently completed restoration project of the city, with its new bulkheading and riverfront park. Site of the Georgia Week pageant every February and monthly "First Saturdays," the street features cotton warehouses which are now craft shops, restaurants, and boutiques.

Drawing by Mark Lindsay.
Copyright© 1973 by Lady Print Shop

CAKES

CAKE MAKING

Cake making should never be attempted unless all the ingredients are at hand. Put on a housekeeping apron, roll the sleeves above the elbows, and remove from the table everything not needed in making the cake. Have a receptacle for the egg shells, and a pan of hot soap-suds in which to throw every knife, fork, spoon and dish as soon as you have finished with them. A cake made with a system is not a Herculean task. It need not disarrange an entire kitchen, and disturb the peace of the whole household as it often does.

First, all the ingredients should be of the best quality. No art can disguise poor ones. . . . The flour and sugar should be sifted. . . . If the recipe calls for baking powder or cream of tartar, sift it in the flour, and dissolve soda in milk. Cream the butter. . . . Raisins should be seeded, currants stemmed, and then cleaned by rubbing in a coarse towel. Slice citron very thin, and then dust all your fruit with flour to prevent its sinking to the bottom.

Never attempt to make a cake while a meal is being prepared. Do not open the stove doors too often, or for too long at a time. . . . You may know when the cake is done, by piercing it with a straw. If it comes out clean, take the cake from the stove. . . . Let your cakes get thoroughly cold before removing to a plate or cake stand. This prevents a damp and sticky undersurface. Keep in a box devoid of any other articles of food. Cake imbibes odors almost as readily as does butter.

House-Keeping In The Sunny South, 1885

LANE CAKE

No Southern cookbook is complete without a recipe for Lane Cake, the tiered, filled specialty of Emma Rylander Lane of Clayton, Alabama. A beautiful young mother of four, Mrs. Lane was the author of the 1898 classic cookbook, *Some Good Things To Eat.* The cake first won her recognition when it took first prize at the state fair in Columbus, Georgia. It was named, she noted in her book, "Not from my own conceit, but through the courtesy of Mrs. Janie McDowell Pruett," a friend from Eufaula, Alabama. It has since been called the South's favorite Christmas cake.

Here is the original recipe, updated by Mrs. Lane's granddaughter, Emma Rylander Law.

3¼	cups sifted cake flour	2	cups sugar
2	teaspoons baking powder	2	teaspoons vanilla extract
¹⁄₁₆	teaspoon salt	8	egg whites
½	pound (2 sticks) butter, at room temperature	1	cup milk

Preheat oven to 375 degrees. On wax paper, sift dry ingredients. Cream butter, sugar, and vanilla. Add egg whites in four additions, beating after each. Fold in flour mixture alternately with milk; begin and end with dry ingredients. Turn into 4 ungreased 9-inch round layer cake pans, lined on the bottom with wax paper.

Bake until edges shrink slightly from sides of pans and tops spring back when gently pressed with finger, or cake tester inserted in the center comes out clean, about 20 minutes. Cool on wire racks about 5 minutes. Turn out of pans; remove wax paper. Turn right side up. Cool completely.

Put layers together with **Lane Cake Filling**. Cover top and sides with **Boiled White Frosting**. Cover, store in cool place. If refrigerated, bring to room temperature before serving for best texture. Cake is better a day or so after making.

Lane Cake Filling

8	egg yolks	1	cup seedless raisins, finely chopped
1	cup sugar		
¼	pound (1 stick) butter, at room temperature	⅓	cup bourbon or brandy
		1	teaspoon vanilla extract

In a 2-quart saucepan, beat the egg yolks. Add the sugar and butter. Cook, stirring constantly, over moderate heat, until quite thick. Remove from heat, stir in raisins, bourbon or brandy, and vanilla. Cool slightly; use as directed in cake recipe.

Boiled White Frosting

½ cup sugar   2 tablespoons water
¼ cup white corn syrup   2 egg whites
⅛ teaspoon salt   ½ teaspoon vanilla extract

In a 1-quart saucepan, mix the sugar, syrup, salt, and water. Stir over moderately low heat several times to dissolve sugar. Boil to thread stage, (see **Candy Stages**) or 242 degrees on the candy thermometer.

Beat egg whites to soft peaks. Gradually beat about half of syrup into beaten whites. Place saucepan with remaining syrup in a skillet of hot water off heat to keep warm. Continue beating egg white mixture until thick and fluffy. Gradually beat in remaining warm syrup and vanilla. Continue to beat, if necessary, until mixture holds stiff, shiny peaks.

LANE CAKE-MAKING HINTS

Strangely enough, Mrs. Lane's own favorite cake was not Lane Cake, but a brown fruit cake of which she warned, "Under no condition should a fruit cake be cut before it is a month old!" Her hint for preserving fruit cake:

Put away in close tin boxes, with three or four sound apples to each box. This will keep the cakes fresh and moist for several months, and they improve with age, only be careful to look often into the boxes to see that the apples do not decay, and as they begin to speck, replace them with sound ones.

In measuring or weighing cake materials, be perfectly accurate, remembering that over or under weight, scant or heaping measure, unless so directed, will nearly always bring failure....

Egg whites should not be whipped until quite ready to use, and must be put into the batter immediately after they are beaten and the whip removed. Allowing them to stand for even one minute will make the cake coarse-grained, and a little tough....No one can expect to do first class work of any description without the necessary implements.

Some Good Things To Eat, 1898

LAW CAKE

Another of Mrs. Lane's recipes, White Pound Cake, used pure alcohol. Emma Rylander Law made it with vodka instead. Her friend, food editor Cecily Brownstone of the Associated Press, renamed it **Law Cake** when she featured it in one of her syndicated newspaper columns. You'll call it unusual!

½ pound crystallized ginger
½ cup finely chopped pecans
3 cups sifted cake flour
3 teaspoons baking powder

½ pound (2 sticks) butter
1¾ cups sugar
8 egg whites from large eggs
¾ cup 80-proof vodka

Line bottom of an 11-by-4½-by-2¾-inch pan with wax paper. Butter paper. Rinse ginger with hot water to soften and remove outside coating of sugar; drain and dry well on paper toweling. With kitchen scissors, snip ginger into tiny pieces, about 1 cup. Mix ginger, pecans, and ½ cup flour.

Sift together remaining flour and baking powder. Cream butter and sugar; beat in egg whites in 4 additions, with medium speed of electric beater, beating ½ minute after each addition. Preheat oven to 300 degrees.

Sprinkle about one-third of the flour mixture over creamed mixture, and fold in with rubber spatula. Gently stir in about half of the vodka. Add another third of the flour and fold in; stir in remaining vodka and fold in remaining flour. Fold in ginger-pecan mixture with any flour that does not stick to the ginger and nuts. Batter will be grainy.

Turn into prepared pan, and flatten top with spatula. Bake until a cake tester comes out clean, or 1 hour and 35 to 45 minutes. Cake will have a crack on top.

Put cake on pan or wire rack for 30 minutes. Loosen edge, turn out on rack, and remove paper. Turn cake right side up; cool completely.

Wrap cold cake in transparent plastic wrap for a few hours, or overnight, before slicing so that flavor can mellow and top crust soften enough for easy slicing.

Emma R. Law

OGLETHORPE'S BIRTHDAY

Oglethorpe once more called for gaiety to celebrate his own birthday, and for this a pint of rum per head was ordered all around, after which Cudgel was played for the coveted prize of a pair of shoes.

Colonial Receipts and Remedies *by Mary H. Freeman*

GATEAU CECILY

"Here is the most elegant French-type layer cake I know how to make," food writer Cecily Brownstone says in her *Associated Press Cook Book.* As a popular columnist as well as food editor of A.P., her recipes are world-famous. In giving one to be reprinted here she added, "Although the cake and frosting recipes are not spanking new, I did evolve this way of assembling them with a filling of apricot preserves and cognac, and so I've named the dessert **Gateau Cecily** out of my own conceit."

1	cup plus 2 tablespoons sifted cake flour	1	cup sugar
1	teaspoon baking powder	¾	teaspoon vanilla extract
½	cup milk	½	cup apricot preserves
4	tablespoons (½ stick) butter	¼	cup cognac
6	egg yolks	⅓	cup slivered toasted blanched almonds

Grease and flour three 8-inch round layer cake pans. Or, if your pans tend to stick, line the bottom of the pans with wax paper; grease and flour the sides of the pans and the paper. On wax paper, sift together the flour and the baking powder.

In a small saucepan, heat milk until bubbles appear around the edge; set aside to cool slightly. In a small skillet melt butter; set aside to cool slightly.

Preheat oven to 350 degrees. In a medium mixing bowl, with electric beater at high speed, beat together egg yolks and sugar until thick and ivory color. Gradually beat in milk and vanilla. At low speed, gradually beat in flour mixture, making sure all flour is moistened. Fold in butter. Turn into prepared pans.

Bake until cake tester inserted in center comes out clean, about 15 minutes. Place pans on wire racks to cool for 10 minutes. With a small spatula, cut around edges of layers, using an up-and-down motion to prevent tearing edges of cake. Turn cakes out of pans onto wire rack to cool completely. Thoroughly mix together preserves and cognac, beating to break up any large apricot pieces; set aside and prepare **Vanilla Butter Cream.**

Vanilla Butter Cream

1 cup sugar	2 egg whites
1 tablespoon light corn syrup	1 tablespoon vanilla extract
¼ cup water	⅔ cup butter, softened slightly

In a 1½-quart saucepan over moderate heat, stir together sugar, corn syrup, and water until sugar dissolves and mixture comes to a boil. Boil gently, without stirring, to 240 degrees on a candy thermometer, or until a small amount of syrup dropped into cold water forms a soft ball that flattens on removal from water. Remove from heat and set aside.

In a medium mixing bowl with electric beater, beat egg whites until they form stiff straight peaks; beat in vanilla. Gradually beat in hot syrup; cool.

In another medium mixing bowl, without washing beater, thoroughly beat the butter. Then beat in the egg white mixture, a few tablespoons at a time.

Place one cake layer upon a cake plate; spread with half of the apricot preserve mixture. Add another cake layer; spread with remaining preserve mixture. Add third layer. Cover top and sides of cake with **Vanilla Butter Cream** and refrigerate. At serving time, sprinkle top of cake with almonds, pressing down firmly; serve at once. Return any left over cake to the refrigerator.

Cecily Brownstone, **Cecily Brownstone's Associated Press Cook Book**

HELEN McCULLY'S CHOCOLATE CAKE
WITH CHOCOLATE GLAZE

Food editor of *House Beautiful* and author of such books as *Cooking With Helen McCully Beside You* and *The Other Half of The Egg,* the late Helen McCully combined wit and taste in her writing about good food. She selected this recipe as her favorite for this collection.

¼ pound (1 stick) butter, at room temperature, cut up	⅔ cup sugar
1 cup (1 5½-ounce bag or can) almonds, skin on	3 eggs grated rind of 1 large orange
4 1-ounce squares semi-sweet chocolate or ¾ cup chocolate pieces	¼ cup very fine dry bread crumbs

Butter the sides of an 8-inch round cake pan. Line the bottom with kitchen parchment. Set aside.

Melt the chocolate in the top of a double boiler over hot, but not boiling, water. Preheat oven to 375 degrees. Work the butter with an electric beater or in an electric mixer until very soft and light. Gradually work in the sugar, beating constantly. Once all the sugar has been added, add the eggs, one at a time, beating hard after each addition. (The batter, at this point, may look curdled, but don't be alarmed!)

Stir in the melted chocolate, ground nuts, orange rind, and bread crumbs thoroughly. Pour into the prepared pan and bake for 25 minutes. Take from the oven and cool for 30 minutes on a cake rack. Turn out on the rack. If the cake doesn't drop out easily, give the pan a good bang with your hands. Lift off, and discard the parchment. Cool completely. The center of the cake will not seem thoroughly cooked; hence its soft texture and exceptionally delicious flavor.

Chocolate Glaze

2	1-ounce squares unsweetened chocolate	4	tablespoons (½ stick) butter, softened and cut up
2	1-ounce squares semisweet chocolate or ¼ cup chocolate pieces	2	teaspoons honey toasted slivered almonds

Combine the two chocolates, the butter, and the honey in the top of a double boiler. Melt over hot water. Take off the heat and beat until cold but still pourable; in other words, until it begins to thicken.

Place the cake on a rack over a piece of waxed paper, and pour the glaze over all. Tip the cake so the glaze runs evenly over the top and down the sides. Smooth sides, if necessary, with a metal spatula. Garland the rim of the cake with toasted slivered almonds, placing them fairly close together.

This cake freezes successfully if wrapped and sealed securely. Bring to room temperature before serving and the glaze will become shiny again.

Helen McCully, New York City

WHITE CHOCOLATE CAKE

This cake, one of the most unique recipes tested, is moist and delicious with pecans and coconut. It may be that "different" recipe you've been looking for, to serve at a special occasion; it's good enough to start a family tradition. White chocolate is available in many specialty stores, such as Gottleib's in Savannah, in imported Tobler 3-ounce bars, half-pound packages of squares, or from a slab. We found the cake rich enough to require no frosting but a sifting of confectioners' sugar over the top for those who wish it. However, a **White Chocolate Frosting** recipe is included, either for this cake or to use separately.

1	3-ounce bar white chocolate, broken in pieces	¾	cup commercial buttermilk
6	tablespoons water	6	ounces (1½ sticks) butter, at room temperature
2	cups plus 3 tablespoons sifted flour	1½	cups sugar
¾	teaspoon baking powder	3	eggs
⅟₁₆	teaspoon salt	1	3½-ounce can (1 cup) flaked coconut
¾	teaspoon vanilla extract	¾	cup finely chopped pecans

Place chocolate and water in a quart saucepan over very low heat. Stir until no lumps remain. Let cool on a rack. Preheat oven to 350 degrees. Sift flour and baking powder together; set aside. Stir salt and vanilla into buttermilk; set aside. Cream butter and sugar together until light and fluffy. Add eggs, one at a time, beating well after each

Beat in cooled chocolate. Gently fold in flour alternately with buttermilk, beginning and ending with dry ingredients. Fold in coconut and pecans. Turn into three prepared 8-inch square layer pans, or one 13-by-9-by-2-inch baking pan. Butter bottoms, or line the bottom of pan with waxed paper, and then butter the paper, but do not butter sides of pan. Bake for 25 to 30 minutes, or until done. Let cool in pans on racks for 10 to 15 minutes. Turn onto racks, remove paper, and turn top side up to finish cooling. Frost when cool with **White Chocolate Frosting** if desired, or finish with a sift of confectioner's sugar. Do *not* use a "7-minute icing" recipe with this cake; it is too soft. If preferred, 8-inch round cake pans may be used instead of square ones.

White Chocolate Frosting

½	cup water	½	teaspoon cream of tartar
¼	cup light corn syrup	1	teaspoon vanilla extract
3	cups sugar	1	cup sifted confectioner's sugar
4	egg whites		

Bring water, syrup, and sugar to a boil in a 2-quart saucepan, and cook until mixture spins a two-inch thread when dropped from a fork or spoon (234 degrees on a candy thermometer). Remove from heat. Whip egg whites with cream of tartar until stiff but not dry. Pour syrup very slowly into whites, beating all the while. Beat in vanilla and confectioner's sugar.

When of spreading consistency, spread over first layer of cake (if making layer recipe), then over second layer, and then third one. With one hand holding layers gently in line, spread icing up and down sides. Lastly, cover top. Enjoy!

Marjorie Wright

MOTHER'S SELF-ICE CAKE

As food editor of *Southern Living* Magazine, Jean Wickstrom sees some of the South's best recipes. This is her personal favorite for an easy to bake and take dessert:

1	cup chopped dates	1	teaspoon vanilla extract
1	cup boiling water	1¾	cups flour
1	teaspoon baking soda	½	teaspoon salt
½	cup vegetable shortening	½	teaspoon cream of tartar
1	cup sugar	1	6-ounce package chocolate
2	eggs		chips
2	teaspoons cocoa	¾	cup chopped nuts

Combine dates, water, soda; let stand until cool. Preheat oven to 350 degrees. Cream shortening and sugar; add eggs and beat well. Add cocoa and vanilla extract; blend well. Slowly add the flour, salt, and cream of tartar; stir until well blended. Add date mixture; mix well. Pour into a greased 13-by-9-by-2-inch pan. Sprinkle chocolate chips and nuts over top of cake. Bake cake for 30 minutes. Cool. Keep cake covered in pan to store. This is especially nice for picnics.

Jean Wickstrom, Food Editor, Southern Living Magazine

ITALIAN CREAM CAKE

Southern Living Magazine's first food editor, Lena Sturges has also tested some of the South's finest foods. One personal favorite is this moist, rich cake.

¼	pound (1 stick) butter or margarine	1	teaspoon baking soda
½	cup vegetable shortening	1	cup buttermilk
2	cups sugar	1	teaspoon vanilla extract
5	egg yolks	1	3½-ounce can grated coconut
2	cups sifted flour	1	cup chopped pecans
		5	egg whites, stiffly beaten

Preheat oven to 350 degrees. Combine margarine and shortening; add sugar and beat until mixture is smooth. Add egg yolks and beat well. Combine flour and soda and add to creamed mixture alternately with buttermilk. Stir in vanilla. Add coconut and chopped nuts. Fold in stiffly-beaten egg whites. Pour batter into three greased and floured 8-inch cake pans. Bake for 25 minutes, or until cake tests done. Cool. Frost with **Cream Cheese Frosting.**

Cream Cheese Frosting

8 ounces cream cheese, at room temperature	1 pound confectioner's sugar
4 tablespoons (½ stick) butter or margarine, at room temperature	1 teaspoon vanilla extract chopped pecans

Beat cream cheese and margarine until smooth; add sugar and mix well. Add vanilla and beat until smooth. Spread between layers and on top and sides of cake. Sprinkle top with pecans.

Lena E. Sturges

FAVORITE STRAWBERRY SHORTCAKE

A *Savannah News-Press* staff writer and author of the popular "Savannah Scene" column, Bette M. Hurst says this is still her all-time choice.

Sponge Cake

1¼ cups sifted flour	6 eggs, separated
1½ cups sugar	1 teaspoon cream of tartar
½ teaspoon baking powder	¼ cup water
½ teaspoon salt	1 teaspoon vanilla extract

Sift together flour, 1 cup sugar, baking powder, and salt. Beat egg whites at high speed until frothy. Add cream of tartar. Gradually add other ½ cup sugar, beating until peaks form, and whites are stiff but not dry.

Preheat oven to 350 degrees. Combine egg yolks, water, vanilla, and dry ingredients. Beat at medium high speed until thick and lemon-colored, about 4 minutes. Gradually fold egg yolk mixture into egg whites. Pour batter into ungreased 10-inch tube pan. Bake for 45 minutes, or until cake tests done when lightly pressed with fingers. While cake is baking prepare **Strawberry Filling and Topping**. Invert tube pan on funnel or bottle to cool. When completely cool, remove from pan.

Strawberry Filling and Topping

2 pints fresh strawberries	2 tablespoons butter or margarine, at room temperature
1 cup sugar	
½ cup heavy cream	
1 teaspoon vanilla extract	

While **Sponge Cake** is baking, gently wash berries in cold water. Drain; hull. Reserve at least 6 large berries for garnish. Slice remaining berries into medium bowl. Add sugar; stir gently. Set aside until ready to use.

In a small bowl, whip cream until stiff but not dry. Stir in vanilla. Split cake in half crosswise. Place bottom half, cut side up, on a serving platter. Spread with butter. Spoon on half the sliced berries. Top with the other half of the cake, cut side down. Spoon on rest of sliced berries and the whipped cream. Garnish with whole berries.

There are many ways to make a strawberry shortcake. Some prefer more of a biscuit dough...but my vote is for a sponge cake, and fresh berries with real cream!

Bette M. Hurst

MARTHA WASHINGTON'S GREAT CAKE

The original recipe of the First Lady, copied in her own hand and passed to her descendants, called for forty eggs! Here is Emma R. Law's adaptation for modern kitchens, but with old-time goodness.

½ pound (2 sticks) butter	¼ to ½ cup brandy
1 cup sugar	2 pounds packaged fruit cake
5 eggs	mix or assorted fruits for fruit
2½ cups sifted flour	cake
¼ teaspoon nutmeg	

Preheat oven to 300 degrees. Cream butter. Add sugar gradually and beat until light and fluffy. Add eggs, one at a time, beating well after each. Fold in about half the flour, sifted with the nutmeg, then ¼-cup brandy and the remaining flour; fold in gently but well. Fold in fruit. Turn into ungreased 9-inch springform ring mold or 9-inch tube pan with slip bottom. (If using a one-piece pan, be sure to grease bottom.)

Bake about one hour and 20 minutes, or until top is golden brown and springs back when touched gently with fingers. Cool in pan on rack about 30 minutes. Remove from pan; continue cooling on rack. Store in air-tight container, or well-wrapped in heavy foil. Optional: for several days, dribble a bit more brandy on top of cake.

Hints: vary spice with mace, cinnamon, or pumpkin pie spice instead of nutmeg. Vary fruit as desired, as long as total weight is two pounds. You may use half fruit and half nuts. Or, bourbon or rum may be used instead of brandy.

NORWEGIAN GOLD CAKE

The mixing directions for this cake are different from that of most tube cakes, but the Downey family says no buffet or family gathering is complete without one...and also, that it keeps well.

½ pound (2 sticks) butter or margarine, at room temperature
1⅓ cups sifted flour
5 eggs
1⅓ cups sugar

1½ teaspoons baking powder
½ teaspoon salt
½ teaspoon almond extract
½ teaspoon vanilla extract
confectioner's sugar (optional)

Preheat oven to 325 degrees. Mix butter and flour for 5 minutes at low speed on electric mixer. Add eggs, one at a time, and beat well after each addition. Add sugar, mixed with baking powder and salt, gradually. Add flavorings. Beat two minutes longer at low speed with the electric mixer. Grease bottom of a 10-inch tube pan. Bake approximately one hour. Let cool 10 minutes or so before removing from pan. After it cools, it may be sprinkled with confectioner's sugar if you wish, but do not frost. Delicious!

Jerry Downey

CHARLESTON WEDDING CAKE

Twenty pounds of butter, twenty pounds of sugar, twenty pounds of flour, twenty pounds of raisins, forty pounds of currants, twelve pounds of citrons, twenty nutmegs, one ounce of mace, four ounces of cinnamon, twenty glasses of wine, twenty glasses of brandy, ten eggs to the pound; add cloves, to your taste. If you wish it richer, add two pounds of currants, and one pound of raisins to each pound of flour.

House and Home, or, The Carolina Housewife,
by a Lady of Charleston, 1855

ONE-EGG APPLESAUCE CAKE

1 16-ounce can applesauce
1 cup quick-cooking oats
1½ cups unsifted flour (stir to aerate before measuring)
1 teaspoon baking soda
¾ teaspoon salt
1 teaspoon cinnamon

¼ teaspoon cloves
¼ pound (1 stick) butter or margarine
¾ cup dark brown sugar, firmly packed
1 egg

Grease and flour an 8-inch square cake pan. In a 1-quart saucepan, heat the applesauce until hot. Remove from heat and stir in the oats. Cover tightly and let stand 20 minutes.

Thoroughly stir together the flour, baking soda, salt, cinnamon, and cloves. Preheat oven to 350 degrees.

In a medium mixing bowl, cream butter and sugar. Add egg and beat well. Gradually and gently beat in flour mixture. Add applesauce-oat mixture. Stir well. Turn into prepared pan. Bake until a cake tester inserted in the center comes out clean, 50 to 55 minutes. Cool in pan on a wire rack. Cover top with **Butter Frosting** and let set. Cover tightly during storage of cake and serve in squares as needed. Keeps up to one week.

If you want cake out of the pan, as soon as it comes from the oven, let it stand on a wire rack for about 30 minutes. Then, loosen sides with a small spatula. Use another rack to turn it out on, and then turn it right side up. Cool completely and then frost. Store in tin box.

Butter Frosting

2 tablespoons butter or margarine	½ teaspoon vanilla extract
2 tablespoons milk	2 cups sifted confectioner's sugar, approximately

Beat together the butter, milk, vanilla and 1 cup of the sugar. Gradually add enough sugar to make a spreading consistency, keeping smooth.

Savannah News-Press

BANANA DATE CAKE

1½ cups diced pitted dates	1 teaspoon vanilla extract
1½ cups water	3 cups sifted flour
1½ cups mashed bananas	2 teaspoons baking powder
4 tablespoons (½ stick) butter or margarine	1 teaspoon baking soda
1 cup sugar	½ teaspoon salt
2 eggs, separated	1 cup chopped walnuts

Preheat oven to 350 degrees. Boil dates in water 5 minutes. Cool. Put in large bowl, and beat in bananas, butter, sugar, egg yolks, and vanilla. Sift together next 4 ingredients and fold into banana mixture. Beat egg whites until stiff, and fold in batter with nuts. Spoon into greased and floured 8-or 9-inch Bundt pan. Bake for 50 minutes, or until a cake tester inserted in the cake comes out clean. Cool in pan 10 minutes. Remove from pan and cool on a rack. Frost with **Powdered Sugar Glaze**.

Powdered Sugar Glaze

Combine 1 cup sifted confectioner's sugar, 1 teaspoon soft butter, and enough hot water (or use orange juice in place of water) to form a thin mixture. Pour over cooled cake.

Savannah News-Press

KENTUCKY BLACKBERRY CAKE

This is a very old Southern family recipe from the Cofer family of Elizabethtown, Kentucky. It was formerly made with home-made blackberry jam from whole berries. If you can't find that, Mrs. Saposnik says, it can be made with the seedless variety.

4 cups flour	2 cups sugar
2 teaspoons ground allspice	6 eggs
2 teaspoons ground cloves	2 cups blackberry jam
2 teaspoons ground cinnamon	1½ cups buttermilk
2 teaspoons ground nutmeg	2 teaspoons baking soda
¾ pound (3 sticks) butter, at room temperature	

Preheat oven to 350 degrees. Into a large bowl, sift the flour and mixed spices. In another large bowl, cream the butter and sugar until fluffy. Beat eggs slightly, and beat eggs and jam into butter mixture. Beat in flour mixture alternately with the buttermilk, in which you have dissolved the soda. Begin and end with flour mixture. Pour batter into 3 buttered and floured 9-inch round cake tins. Bake for 35 minutes, or until a cake tester inserted in the center comes out clean. Transfer the tins to racks, let the layers cool, and invert them onto the racks. Frost with **Walnut Frosting.**

Walnut Frosting

2 cups sugar	¼ pound (1 stick) butter
2 cups brown sugar, firmly packed	2 egg yolks
1½ cups light cream	1 cup coarsely chopped walnuts
	½ teaspoon vanilla extract

In a large saucepan, combine the sugars and light cream, butter, and egg yolks. Cook over moderate heat, stirring and washing down any sugar crystals which cling to the side of a pan with a brush dipped in cold water, until the sugar is dissolved. Bring mixture to a boil, stirring, and cook over moderate heat, continuing to stir it as necessary, until it is thickened, about 10 minutes. Remove the pan from the heat and stir in walnuts and vanilla; then let frosting cool until of spreading consistency. With a metal spatula, spread frosting on cooled cake. Store in an airtight container.

Mrs. Saposnik adds that this is their family's favorite cake. If she happens to be in a place where she can't get blackberry jam, she has even been known to buy canned or frozen berries and make her own jam, (following the basic recipe in the **Jellies and Preserves** chapter) in order to make the cake!

Marlene Taber Saposnik, Atlanta, Georgia

DARIEN CARROT CAKE

2 cups sugar	1 cup chopped pecans
1¼ cups vegetable oil	2½ cups cake flour
4 eggs	2¼ teaspoons baking soda
3 cups finely shredded carrots	2 teaspoons cinnamon

Preheat oven to 350 degrees. Combine sugar and oil, beating thoroughly. Add eggs, one at a time, beating well after each addition. Stir in carrots; add nuts. Sift together dry ingredients. Stir into mixture. Turn into 3 greased and floured 9-inch cake pans. Bake for 30 to 35 minutes. Cool before frosting. Good with a lemon butter icing, or try **Cream Cheese-Coconut Icing.**

Mrs. William J. Ward, Darien, Georgia

CREAM CHEESE-COCONUT ICING

8 ounces cream cheese	2 teaspoons vanilla extract
1 pound confectioner's sugar	1 cup chopped pecans
¼ pound (1 stick) butter or margarine	1 cup grated coconut

Mix first 4 ingredients then add nuts and coconut.

Diane Harvey Johnson
Savannah News-Press

RUM AND BRANDY CAKE

This "self-finishing" cake requires no frosting.

⅓ cup chopped pecans	1 teaspoon vanilla extract
¼ teaspoon salt	1 teaspoon almond extract
½ pound (2 sticks) butter	2 tablespoons brandy
1½ cups sugar	1 tablespoon rum
4 eggs	
1½ cups sifted self-rising flour	

Line bottom and sides of an 8½-by-4½-by-2½-inch loaf pan with heavy waxed paper. Sprinkle bottom of pan evenly with pecans, then with salt; set aside. Preheat oven to 350 degrees. Cream butter and sugar together until light and fluffy. Add eggs, one at a time, beating well after each. Combine extracts, brandy, and rum. Fold in flour alternately with mixture of extracts, beginning and ending with flour. Turn into prepared pan. Bake for 1 hour and 10 minutes. Cool in pan on rack for 20 minutes. Carefully turn pan onto rack, and remove from loaf. Gently remove wax paper. Let cake cool completely. Store in airtight container, or wrapped well in heavy foil. If desired, dribble more brandy and rum over top and sides. A few punctures with a skewer will help to get liquid inside cake!

Irving Herschbein

EMMA'S FAVORITE BOURBON CAKE

1	8-ounce package pecans, finely chopped	½	pound (2 sticks) butter, at room temperature
1	11-ounce package dried black currants	2	cups sugar
3	cups sifted flour	4	eggs
3	teaspoons baking powder	1	cup bourbon whisky
¾	teaspoon mace		

Preheat oven to 325 degrees. Toss nuts and currants together. Sprinkle with ½ cup flour and toss to cover. Set aside.

Sift remaining flour well with baking powder and mace. Set aside. Cream butter and sugar together until light and fluffy. Add eggs one at a time, beating well after each. Fold in remaining flour and bourbon, alternately, beginning and ending with the dry material. Fold in nut and currant mixture. Distribute evenly in ungreased 9-or 10-inch tube pan. Bake about an hour and 25 minutes. Cool on rack in pan for 25 minutes. Remove from pan and continue cooling on rack. When completely cool, wrap well in foil and store in cool, dry place or in air-tight container. If necessary to refrigerate, let come to room temperature before serving. A bit more bourbon may be dribbled over top and sides of cake as it cools. Tedious but worth the effort: thinly cross-cut pecans with a sharp knife. This makes prettier slices.

You may also want to try this cake with seedless gold or dark raisins. Snip the raisins into small pieces; this helps to make prettier slices. Try rum or brandy instead of bourbon, or allspice or cinnamon instead of mace. Make your own combinations!

Emma R. Law

GEORGIA NUT CAKE

3¾ cups cake flour
1 teaspoon baking powder
2 cups sugar
½ pound (2 sticks) butter or margarine
6 eggs

6 cups coarsely chopped pecans
⅓ cup bourbon, wine, sherry, brandy, or orange juice
1 teaspoon butter flavoring
1 teaspoon rum extract
1 teaspoon vanilla extract

Preheat oven to 275 degrees. Sift flour and baking powder; set aside. Gradually add sugar to butter or margarine in a large bowl, beating until fluffy. Add eggs two at a time, beating after each addition. Measure ½ cup of flour mixture, and add to nuts in small bowl; mix thoroughly. Add the remainder of the flour mixture to the creamed mixture alternately with the liquid, mixing well after each addition, until blended. Add nuts and mix thoroughly but lightly. Pour batter in an oiled 10-inch tube pan; bake about 2 hours, or until cake pulls away from the pan slightly, and is springy to the touch.

Martha Kemp, Lyons, Georgia
Savannah News-Press

HAZEL FRANKLIN'S POUND CAKE

One of Savannah's most popular cooks is Hazel Franklin, a retired home economist who hosted a local television cooking show for several years. She says this is her favorite recipe for sour cream pound cake, and suggests a maple flavoring variation as well. For extra variety, she says you can also make a half-and-half cake!

½ pound (2 sticks) butter
3 cups sugar
6 eggs
1 teaspoon vanilla extract

1 cup commercial sour cream
3 cups flour
¼ teaspoon baking soda

Preheat oven to 325 degrees. Cream butter; add sugar, ¼ cup at a time, and beat until light and fluffy. Add eggs, one at a time. Continue beating. Combine vanilla and sour cream, and beat into creamed mixture. Add sifted flour and soda and beat two minutes. Pour batter into an oiled tube pan. Bake 1 hour and 20 minutes. Cool on a rack 10 minutes, then remove from pan to finish cooling.

Maple Pound Cake

Add ½ teaspoon maple flavoring and ¾ cups finely chopped pecans to the batter of **Hazel Franklin's Pound Cake**. Mix and bake as usual.

Half-and-Half Cake

Pour one half of **Hazel Franklin's Pound Cake** batter in one side of an oiled tube pan. Add 3 ounces finely chopped pecans and ¼ teaspoon maple flavoring to the other half of the batter, and pour it in the opposite side of the pan. (With a spatula, push the plain batter back as you pour in the second.) Bake as directed above. Especially nice with weekend guests...it's like having two cakes in the house! This cake is best served warm. And it freezes well.

Hazel Franklin

PEACH BRANDY POUND CAKE

½ pound (2 sticks) butter or margarine	1 cup commercial sour cream
3 cups sugar	½ teaspoon lemon extract
6 eggs	½ teaspoon orange extract
3 cups flour	¼ teaspoon rum extract
¼ teaspoon salt	1 teaspoon vanilla extract
¼ teaspoon baking soda	½ cup peach brandy

Preheat oven to 325 degrees. Cream butter and sugar until light and fluffy. Add eggs, one at a time, beating well after each addition. Sift dry ingredients together. Combine sour cream and extracts with brandy. Fold dry ingredients in batter alternately with cream mixture, ending with dry ingredients. Bake in a well-oiled 10-inch tube pan for 70 minutes. Let cool in pan 10 minutes before removing, then remove and cool completely on wire rack.

Mrs. Sally J. Brown, Beaufort, South Carolina

SAVANNAH WHITE FRUIT CAKE

One pound sugar, three-fourths pound butter, one pound flour, whites of 12 eggs, one grated coconut, two pounds almonds blanched and cut fine, one pound citron cut fine; use a little milk if necessary.

Hints From Southern Epicures, *circa 1890*

LAZY DAISY OATMEAL CAKE

1¼ cups boiling water
1 cup uncooked quick or old-fashioned oatmeal
4 tablespoons (½ stick) butter or margarine, at room temperature
1 cup sugar
1 cup brown sugar, firmly packed
1 teaspoon vanilla extract
2 eggs
1½ cups sifted flour
1 teaspoon baking soda
½ teaspoon salt
¾ teaspoon cinnamon
¼ teaspoon nutmeg

Pour boiling water over oatmeal. Let stand 20 minutes. Preheat oven to 350 degrees. Beat butter until creamy. Gradually add sugars, and beat until fluffy. Blend in vanilla and eggs. Add oatmeal mixture; mix well. Sift together flour, soda, salt, and spices. Add to creamed mixture; mix well. Pour into well-greased and floured 9-inch square pan. Bake for 50 to 55 minutes. Frost cake in pan while it is still warm, with **Broiled Frosting.**

Broiled Frosting

4 tablespoons (½ stick) butter or margarine, melted
½ cup brown sugar, firmly packed
1 tablespoon half-and-half cream
⅓ cup chopped pecans
¾ cup grated coconut

Mix well. Spread over warm cake. Broil under medium heat until brown and bubbly, taking care not to burn.

Sandra Jones

MISSISSIPPI MUD CAKE

One of the most popular recipes ever printed in the famous "Swap Shop" column of the *Savannah News-Press* Food section.

2 cups sugar
½ pound (2 sticks) butter
4 eggs
1½ cups flour
½ cup cocoa
1½ cups chopped pecans
⅛ teaspoon salt
1 teaspoon vanilla extract
miniature marshmallows to cover cake

Preheat oven to 350 degrees. Cream together sugar and butter. Add eggs, one at a time, and blend well. Add remaining ingredients and mix well. Pour into a greased and floured pan, 13-by-9-by-2-inches. Bake for 35 minutes. When the cake is done, immediately cover the top with miniature marshmallows. Do not remove from pan. Pour **Mud Icing** over marshmallows after the cake is completely cooled.

Mud Icing

1 pound confectioner's sugar
⅓ cup cocoa
½ teaspoon vanilla extract
6 tablespoons milk

Sift sugar and cocoa together. Add other ingredients and blend well. Pour over marshmallows on **Mississippi Mud Cake**. Delicious!

Mrs. Clark F. Branch, Garden City, Georgia
Mrs. Eschol Dixon, Vidalia, Georgia
Savannah News-Press

COFFEE ANGEL CAKE

What to do with the egg yolks left from making an angel food? Emma R. Law developed these two cakes as an answer to that question: one uses 10 egg whites, and the other the yolks... deliciously.

1 cup sifted flour	¼ teaspoon salt
½ cup sugar	1½ teaspoons cream of tartar
½ teaspoon ground cardamom	2 tablespoons dry instant coffee
¼ teaspoon ground cloves	1 cup sugar
1⅓ cups (about 10) egg whites, at room temperature	

Preheat oven to 375 degrees. Sift flour, ½ cup sugar, cardamom and cloves together several times. Set aside. In a large bowl, combine the egg whites, salt, cream of tartar, and coffee. Beat until stiff enough to hold soft peaks. Add other 1 cup sugar gradually, beating constantly, until sugar is well-blended and mixture holds stiff peaks. Gently fold in the flour mixture, blending well. Distribute batter evenly into ungreased 9-or 10-inch slip-bottom tube pan. Cut through batter several times with knife. Bake for 30 to 35 minutes, or until top springs back when gently pressed with tips of fingers. Invert pan and let cake cool upside down. Remove cake from pan; store in cake box. When ready to serve, sprinkle top with confectioner's sugar, if desired.

Emma R. Law

TEA NUT CAKE

Now to use those left-over egg yolks.

½ pound (2 sticks) butter or margarine, at room temperature	1 teaspoon ground allspice
	2 tablespoons dry instant tea
	¾ cup water
1½ cups sugar	2 cups or 1 7-ounce can flaked coconut
10 large egg yolks, at room temperature	3 cups coarsely chopped walnuts, or 1 12-ounce package shelled nuts
2½ cups sifted flour	
1½ teaspoons baking powder	

Preheat oven to 300 degrees. Cream butter. Add sugar gradually, and beat until light and fluffy. Add egg yolks, about 2 at a time, beating well after each addition. Sift flour with baking powder and allspice several times; fold in alternately with the tea dissolved in water, beginning and ending with the dry material. Mix coconut with nuts and fold in batter. Distribute evenly in ungreased 9-or 10-inch slip-bottom tube pan, smoothing top with back of spoon. Bake for about 1½ hours, or until top springs back when gently pressed with fingers. Cool about 30 minutes in pan on rack. Remove cake from pan and continue cooling on rack. Store in cake box. If desired, sprinkle with confectioner's sugar when ready to serve.

Emma R. Law

JOAN'S PINEAPPLE CAKE

2 cups flour	2 tablespoons melted butter or
2¼ cups sugar	margarine
2 teaspoons baking soda	¾ cup evaporated milk
1 teaspoon salt	¼ pound (1 stick) butter or
1 16-ounce can crushed	margarine
pineapple	¼ cup chopped pecans
1 egg, beaten	¼ cup grated coconut

Preheat oven to 350 degrees. Sift together flour, 1½ cups of the sugar, soda, and salt. Stir in pineapple, egg, and butter. Mix well. Bake in 11-by-15-inch pan for 30 minutes. Mix remaining sugar, milk and butter or margarine, and cook for 10 minutes. Remove from heat; add pecans and coconut. Spread over cake. This is good for picnics and covered-dish dinners.

Mrs. Joan Christian
Savannah News-Press

WESLEY GINGERBREAD

In 1736 the young Reverend John Wesley arrived in Savannah and spent nearly two years as an Anglican minister at Christ Church. Discouraged after the young woman he loved married another man, and embroiled in a theological-civil debate, he left the colony by boat for South Carolina one rainy December night. A few friends came out in secret to see him go. One of these, Margaret Burnside, gave him as a parting gift a small loaf of warm gingerbread, and a pint of rum to cheer his departure. Ahead of him, though none could have known it then, lay enduring fame as a founder of Methodism.

JOHN WESLEY

This statue of John Wesley was dedicated in Reynolds' Square
by the Methodists of Georgia in 1969. The John Wesley Hotel
behind it stands on the site of what was once his parsonage.
The hotel was built in 1913. Since it has always been frequented
by railroad men, it recently opened the Nancy Hanks Restaurant in honor of the famous train which ran for many years
between Atlanta and Savannah.

Drawing courtesy of John Wesley Hotel

½ cup vegetable shortening
½ cup brown sugar, firmly
    packed
1 tablespoon grated orange peel
3 eggs
1 cup dark molasses
¾ cup hot water
2 teaspoons dry instant coffee
⅓ cup orange juice

3 cups sifted flour
2 teaspoons ginger
1 teaspoon cinnamon
1 teaspoon baking soda
1 teaspoon baking powder
1 teaspoon salt
1 teaspoon nutmeg
½ cup currants
½ cup finely chopped pecans

Preheat oven to 350 degrees. Cream together shortening, sugar, orange peel, and eggs. Blend in molasses, water, coffee, and juice. Sift dry ingredients into batter. Beat until smooth. Stir in currants and pecans. Pour into greased and floured 13-by-9-inch pan. Bake for 40 to 45 minutes. Serve warm or cold, with whipped cream or an orange or lemon sauce.

John Wesley Hotel

QUICK CARAMEL FROSTING

Yield: enough for 2 8- or 9-inch
layers or a 13-by-9-inch cake

⅔ cup butter or margarine
1 cup light brown sugar,
    firmly packed

⅓ cup milk
3 cups sifted confectioner's
    sugar

Melt butter in saucepan. Add brown sugar; cook over low heat two minutes, stirring constantly. Add milk; cook and stir until mixture boils. Remove from heat and cool about 10 minutes. Place in mixer bowl and beat while gradually adding sugar. Beat until ready to spread.

LEMON FROSTING

It is a great improvement to squeeze a little lemon juice into the egg and sugar prepared for frosting. This gives a fine flavor, and makes it extremely white.

The American Frugal Housewife, 1838

ROSSIE'S LEMON BUTTER FROSTING

Yield: enough for a 9-inch square
or 2 8- or 9-inch layers

⅓ cup (about ⅔ stick) butter, at
    room temperature
⅛ teaspoon salt
3 cups sifted confectioner's
    sugar

juice and grated rind of one
  lemon

Mix butter with salt and 1 cup of the sugar until light and fluffy. Gradually add remaining sugar, lemon rind, and juice, beating smooth after each addition.

Rossie Shuman Adams

PLAINS FROSTING

Yield: enough for 2 8- or 9-inch layers

⅓ cup butter, at room
    temperature
⅓ cup creamy peanut butter
⅓ cup milk

1 teaspoon Angostura bitters
1 pound sifted confectioner's
    sugar

Cream butter and peanut butter together; stir in milk and bitters. Gradually stir in sifted confectioner's sugar; beat until smooth. Spread on cooled cake layer. Top with second layer, and cover sides and top. Chill until serving time.

PIES

OLD-FASHIONED PIE CRUST

One pint flour, two table-spoonfuls of lard, pinch of salt, one tablespoonful butter. Mix with ice water, using a fork. Mix dough stiff. Roll thin.

Hints From Southern Epicures, *circa 1890*

ALL-AMERICAN APPLE PIE

6-8 cooking apples or 1 16-ounce
    can apples for pie
  ½ cup sugar
  ½ cup brown sugar
  ¼ teaspoon cinnamon
  ¼ teaspoon nutmeg

  ⅛ teaspoon ginger
  ⅛ teaspoon allspice
1   tablespoon orange juice
2   teaspoons grated orange
    rind
1   9-inch unbaked pie shell

Fruit Pie Topping

½ cup flour
⅓ cup butter or margarine, at
    room temperature

⅓ cup sugar

INDEPENDENT PRESBYTERIAN CHURCH

One of the city's most historic churches is Independent
Presbyterian Church at 207 Bull Street. This 1878 print shows
the original structure, which was built in 1816, burned in 1889,
and rebuilt to duplicate the first house of worship. *Hints From
Southern Epicures*, the cookbook quoted frequently here, was
compiled by the Flower Committee of the church in 1890 to help
raise money to restore the building. Its introduction said: "It
has been the effort of the young ladies who have undertaken
this work, to send out a book that will combine the practical
with the dainty. These recipes have been given by some of the
leading Southern epicures, and have been tried and proven."

If using fresh apples, peel, core them, and slice thin. Preheat oven to 425 degrees. Mix the sugar and spices in a large bowl. Blend with the orange juice and grated rind; mix with apples and pour into pie shell. Combine flour and butter in **Fruit Pie Topping** recipe until crumbly and gradually add sugar. Sprinkle this crumb mixture over apples. Bake in preheated oven for 10 minutes, and then in 350 degree oven for 40 minutes. Serve with sharp Cheddar cheese or ice cream if desired.

    Fruit Pie Topping can be used with other fruit pies. It has much more flavor than the standard 2-crust pie.

SPICY APPLE CREAM PIE

Easy and unusual version of a traditional favorite.

¾ cup sugar	1 8-inch unbaked pie shell
2 tablespoons flour	4 crisp, tart cooking apples
¾ teaspoon allspice	(about 1½ pounds)
½ teaspoon salt	½ cup heavy cream

Preheat oven to 450 degrees. Mix first four ingredients well together. Sprinkle half of mixture evenly over bottom of pie shell. Pare, core, and slice apples. Add them evenly over pie shell. Sprinkle remaining sugar mixture over apples. Pour cream evenly over top. Bake for 15 minutes; reduce heat to 350 degrees and cook about 45 minutes longer.

SLICED APPLE PIE

Pare and slice your apples thin; sprinkle a pint of sugar over a quart of apples, cover with water, and add a tablespoon of butter. The butter seasons them highly, and prevents them from falling to pieces; put in a bit of cinnamon, mace, and grated nutmeg. Do not cook too long. Remove to a pan, lined with rich pastry, cover, and bake. If there is too much juice to put in the pies, pour into a small pitcher, and use with the pies when served.

Miss Mollie Downey, **House-Keeping In The Sunny South,**
1885

NUT-BUTTERSCOTCH PIE

1¼ cups dark brown sugar
⅓ cup flour
¼ teaspoon salt
3 egg yolks
2 cups milk

1 teaspoon vanilla extract
1 tablespoon butter
½ cup pecans
1 baked 9-inch pie shell

Blend sugar, flour, and salt. Add egg yolks and milk. Cook in a double boiler over hot water until thick and creamy. Stir frequently. When filling is thick, add rest of ingredients. Mix and pour into baked pie shell. Top with **Basic Meringue.**

Basic Meringue

3 egg whites
¼ teaspoon cream of tartar

6 tablespoons sugar

Preheat oven to 400 degrees. Beat egg whites until frothy. Add cream of tartar and continue to beat until stiff and glossy, but not dry. Add sugar, a little at a time, and beat until mixture holds peaks. Spread evenly over pie, all the way to the edge of the crust. Bake 8 to 10 minutes. Cool before serving.

PEANUT BUTTER PIE

3 eggs
1 cup dark corn syrup
½ cup sugar
½ cup creamy peanut butter

½ teaspoon vanilla extract
1 cup salted peanuts
1 unbaked 9-inch pie shell

Preheat oven to 400 degrees. Beat eggs in a large bowl. Add the next 4 ingredients; beat until smooth. Stir in peanuts. Pour in pie shell, and bake for 15 minutes; then, lower heat to 350 degrees and bake for 30 to 35 minutes more. Cool on rack before serving.

Artist, author, gardener and expert cook Idalee Vonk and her husband, Paul, live in this West Jones Street townhouse which they restored after arriving in Savannah from Atlanta.

NO-CRUST CHEESE CAKE

16 ounces cream cheese,
    at room temperature
3 eggs
⅔ cup sugar

⅛ teaspoon almond extract
1 cup commercial sour cream
3 tablespoons sugar
1 teaspoon vanilla extract

Preheat oven to 325 degrees. Beat cheese until fluffy. Add eggs, one at a time, beating thoroughly after each addition. Add 2/3 cup sugar and almond extract. Beat about 5 minutes. Pour into oiled 9-inch pie pan. Bake for 50 minutes. (Don't open door to check!) Cool 20 minutes.

Beat together sour cream, 3 tablespoons sugar, and vanilla. Spoon over pie, and return to oven for 15 minutes. Cool to room temperature, and then refrigerate before serving. Pie may be glazed if desired (see **Strawberry Glaze**).

Idalee (Mrs. Paul Kenneth) Vonk

STRAWBERRY GLAZE

1 cup sliced strawberries
½ cup sugar
⅛ teaspoon salt
¼ cup water

1½ tablespoons cornstarch
¼ cup cold water
1 tablespoon lemon juice

Place berries in a large saucepan with sugar, salt, and water. Bring to a boil and cook 3 minutes. Mix cornstarch and cold water together; stir into berries and cook, stirring, until thick. Add lemon juice. This glaze is delicious as a topping for cheesecake, filling for a layer cake, or in tarts.

GRAHAM NUT PIE

This pie makes its own crust.

3 eggs, separated
1 cup sugar
1 tablespoon maple flavoring
1 cup graham cracker crumbs

1 cup coarsely chopped pecans
8 ounces whipping cream,
    whipped and sweetened
    (optional)

Preheat oven to 350 degrees. Beat egg whites until stiff. Add ½ cup sugar; fold in gradually. Beat egg yolks until light; add remaining sugar and maple flavoring. Mix in graham cracker crumbs and pecans. Blend thoroughly; fold into egg white mixture. Pour into a well-buttered 9-inch pie plate. Bake 30 minutes. Cool; top with sweetened whipped cream, if desired.

Savannah News-Press

MOCHA PIE

A rich and unusual pie in both filling and pastry.

Nut Pastry

1 cup sifted flour
½ teaspoon salt
⅓ cup vegetable shortening
2 tablespoons water
¼ cup light brown sugar, firmly
  packed

¾ cup finely chopped walnuts or
  pecans
1 square unsweetened
  chocolate, grated
1 tablespoon water
1 teaspoon vanilla extract

Combine flour with salt; cut in shortening with pastry blender. Add water and gather dough together; work in sugar, walnuts, and grated chocolate. Add water and vanilla and mix with fork until well blended. Preheat oven to 375 degrees. Roll out dough and place in well-greased 9-inch pie pan; press firmly against bottom and sides. Bake 15 minutes. Cool shell in pie pan on wire rack.

Mocha Filling

1 cup water
2½ teaspoons instant coffee
  powder
1 cup sugar
1 square unsweetened
  chocolate, melted

1 tablespoon (1 envelope)
  unflavored gelatin
1 pint heavy cream
1 teaspoon vanilla extract
  sweetened chocolate, shaved
  or grated (optional)

Boil ½ cup water; pour over instant coffee and ¾ cup sugar in mixing bowl. Stir to dissolve. Add melted chocolate and blend well. Dissolve gelatin in remaining ½ cup cold water, then melt over hot water and combine with coffee-chocolate mixture. Chill until slightly set, but not stiff. (Watch carefully!) Beat with an electric mixer until thick and foamy and creamy-light in color. Scrape bottom and sides of bowl often. Whip cream and add remaining ¼ cup sugar and vanilla. Fold into mocha mixture. Fill cooled **Nut Pastry** shell. Chill at least 4 hours, or overnight. Decorate with shaved or grated chocolate as desired.

Savannah News-Press

OLD-FASHIONED LEMON PIE

For a richer taste in lemon pies, use hot, but not boiling tea in place of the boiling water. Allow one tea bag to each cup of water; remove tea bag before adding to recipe. This really brings out the lemon taste!

1½ cups sugar	⅓ cup lemon juice
4 tablespoons flour	grated rind of two lemons
4 tablespoons cornstarch	1 9-inch baked pie shell
½ teaspoon salt	4 egg whites
2 cups boiling water	½ teaspoon sugar
4 egg yolks, beaten	¼ teaspoon salt

Mix 1½ cups sugar, flour, cornstarch, and salt. Add boiling water gradually, stirring constantly, and cook over medium heat for a few minutes until mixture begins to thicken. Still stirring, reduce heat to low and continue to cook until thickened. Stir a little of the hot mixture into the egg yolks, and then stir yolks back into remaining hot mixture, stirring well. Continue to cook two minutes longer, still stirring. Add lemon juice and rind and blend well. Cool for 5 minutes, then pour into baked pie shell.

Preheat oven to 350 degrees. Make a meringue from the remaining egg whites, sugar, and salt, following the directions for **Basic Meringue**. Bake until brown, approximately 12 minutes.

Mrs. Lehman Lanier, Alma, Georgia
Savannah News-Press

BIRTHDAY LIMEADE MERINGUE PIE

If the guest of honor likes pie better than cake, make a pie and cover it with meringue for a family birthday party. If desired, meringue can be swirled on pie in a pattern to surround candles. Do not add candles until meringue is baked.

3 eggs, separated	⅓ cup frozen limeade, thawed
1⅓ cups sugar	and undiluted
¼ cup cornstarch	1 tablespoon butter
¼ teaspoon salt	1 baked 9-inch pie shell
1½ cups boiling water	

Beat egg yolks slightly. Mix 1 cup sugar, cornstarch, and salt together in saucepan. Add water gradually, stirring constantly to keep mixture smooth. Bring to a boil and cook over moderate direct heat, stirring constantly, until mixture is thick and clear, about 1 minute. Blend part of hot mixture with beaten egg yolks; pour egg mixture back into remaining hot mixture, stirring well. Cook 2 minutes longer over low heat, stirring constantly. Remove from heat; add limeade gradually, stirring all the while. Blend in butter, and allow to cool slightly. Pour into cooked pastry shell. Cool. Preheat oven to 350 degrees. Beat egg whites until stiff but not dry. Add the remaining sugar gradually, beating well after each addition. Pile beaten whites over filling, making sure that mixture touches pie crust all around. Bake until meringue is golden brown, about 12 to 15 minutes. Allow to cool on a rack before cutting.

GEORGIA PEACHES

"Tybee, Where The Georgia Peaches Go," was a popular song first played in the 1920s era of the big bands at Tybee. The song celebrated the association in American minds between Georgia and peaches.

A native of China, the peach tree came to America via Europe, and was introduced by the Spanish at Fort Augustine. The first Georgia peach trees were part of plantation orchards. Georgians, anxious to sell their fruit in the North before Yankee fruit was ripe enough to compete, found transportation a problem. Then they realized the ripe peaches could be shipped in refrigerated steamer boxes out of the port at Savannah, and re-iced en route. Later, refrigerated railroad cars were used.

The most famous Georgia peach variety, the Elberta, was first grown at Marshallville. Because of the number of varieties grown in the Peach State now, "peach season" lasts several months. The results are delicious...from eating out-of-the-hand and in fresh fruit cups, to baked in pies, tarts, and cobblers, stewed in sauces and jellies, broiled or glazed as a garnish, and frozen in ice creams.

SAVANNAH PEACH PIE

Make one rich crust and bake it, laying a folded towel in the plate at first to prevent the crust from puffing too much. Stew a can of peaches in their own juice, adding more sugar if necessary, and fill the empty crust. Beat the whites of three eggs very stiff, and add three tablespoonfuls sugar and a little almond extract. Put back in the oven until the meringue is well set.

Hints From Southern Epicures, *circa 1890*

GEORGIA PEACH PIE

½ cup brown sugar
½ cup sugar
⅛ teaspoon salt
3 tablespoons tapioca
5 cups sliced fresh peaches (5 to 6 medium peaches)

⅛ teaspoon almond extract
pastry for two-crust 9-inch pie
1 tablespoon butter
small amount cold water (optional)
½ teaspoon sugar (optional)

Preheat oven to 450 degrees. Mix sugars, salt, and tapioca. Pour over sliced peaches, and mix gently. Sprinkle mixture with almond extract. Line a 9-inch pan with pastry. Pour in fresh peach mixture. Dot with butter. Cover with top crust. Seal edges by fluting (pinching between your fingers at regular intervals). Prick top with fork. Top crust may be brushed with cold water and sprinkled with a small amount of sugar before putting pie in oven. Bake at 450 degrees for 10 minutes; reduce heat to 375 degrees and continue to bake for 40 minutes, or until a golden brown.

SPECIAL PECAN PIE

The first pecans in Georgia were grown about 1840 from pecan nuts found floating at sea by Captain Samuel F. Flood and his wife, Rebecca Grovenstine Flood. Some of the nuts were also planted by St. Joseph Sebastian Arnow nearby, all in Camden County. The first plantings produced large and heavy-bearing trees, as did their nuts and shoots in turn. Taken from St. Mary's to distant points throughout the southeastern states, they became famous before the Texas pecan was generally known.

3 eggs
½ cup heavy cream
½ cup dark corn syrup
1 teaspoon vanilla extract
3 tablespoons bourbon or rum

1 cup sugar
⅛ teaspoon salt
2 tablespoons melted butter
2 cups thinly sliced pecans
1 unbaked 9-inch pie shell

Preheat oven to 400 degrees. Beat eggs well. Stir in remaining ingredients and pour into unbaked pie shell. Since pecan pie filling is thin before it is baked, the easiest way to get it into a pie is to mix it in a wide-mouth measuring pitcher, and pour it directly in the pie crust after the crust has been placed on the oven rack, pulled toward you. Then, gently slide the pie back into the oven on the rack, and close the door. Saves spilling pie filling! Bake for about 35 minutes, or until crust is browned and filling slightly puffy. Cool on rack to room temperature. Top with **Pecan Pie Topping**, if desired.

Pie may be cooled, wrapped in foil, and frozen after cooling. If frozen, bring to room temperature before serving.

Pecan Pie Topping

½ cup heavy cream, whipped
  sugar to taste

½ teaspoon (about 4 dashes)
  aromatic bitters

Blend, giving a dollop to each pie wedge before serving.

Emma R. Law

TIM'S CHRISTMAS RUM PIE

6 egg yolks
¾ cup sugar
1½ envelopes unflavored gelatin
½ cup Myer's Jamaican rum
  mixed with ¼ cup water

3 cups cold heavy cream,
  whipped
¼ cup Myer's Jamaican rum
2 prepared 9-inch graham
  cracker crumb pie shells

In a mixing bowl, blend the egg yolks and sugar until thick and creamy. Dissolve the gelatin in the water and rum mixture and heat for 10 minutes. Cool slightly, and gradually add to the egg mixture. Allow this to cool again. Fold into this the whipped cream until completely blended. Then, mix in the final quarter cup of rum. Pour into pie shells, and refrigerate until set.

Kenneth T. Williams, Savannah News-Press

PUMPKIN ICE CREAM PIE

A refreshing treat, especially during the holiday season.

1 9 or 10-inch graham cracker
  crumb pie shell
1 cup mashed, cooked pumpkin
½ cup brown sugar, firmly
  packed
½ teaspoon salt

1 tablespoon pumpkin pie spice
1 quart vanilla ice cream,
  softened
1 cup sweetened whipped cream
  (optional)
  pecan halves (optional)

Place cracker crust in freezer to chill. Blend together pumpkin, sugar, salt, and spice. Fold in softened ice cream. Fill crust and place in freezer to freeze. Make a border around edge with sweetened whipped cream before serving, if desired. Garnish with pecan halves, if desired.

CAROLINA STRAWBERRY PIE

Related to the rose family, strawberries are a wonderful blend of color, scent, and flavor. The Indians used wild berries for wine and in breads as well as for eating as a fruit. The present cultivated strawberry is a hybrid of American and European varieties.

225

1	quart fresh or frozen whole strawberries	2	tablespoons lemon juice
1½	cups sugar	1	baked 9-inch pie shell
1	tablespoon (1 envelope) unflavored gelatin	8	ounces whipping cream, whipped and sweetened (optional)
¼	cup cold water		

Wash and cap berries, if using fresh ones. Sprinkle with 1 cup sugar. Let stand in refrigerator for several hours. Soften gelatin in cold water. Press half the berries, and all the berry juice, through a sieve to make 1½ cups of berries and juice. If necessary, add water to make up full amount. Add remaining ½ cup sugar and lemon juice. Heat to the boiling point. Dissolve gelatin in hot mixture. Chill until mixture thickens. Place remaining whole berries in pie shell, saving a few for top garnish if desired. Cover berries in shell with gelatin mixture. Chill until firm. Top with sweetened whipped cream, if desired.

Mrs. R. A. Travis, Ridgeland, South Carolina
Savannah News-Press

STRAWBERRY-RICE PIE

Another use for left-over rice! An old Isle of Hope recipe.

1	cup heavy cream	1½	tablespoons (1½ envelopes) unflavored gelatin
8	ounces cream cheese at room temperature	4	tablespoons juice from the berries, or other fruit juice
½	cup sugar	1	cup cooked white rice
1½	cups strawberries (if frozen, thaw and drain)	1	baked 9-inch pie shell

Whip cream; set aside. In a mixing bowl, combine cream cheese with sugar until light and fluffy. Add strawberries. Put gelatin in the juice; heat until gelatin is dissolved. Combine with cheese mixture. Add rice and mix well. Fold in whipped cream. Turn into pie shell; chill and serve.

Savannah News-Press

GEORGIA SWEET-POTATO PIE

Boil, peel, and mash in milk the potatoes; allow one pint of warm milk or cream to every pint of potatoes; three eggs, sugar and spice to taste; one crust; frost.

Mrs. C. R. Upson, **House-Keeping In The Sunny South,** *1885*

OLD SOUTH GEORGIA VINEGAR PIE

The old fashioned chess, or custard pie, is said to have been a favorite dessert of Confederate President Jefferson Davis.

¼ pound (1 stick) butter, at room temperature	3 eggs
1½ cups sugar	2 tablespoons cider vinegar
	1 8-inch unbaked pie crust

Preheat oven to 375 degrees. Cream butter and sugar together until light and fluffy. Add eggs one at a time, beating well after each. Stir in the vinegar. Turn into pie shell. Bake for about an hour, or until "set." Let cool before serving.

For a crisper crust, brush about 1 teaspoon of unbeaten egg white over bottom and sides of shell, before adding filling. This will not affect the recipe.

Since this is a very thin filling, pie shell may be placed on oven rack, and then filling gently poured in, to prevent spilling.

Betty Chamlee

CHOCOLATE COOKIE CRUST

4 tablespoons melted butter
1¼ cups ground chocolate
    cookies

Mix together and press into 9-inch pie pan. Chill in refrigerator until needed.

Pirates' House Cook Book

COCONUT CRUST

1⅓ cups flaked coconut
1 teaspoon soft butter

Mix butter and coconut in 9-inch pie pan, and press to bottom and sides. Bake 10 minutes in a preheated 325 degree oven.

Pirates' House Cook Book

GINGER SNAP CRUST

1½ cups crushed ginger snap crumbs	4 tablespoons (½ stick) butter, at room temperature
2 tablespoons sugar	

Combine ginger snap crumbs and sugar. Blend in butter. Press mixture into 9-inch pie pan. Bake in a preheated 350 degree oven for 10 minutes. Cool.

Pirates' House Cook Book

COCO-CHOCOLATE CRUST

An interesting flavor, and easy to make.

2 squares (1 ounce each) unsweetened chocolate
2 tablespoons butter or margarine
¾ cup unsifted confectioner's sugar
2 tablespoons hot water
1½ cups flaked coconut

Melt chocolate and butter over low heat. Add to sugar in a mixing bowl, and stir in hot water. Blend together until smooth. Stir in coconut, and press on the bottom and sides of a buttered 9-inch pie plate. Chill. Fill with any pie filling which does not require more baking.

Savannah News-Press

WHEAT GERM CRUST

A different and delicious crust for any recipe requiring a baked pie shell; more nutritious, too, than the usual pastry crust.

3 egg whites
1 teaspoon vanilla extract
1 cup sugar
¼ teaspoon baking powder
1 cup regular wheat germ butter

Preheat oven to 325 degrees. Beat egg whites until stiff, but not dry. Add vanilla slowly; beat in sugar mixed with baking powder. Fold in wheat germ. Spread evenly against bottom and sides of a buttered 9-inch pie pan. Bake 30 minutes. Cool, and fill with any custard or ice cream pie filling which requires a baked crust. Chill pie until firm. If desired, garnish with 1 tablespoon grated semi-sweet chocolate mixed with 1 tablespoon wheat germ.

Savannah News-Press

VANILLA WAFER CRUST

2 cups ground vanilla wafers
4 tablespoons melted butter

Mix wafers and butter. Press into 9-inch pie pan, and chill in refrigerator until needed.

Pirates' House Cook Book

STIR-N-ROLL PIE CRUST

2 cups sifted flour
1½ teaspoons salt
½ cup vegetable oil
¼ cup milk

DR. DAVID WESSON AND HIS OIL

It was once thought that cottonseed caused sickness, and its oil fostered pellagra. The government warned against feeding it to cattle. In 1899 Dr. David Wesson was employed by the Southern Cotton Oil Company at Savannah as plant chemist. In early 1900, a cottonseed oil and other shortening products were presented to the consumer market. Later, during World War I, Dr. Wesson was instrumental in the manufacturing of glycerine from cottonseed soapstock. In 1930 he was successful in producing synthetic beef steak, sausage, and flour from cottonseed. He received many honors prior to his death in New Jersey in 1934, but he is best remembered by the oil which bears his name. The company which brought him to Savannah is now part of Hunt-Wesson Foods, Inc. One early recipe developed by the company was **Stir-N-Roll Pie Crust.**

Combine flour and salt in mixing bowl. Measure oil and milk in the same measuring cup. Do not stir. Pour directly on the flour-salt mixture. Mix until dry ingredients are moist. Shape into a ball. Cut in two. Flatten halves slightly.

Roll one half between 2 sheets of waxed paper until you have a 12-inch circle. Take off top layer of waxed paper. Turn crust-side down into pie pan. Remove waxed paper from top.

If you need a baked pie crust, bake in a preheated 425 degree oven for 20 minutes, or until brown. Some recipes call for uncooked pie crust. The other half of the crust may be used for the top crust, rolled out the same way. Or, save it for a single baked or unbaked one-crust pie.

Hunt-Wesson Foods, Inc.

SPICY TOPPING

Quick and tasty for fruit pies.

½ cup flour
½ cup sugar
⅓ cup butter or margarine
½ teaspoon ground ginger
½ teaspoon cinnamon
¼ teaspoon nutmeg

Mix and sprinkle on filled pie shell. Bake in preheated 400 degree oven for 45 minutes.

GIRL SCOUT HEADQUARTERS

This building at 330 Drayton Street was the carriage house of the elegant home of Juliette Gordon Low when she spent her last years in Savannah at 325 Abercorn Street, now the Colonial Dames House. Here she founded the Girl Scouts of America in 1912. She bequeathed the carriage house to the Girl Scouts of Savannah in her will, and it is now council headquarters as well as a "must see" for scouts from all over the world who visit Savannah.

COOKIES

GIRL SCOUT BROWNIES

A favorite cookie at Night In Old Savannah, the annual festival in Johnson Square sponsored by the Girl Scout Council of Savannah.

Yield: 32

4	ounces unsweetened chocolate	1	teaspoon vanilla extract
⅔	cup vegetable shortening	1¼	cups flour
2	cups sugar	1	teaspoon baking powder
4	eggs	¼	teaspoon salt
		1	cup chopped nuts

Preheat oven to 350 degrees. Melt chocolate and shortening in large saucepan over low heat. Remove from heat. Mix in sugar, eggs, and vanilla. Stir in remaining ingredients, sifting dry ingredients together into the mixture and then stirring in the nuts. Spread in oiled, floured 9-inch square baking pan. Bake 30 minutes, or until brownies start to pull away from sides of pan, and a cake tester inserted in the dough comes out clean. Do not overbake.

Girl Scout Council of Savannah

BENNE SEED COOKIES

One of Savannah's most famous cookie recipes is this one for **Benne Seed Cookies,** a "receipt" of the Gordon family. It is now baked frequently by Girl Scouts in the restored kitchen of the Gordon home.

Yield: 3 dozen

¾ cup (1½ sticks) butter
1½ cups light brown sugar, firmly
    packed
2   eggs

1¼ cups flour
½ cup **Toasted Benne Seed**
1   teaspoon vanilla extract
¼ teaspoon baking powder

Preheat oven to 325 degrees. Cream butter and sugar together and mix with other ingredients in order given. Line unoiled cookie sheets with waxed paper. Drop cookie dough with a teaspoon onto waxed paper about 2 inches apart, to allow for spreading. Bake for 15 to 20 minutes. Cool on waxed paper until cookies can be peeled off. (Bonus: no pans to wash!)

These cookies burn easily, so it would be best, as with all baking recipes, to time them carefully in your own oven, and adjust directions accordingly.

Juliette Gordon Low Girl Scout National Center

APRICOT REFRIGERATOR COOKIES

Adapted from a favorite recipe of Betty Bird Foy (Mrs. Carl) Sanders, former first lady of Georgia. Other dried fruit, such as peaches or prunes, may be used instead of apricots if desired.

Yield: about 5 dozen

¾ pound (1½ sticks) butter,
    at room temperature
1½ cups light brown sugar, firmly
    packed
1   egg
2½ cups sifted flour

3   teaspoons baking powder
¼ teaspoon salt
¼ cup milk
1   cup minced dried apricots
1   cup chopped pecans

Preheat oven to 400 degrees. Cream butter and sugar together until light and fluffy. Add egg and beat well. Sift flour, baking powder, and salt together. Add to first mixture alternately with dry ingredients; start and finish with the dry mixture. Work in apricots and pecans. Shape into rolls about 2 inches in diameter. Wrap in waxed paper and chill or freeze until ready to use. Cut into slices ¼-inch thick and bake for about 12 to 14 minutes. Do not let brown. Cool on racks. Store in air-tight containers in a cool place.

DATE BROWNIES

Yield: 32

6 tablespoons butter or vegetable shortening
1½ cups dark brown sugar, firmly packed
2 eggs
1½ cups flour

2 teaspoons baking powder
¼ teaspoon salt
1 teaspoon vanilla extract
1 cup chopped pitted dates
½ cup chopped nuts or grated coconut (optional)

Preheat oven to 350 degrees. Melt butter in a saucepan. Stir in sugar, and cool. Beat in eggs. Sift together flour, baking powder, and salt. Fold in sifted dry ingredients, vanilla, and dates (also nuts or coconut if desired). Spread mixture in a well-oiled 9-inch square pan. Bake for 25 minutes. Cool in pan, or cut in squares or bars with a sharp knife and serve warm.

Savannah News-Press

CHOCOLATE-SWIRLED PEANUT BUTTER BROWNIES

One of Georgia's most famous products, swirled into delicious brownies.

Yield: 50

¾ cup peanut butter, crunchy-style preferred
¼ pound (1 stick) butter or margarine
1½ cups sugar
1½ cups light brown sugar, firmly packed

4 eggs
2 teaspoons vanilla extract
3 cups sifted flour
1 tablespoon baking powder
¼ teaspoon salt
2 2-ounce squares semi-sweet chocolate

Preheat oven to 350 degrees. Cream peanut butter and butter until soft and creamy. Gradually blend in sugar and brown sugar. Beat in eggs one at a time, stirring well after each addition. Stir in vanilla. Sift flour, baking powder, and salt. Add all at once, and beat until smooth and well blended. Spread mixture into a greased and floured 13-by-9-by-2-inch pan. Melt chocolate in top of double boiler over hot (not boiling) water. Drizzle melted chocolate over the top of the batter. With the tip of a knife, swirl chocolate into the batter. Bake for 35 to 40 minutes, or until brownies feel firm to the touch. Cool in pan, and then cut into squares.

Georgia Peanut Commission

PEA-NUTS

This sketch of "Pea-nut sellers in Savannah" from a July 1870 *Harper's Weekly*, was accompanied by an article in which the correspondent complained:

The pea-nut, though almost universally liked, is considered very "ungenteel." Its cheapness, and the ease with which its shell is broken, make it a favorite with boys....Pea-nuts impart a pungent odor to the breath, which makes the eater almost as great a nuisance in a crowd as one who indulges in the luxury of Limburger chese....

The pea-nut is not recognized in polite society. It is never found at dessert....Thus pea-nuts, like prophets, are not without honor save in their own country, and it is not likely they will ever rise above their present position here.

Happily, the recipes in this and other modern Southern cookbooks have proved that correspondent wrong!

Courtesy of Rita Trotz

SAVANNAH NUT BARS

Even Hard-Hearted Hannah's disposition might have been changed by these.

Yield: 32

⅔ cup vegetable shortening
1 cup light brown sugar, firmly packed
1 egg

2 cups sifted flour
½ teaspoon cinnamon
1/16 teaspoon salt

Topping

1 egg, lightly beaten
½ cup light brown sugar, firmly packed

¾ cup chopped pecans

Preheat oven to 350 degrees. Cream shortening and sugar together. Add egg; beat until light and fluffy. Sift dry ingredients together and fold into creamed mixture. Press over the bottom of oiled 11-by-16-by-½-inch pan. To make the topping, brush top of dough with egg. Sprinkle evenly with the sugar and pecans. Bake for 20 to 25 minutes. Cool in pan on rack for 20 to 25 minutes. Cut into 32 bars. Remove from pan and continue cooling on rack. Store in air-tight container. Suggested variations: use all white sugar or all dark brown sugar; walnuts, almonds, or untoasted benne (sesame) seed; or ginger or pumpkin pie spice mix in place of cinnamon.

RASPBERRY COCONUT SQUARES

Yield: 3 dozen

1 cup sifted flour
1 teaspoon baking powder
6 tablespoons butter or margarine

1 egg, well beaten
1 tablespoon milk
½ cup raspberry jam

Preheat oven to 350 degrees. Combine and sift flour and baking powder. Cut in butter or margarine until mixture is like coarse corn meal. Combine egg and milk. Add to flour mixture. Press into ungreased 9-inch square cake pan. Bake for 10 to 12 minutes, or until lightly brown. Spread with raspberry (or any favorite flavor) jam. Spread with **Walnut Coconut Topping**. Bake at same temperature 30 minutes longer. Cool and cut into 1½-inch squares.

Walnut Coconut Topping

1	egg, well beaten	1½	cups moist, finely chopped coconut
4	tablespoons (½ stick) butter or margarine, melted	½	cup chopped nuts
1	cup sugar	1	teaspoon vanilla extract

Combine egg, butter or margarine, and sugar. Stir until moistened. Add remaining ingredients. Spread as directed on **Raspberry Coconut Squares**. These cookies may be stored in the freezer for up to 6 months. A pretty and different holiday cookie!

Jerry Downey

BARNEY'S BUTTERSCOTCH COOKIES

This recipe from staff writer Sally Swartz of the *Savannah News-Press* is an old family one named for her grandfather's cook.

Yield: 4 to 6 dozen

4	cups light brown sugar, firmly packed	6	cups flour
½	pound (2 sticks) butter	1	tablespoon baking soda
4	eggs	1	teaspoon salt
1	tablespoon vanilla extract	1	tablespoon cream of tartar
		1	or 2 cups chopped pecans

Cream sugar and butter together. Add eggs one at a time, beating well after each. Add vanilla with last egg. Sift together dry ingredients and fold into creamed mixture. Stir in nuts. Form into rolls about 1½ inches in diameter. Refrigerate until firm, or place in freezer until firm enough to slice.

Preheat oven to 375 degrees. Cut dough into slices about ¼-inch thick, for a crisp cookie. Place a little apart on ungreased baking sheet. Bake for about 8 minutes, or until lightly browned. This recipe makes 3 or 4 rolls of dough, and 4 to 6 dozen cookies. If you don't want to bake them all at once, extra rolls of dough may be stored in freezer, and sliced directly from freezer for baking. Use dark brown sugar if you prefer a darker-colored cookie.

Sally Swartz

SPICY CREAM CHEESE COOKIES

Yield: about 3 dozen

¼ pound (1 stick) butter, at room temperature
3 ounces cream cheese, at room temperature
1 egg, beaten
1 teaspoon vanilla extract
1 cup sifted flour
2 teaspoons baking powder
½ teaspoon salt
1 teaspoon allspice

Preheat oven to 375 degrees. Cream butter and cheese together. Beat in egg and vanilla. Sift dry ingredients together. Add to first mixture, stirring until smooth. Drop by heaping teaspoonfuls onto lightly oiled cookie sheets, about 1 inch apart. Bake until lightly browned, about 10 minutes. Remove from sheets and cool on racks. Store in air-tight container.

GINGER SNAP COOKIES

Yield: about 7 dozen

1½ cups vegetable shortening
2 cups sugar
2 eggs
½ cup light molasses
4 cups flour
2 teaspoons baking soda
2 teaspoons cinnamon
2 teaspoons cloves
2 teaspoons ground ginger
sugar

Preheat oven to 375 degrees. Cream shortening and 2 cups sugar. Beat in eggs and molasses. Sift dry ingredients together and add to creamed mixture. Mix thoroughly. Take a teaspoon of dough and roll in a ball; then roll in granulated sugar. Place on a greased cookie sheet. Flatten lightly and bake for about 15 minutes. A good after-school snack with cold milk!

Liz Connealy
Savannah News-Press

JEFF DAVIS JUMBLES

One teacupful of sugar, one teacupful of butter, one tablespoonful of thick cream, one egg (white only), fourth of a teaspoonful of soda; flour to roll out. Dip the cakes in sugar before baking.

*Mrs. J. W. Baker, **House-Keeping In The Sunny South**, 1885*

TELFAIR ACADEMY OF ARTS AND SCIENCES

One of Savannah's most beautiful homes turned house museums is the Telfair Academy of Arts and Sciences at 121 Barnard Street, completed in 1819 for Alexander Telfair, son of Georgia Governor Edward Telfair. The Regency mansion was bequeathed to the Georgia Historical Society in 1875, and later remodeled to become the city's major art museum. It includes a restored kitchen in the basement as the Telfairs might have used it prior to 1875. Another treasure is the recipe collection of Sarah Gibbons (Mrs. Edward) Telfair, and her daughter, Mary Telfair, who bequeathed the home to the society. A sample is included from this collection, now at the Georgia Historical Society.

Drawing by Lyda Keller from
The Pirates' House Cook Book
Copyright© 1964 by Frances McGrath

MARY TELFAIR'S DERBY, OR SHORT, CAKES

Rub in with the hand one pound of butter into two pounds of sifted flour. Put in one pound of currants, one pound of good, moist sugar, and one egg; mix all together with half a pint of milk, roll it out thin, and cut them into round cakes with a cutter; lay them on a clean baking plate, and put them into a midling heated oven, for five minutes.

EMMA'S FRUIT DROPS

Yield: 6 to 9 dozen

1 pound (about 2 cups) ready-to-use fruit cake mix	1 teaspoon vanilla extract
4 cups sifted flour	1½ teaspoons baking powder
1 cup butter or margarine	½ teaspoon baking soda
1 pound light brown sugar	½ teaspoon salt
3 eggs	1 teaspoon allspice
1 cup commercial sour cream	pecan halves (optional)

Preheat oven to 400 degrees. Dredge fruit with ½ cup flour, tossing to coat well. Set aside. Cream butter and sugar together. Add eggs, one at a time, beating well after each. Blend in sour cream and vanilla. Sift remaining 3½ cups flour with baking powder, soda, salt, and allspice. Gradually fold dry ingredients into creamed mixture. Fold until smooth. Fold in fruit. Drop by teaspoon or tablespoon, about 2 inches apart on oiled or non-stick cookie sheets. Top each with a pecan half, if desired. Bake until lightly browned, about 10 to 12 minutes. Remove and cool on wire racks.

LIZZIES

In some households, **Lizzies** are the traditional Christmas cookie, easier to serve than fruitcake, and an excellent gift. Hardy to mail or to store, they also freeze well.

Yield: 7 to 8 dozen

3 cups white seedless raisins	½ cup light brown sugar, firmly packed
½ cup bourbon whisky	2 eggs
1½ cups sifted flour	4 cups pecan halves
1½ teaspoons baking soda	½ pound chopped citron
1½ teaspoons cinnamon	1 pound whole candied cherries
½ teaspoon nutmeg	
½ teaspoon cloves	
¼ pound (1 stick) butter, at room temperature	

Johnson Square, showing the General Nathanael Greene
monument and the Cotton Exchange beyond it on Bay Street.

Drawing by Lyda Keller from
The Pirates' House Cook Book
Copyright© 1964 by Frances McGrath

Preheat oven to 325 degrees. Put raisins and bourbon in a bowl. Mix well and let stand 1 hour or more. Snip raisins in half if desired. Sift together the flour, soda, and spices. Cream butter, sugar, and eggs. Beat with mixer or wooden spoon until light and fluffy. Beat dry ingredients into butter mixture until smooth. Stir in nuts, citron, cherries, and raisins. Drop from teaspoon onto oiled cookie sheet. Bake 15 minutes, or until firm. Cool on a wire rack. Store in an air-tight container.

Helena DeBolt

HOLIDAY MINCEMEAT COOKIES

A nice change from mince pies, and more versatile.

Yield: about 3 dozen

1¾ cups sifted flour	1 egg
1½ teaspoons baking powder	1 teaspoon vanilla extract
¼ teaspoon salt	1 9-ounce package or 1 cup
¼ pound (1 stick) butter or	canned mincemeat
margarine	3 tablespoons orange juice
⅓ cup sugar	1 cup chopped nuts (optional)
⅓ cup light brown sugar, firmly	
packed	

Preheat oven to 350 degrees. Sift dry ingredients together. Cream butter or margarine, sugar, egg, and vanilla. Crumble mincemeat and add to creamed mixture along with dry ingredients. Stir in orange juice; add nuts. Drop by teaspoon-fuls on oiled cookie sheet. Bake for 10 to 15 minutes.

OATMEAL COOKIES JOHNSON SQUARE

Another "Night In Old Savannah" recipe.

Yield: about 3½ dozen

1 cup flour	2 eggs
¾ teaspoon baking soda	1⅓ cups light brown sugar, firmly
½ teaspoon salt	packed
1 teaspoon cinnamon	1 teaspoon vanilla extract
¼ teaspoon nutmeg	2 cups uncooked oatmeal
6 ounces (1½ sticks) butter or	1 cup raisins
margarine	

Preheat oven to 350 degrees. Sift first five ingredients together. Cream butter or margarine and eggs together. Add dry and other ingredients, mixing well after each addition. Drop batter by teaspoonfuls onto greased cookie sheet. Bake for 12 to 15 minutes.

Girl Scout Council of Savannah

ORANGE COOKIES

When selecting oranges to grate for fresh orange peel, try to select those which do not have color added, but are a natural yellow-orange.

Yield: about 8 dozen

1	cup vegetable shortening	1	teaspoon baking powder
2	cups sugar	4½	cups flour
2	eggs	1	teaspoon baking soda
	grated rind and juice of one orange (about 2½ inches in diameter)	⅛	teaspoon salt
		1	cup sour milk

Preheat oven to 400 degrees. Cream shortening and sugar. Add eggs, orange rind, and juice. Sift dry ingredients together and add to first mixture. Blend in milk. Drop by teaspoonfuls on oiled cookie sheet. Bake 10 to 12 minutes. Frost with **Miami Frosting.**

Miami Frosting

1	pound confectioner's sugar, sifted	1	tablespoon melted butter
	grated rind and juice of 1 orange (about 2½ inches in diameter)		

Mix together, and use to frost warm **Orange Cookies.**

Alice Terrill and Margaret Allen Wayt

KATE SMITH'S PEANUT BUTTER COOKIES

Once a year, at Night In Old Savannah in Johnson Square, Girl Scouts sell cookies of their own baking. These, named for the famous entertainer who sang in the square in 1976, are a perennial favorite.

Yield: about 3 dozen

¼ pound (1 stick) butter or margarine	1 egg
½ cup peanut butter	1¼ cups flour
½ cup sugar	½ teaspoon baking powder
½ cup light brown sugar, firmly packed	½ teaspoon baking soda
	¼ teaspoon salt

Preheat oven to 375 degrees. Mix butter or margarine, peanut butter, sugars, and egg thoroughly. Blend with sifted dry ingredients. Roll into 1¼-inch balls. Place 3 inches apart on oiled baking sheet. Flatten criss-cross style with fork dipped in flour. Bake 10 to 12 minutes.

Girl Scout Council of Savannah

The Cookie Shanty on Norwood Avenue is not only the present location of the famous Byrd Cookie Company, but is also a museum of the early days of the baking industry in Savannah. Here are displayed the vintage cookie cutters, black iron pans, wooden delivery boxes, and other items used by the company when it was founded in 1924 in the Old Fort section of the city at St. Julian and Habersham Streets.

GEORGIA PECAN STICKS

Yield: 40 to 50

½ pound (2 sticks) butter, at
    room temperature
1 teaspoon vanilla extract
1 cup finely ground pecans
    (better if done in blender)

½ cup sifted confectioner's sugar
2 cups sifted flour
    extra confectioner's sugar

Preheat oven to 325 degrees. Cream butter well. Stir in vanilla, pecans, sugar, and flour. Knead well. Mold dough into pieces about the size and shape of cigarettes. Place on ungreased cookie sheets about ½ inch apart. Bake until lightly browned, about 15 to 20 minutes. Cool on racks and sift with more sugar.

PILGRIM PUMPKIN COOKIES

Yield: about 7 dozen

⅓ cup vegetable shortening
1⅓ cups sugar
2 eggs, well beaten
1 cup cooked pumpkin
1 teaspoon vanilla extract
1 teaspoon lemon extract
1 teaspoon grated lemon rind
2½ cups sifted flour
4 teaspoons baking powder

1 teaspoon salt
¼ teaspoon ginger
½ teaspoon allspice
1 teaspoon nutmeg
1 teaspoon cinnamon
1 cup raisins
½ cup chopped nuts
    sugar and cinnamon (optional)

Preheat oven to 400 degrees. Cream shortening and sugar thoroughly. Add eggs, pumpkin, and flavorings, mixing well. Sift together dry ingredients and stir into creamed mixture. Add raisins and nuts; mix well. Drop by teaspoonfuls onto an oiled baking sheet; these spread very little. Sprinkle equal amounts of sugar and cinnamon, mixed together in a shaker, over cookies if desired. Bake about 15 minutes.

YULE POMANDERS

A good make-ahead holiday treat!

Yield: 4½ dozen

1 cup (1 6-ounce package) semi-
    sweet chocolate morsels
½ cup sugar
¼ cup light corn syrup
¼ cup water
2½ cups finely crushed vanilla
    wafer crumbs (1 7¼-ounce
    box)

1 cup finely chopped pecans or
    walnuts
1 teaspoon orange extract
    confectioner's or granulated
    sugar (optional)

Melt chocolate morsels over hot (not boiling) water. Remove from heat. Stir in sugar and syrup. Blend in water. Combine wafer crumbs and nuts. Add the chocolate mixture and orange extract. Form into one-inch balls. Roll in sugar if desired. Place in a tightly closed container in a cool place for at least several days. These will keep 3 to 4 weeks and improve with age.

Marilyn Whelpley

BOURBON BALLS

Make **Yule Pomanders**, using ¼ cup bourbon whisky instead of water, and omit orange extract.

Frances P. Caire

SASSY ORANGE FROSTING

Yield: about 1 cup

4 tablespoons (½ stick) butter	¼ cup frozen orange juice,
2½ cups sifted confectioner's sugar	concentrate, thawed, undiluted

Cream butter; add sugar alternately with concentrate until well-blended and smooth.

CHOCOLATE CHIP FROSTING

Yield: 1¼ cups

1 cup (1 6-ounce package) semi-sweet chocolate morsels	2 tablespoons butter
	¼ cup milk or cream

Melt chocolate morsels and butter over hot (not boiling) water. Remove from heat and blend in milk. For variation, butter-scotch or coconut morsels may be used.

Savannah News-Press

Rice Mill on Ogeechee River, from which General Sherman watched the storming of Fort McAllister. (From "The Story of the Great March," by Brevet Mayor George Ward Nichols, aide-de-camp to General Sherman. Harper & Brothers, New York, 1865.)

Courtesy of Savannah Public Library

CANDY

CANDY STAGES

The art of making candy is far older than candy thermometers. For those who do not own the latter, and for help in deciphering recipes still written in this manner, the following chart is included.

Thread Stage (230 degrees to 234 degrees): hot candy syrup spins a 2-inch thread when dropped from a fork or spoon into very cold water.

Soft Ball (234 degrees to 240 degrees): syrup forms a soft ball when dropped into very cold water, which flattens on removal from water.

Firm Ball (244 degrees to 248 degrees): syrup, when dropped into very cold water, forms a firm ball which does not flatten on removal from water.

Hard Ball (250 degrees to 266 degrees): syrup forms a hard ball when dropped into very cold water, one which holds its shape and yet is plastic.

Soft Crack (270 degrees to 290 degrees): syrup, when dropped into very cold water, separates into threads which are hard but not brittle.

Hard Crack (300 degrees to 310 degrees): syrup, when dropped into very cold water, separates into threads which are brittle and hard.

THE SAVANNAH SUGAR REFINERY

The Savannah Sugar Refinery, a division of Savannah Foods and Industries, Inc., has been an important Savannah business since 1917. In that year the Sprague and Oxford families, who had a sugar concern in New Orleans, were given permission by the federal government to build a new refinery somewhere between Philadelphia and New Orleans. Savannah was chosen after master pilot Frank W. Spencer demonstrated that the upper Savannah River was navigable as far as Port Wentworth. At the time, it was the only sugar refinery between the two cities mentioned. Nearly four hundred employees and their families made the move from New Orleans; some of these families still work for the refinery. It was the first large industry in the upper harbor of Savannah; records show that its first sale was to A. Ehrlich and Brothers Grocery of Savannah. The refinery's famous "Dixie Crystals" are used in **Georgia Nuggets**.

GEORGIA NUGGETS

Yield: about 2 pounds

3 cups light brown sugar, firmly packed	½ teaspoon vanilla extract
⅛ teaspoon salt	1½ tablespoons butter or margarine
1 cup light cream	2 cups coarsely chopped pecans

Dissolve sugar and salt in cream in a 4-quart saucepan. Cook over moderate heat, stirring occasionally, until mixture reaches soft ball stage (see **Candy Stages**) or 236 degrees on candy thermometer. Remove from heat and cool on rack until bottom of pan is comfortably warm on palm of hand, or 110 degrees on candy thermometer. Add vanilla, butter, and pecans. Beat until mixture is creamy and thick. Drop by tablespoonfuls onto heavy waxed paper. When "set" and cool, store in air-tight container in a cool place.

Georgia's oldest Jewish congregation, Mickve Israel traces its history back to 1733 and the founding of Savannah. President George Washington once wrote them a letter. The present temple was consecrated in 1878.

Drawing by Jemison Hoskins,
Copyright© 1976 by J. Hoskins

ANGEL SWEETS

Yield: about 4½ dozen

1 6-ounce package chocolate chips	1 cup chopped walnuts or pecans
2 tablespoons butter	2 cups miniature marshmallows
1 egg	½ cup flaked coconut
1 cup sifted confectioner's sugar	

Melt chips and butter together over low heat. Remove from heat and cool. Beat in egg. Stir in sugar, nuts, and marshmallows. Shape into small balls. Roll in coconut. Chill until served.

Wanda Duggar

OLD-FASHIONED BENNE CANDY

Benne seed, first brought from Africa with the slave trade, gives a distinctive flavor to Savannah cookies and candy.

Yield: more than 1 pound

1 pound light brown sugar	1 tablespoon cider vinegar
2 tablespoons butter	1½ cups **Toasted Benne Seeds**
½ cup milk	1 teaspoon vanilla extract

Combine first four ingredients in a large, heavy saucepan and bring to a boil. Continue to cook until soft ball stage (see **Candy Stages**) or 236 degrees on the candy thermometer, stirring very little. Take off the stove and cool until bottom of pan is comfortably warm on palm of hand, or to 110 degrees on the candy thermometer. Beat in benne seeds. Add vanilla and beat until creamy and slightly thick. Drop by teaspoonfuls onto a buttered dish or paper, and let stand until firm. Store in an air-tight container in a cool place.

PEANUT-POPCORN CANDY

Make the childhood favorite at home for a fresher taste: fun for the entire family.

Yield: about 6 cups

1 cup whole Spanish peanuts, skins removed	1 tablespoon butter
4 cups popped popcorn	2 cups sugar
1 cup New Orleans molasses	2 tablespoons vinegar
	1 teaspoon baking soda

Combine the nuts and popcorn in a large bowl; set aside. Combine the molasses, butter, sugar, and vinegar in a heavy 1-quart pan. Bring to a boil, and boil to the hard crack stage (see

Candy Stages) or 300 degrees to 310 degrees on the candy thermometer, stirring constantly. Remove from heat and add soda. Stir briskly. Pour over nuts and popcorn; mix well. Let cool, and serve.

Mrs. R. C. Ruckman

ORANGE CARAMELS

This recipe involves some stirring, but its flavor is worth it.

Yield: about 2½ pounds

2 cups sugar	¼ pound (1 stick) butter
⅛ teaspoon salt	1 cup heavy cream
2 cups clear corn syrup	
1 6-ounce can frozen orange juice, thawed and undiluted	

Mix sugar, salt, syrup, and juice in a 3-to 4-quart saucepan. Bring to a boil over moderate heat. Cook to the firm ball stage (see **Candy Stages**) or 245 degrees on the candy thermometer, stirring occasionally. Gradually add butter and cream so that mixture does not stop boiling. Cook rapidly, stirring constantly, to firm ball stage, or 245 degrees on the candy thermometer. Remove from heat. Let cool until bubbles stop. Pour into a well-buttered 9-inch square layer pan. Allow to cool completely. Turn out on a cutting board. Cut with a heavy knife into strips about an inch wide. Finish with kitchen shears cutting into bite-sized pieces. Wrap each piece individually in heavy waxed paper.

Variations: use frozen apple juice plus 1 teaspoon Angostura Bitters, pineapple-grapefruit juice, limeade, lemonade, or grapefruit juice instead of the orange juice. Grape juice is good, but an ugly color!

LORNA'S PEANUT FUDGE

Yield: 5 pounds

4⅔ cups sugar	2 cups marshmallow creme
1 13-ounce can evaporated milk	2 cups peanut butter
¼ pound (1 stick) butter	

Combine sugar and milk in a large, heavy saucepan, and gently bring to a boil. Add butter, and cook to soft ball stage (see **Candy Stages**) or 234 degrees to 240 degrees on the candy thermometer. Remove from heat. Stir in marshmallow creme and peanut butter. Beat until mixture starts to thicken. Pour into lightly buttered shallow pans. Let cool until firm. Cut in squares, and store in air-tight container.

Mrs. Lorna Williams

DATE-NUT ROLL

Rich and absolutely delicious!

Yield: about 2¼ pounds

2 cups sugar
¾ cup milk
1 16-ounce box dates, seeded and chopped

2 cups chopped pecans

Cook sugar and milk over moderate heat until it reaches the soft ball stage (see **Candy Stages**) or 236 degrees on candy thermometer. Do not stir, if possible. Remove from heat, but keep warm. Add dates and let heat through. Add pecans and stir very gently. Pour mixture onto a heavy, damp dish towel. Roll gently until mixture forms a long roll. Roll in foil or heavy waxed paper and refrigerate. Slice as needed.

Mary Osteen

COFFEE-BREAK PECANS

An unusual candied pecan recipe by Emma R. Law, nice for holiday open houses or as gifts for special people.

Yield: about 2 cups

2 teaspoons dry instant coffee powder
¼ cup sugar
¼ teaspoon ground allspice

2 tablespoons water
⅛ teaspoon salt
2 cups pecan halves

Combine all ingredients in a one-quart saucepan and bring to a boil over medium heat. Cook three minutes, stirring constantly. Spread over waxed paper and separate nuts as they cool. Pecans will be sugared, but not sticky.

ORANGE-CANDIED PECANS

Yield: about 3 cups

3 cups light brown sugar
1 cup orange juice
1½ tablespoons butter

1 teaspoon grated orange peel
3 cups pecan halves or chopped English walnuts

Now a gift and book shop, The Little House at 107 East Gordon Street was originally built as a carriage house in 1856. The upstairs is now a rare books and prints shop, The Printed Page, which has also re-issued some out-of-print Savannah books.

Drawing courtesy of The Little House

Place sugar and juice in a 2-quart saucepan. Gently cook to soft ball stage (see **Candy Stages**) or 236 degrees on the candy thermometer. Remove from heat and add butter and orange rind. Beat until mixture is ready to set. Stir in pecans and continue beating until mixture is quite thick. Turn into a buttered, shallow baking pan or platter. While cooling, separate nuts with 2 table forks. Store, covered, in a cool place. It's nice to double this recipe, and have some for friends.

Emma R. Law

PRESIDENT STREET PENUCHE

Yield: about 2½ pounds

¾ cup milk	⅛ teaspoon salt
¾ cup light brown sugar	1 tablespoon light corn syrup
1½ cups sugar	1 teaspoon vanilla extract
1 tablespoon butter	1 cup chopped pecans

Combine all ingredients except vanilla and nuts. Stir over moderate heat only until sugar dissolves. Cover and simmer, very briefly, to dissolve any sugar sticking to sides of pan. Uncover, bring to a boil, and cook gently, without stirring, until soft ball stage (see **Candy Stages**) or 238 degrees on the candy thermometer. Cool, without stirring, until bottom of pan is comfortable on palm of hand (about 110 degrees on the candy thermometer). Add vanilla and nuts. Beat until mixture begins to slightly hold its shape. Quickly pour into buttered 9-inch square pan. Cool on a rack. Cut into squares. Store in air-tight container in a cool place.

SOUTHERN PRALINES

Pralines, the most famous candy of New Orleans, were created by a French marshall's chef, who knew his employer had a sweet tooth. He coated almonds with sugar and named the sweet after the official, Cesar du Plessis Prasline (pronounced pralin). Later, other Southern cooks made a confection of native pecans and brown sugar, using several nuts to each patty.

Yield: 15 to 18

3 cups light brown sugar, firmly packed	¼ teaspoon cinnamon or allspice
¼ cup lightly salted butter	1½ cups chopped or whole pecans
1 cup heavy cream	

Combine sugar, butter, and cream in heavy 3-quart saucepan. Cook over moderate heat, stirring as little as possible, to soft ball stage (see **Candy Stages**) or 236 degrees on a candy thermometer. Remove from heat, place on a rack, and sprinkle with cinnamon. Let cool, without stirring, until bottom of pan is comfortably warm on palm of hand, 110 degrees on candy thermometer. Beat until nearly cool. Stir in nuts. Quickly drop by teaspoonfuls onto heavy waxed paper. Store, covered, when completely cool.

TIFTON PEANUT BRITTLE

Yield: about 2½ pounds

2 cups sugar	2 or 3 cups uncooked Spanish peanuts
1 cup light corn syrup	1 teaspoon baking soda
½ cup water	
½ pound (2 sticks) butter or margarine, at room temperature	

In a three-quart saucepan, combine sugar, syrup, and water. Cook over moderate heat, stirring until sugar dissolves. When mixture boils, blend in butter, and cook until syrup reaches thread stage (see **Candy Stages**) or 230 degrees on candy thermometer. Add peanuts and continue to cook until mixture reaches soft crack stage (280 degrees). Stir mixture constantly at this point until it reaches the hard crack stage, 305 degrees.

Remove from heat. Stir in soda until mixture foams. Pour quickly onto 2 buttered cookie sheets with sides. Cool on racks until hardened. Break into pieces. Store in tightly closed container.

Georgia Peanut Commission

PEANUT BUTTER SWIRL FUDGE
Yield: 64 pieces

2 cups sugar	1 cup crunchy peanut butter
⅔ cup milk	1 teaspoon vanilla extract
½ 7-ounce jar marshmallow creme	½ cup semi-sweet chocolate chips

Combine sugar and milk. Bring to a boil, and cook to soft ball stage (see **Candy Stages**) or 234 degrees on the candy thermometer. Remove from heat and stir in marshmallow creme, peanut butter, and vanilla. Turn into buttered 8-inch square pan. Place on rack to cool. Melt chocolate chips over hot (not boiling) water. Spoon melted chocolate over top, and swirl into fudge. While still warm, cut into one-inch squares. Cool until set.

DOUBLE PEANUT CLUSTERS
Yield: about 2 dozen

½ cup creamy peanut butter	1 cup parched peanuts
1 cup (16-ounce package) semi-sweet chocolate chips	

Combine chocolate chips and peanut butter in top of double boiler over hot (not boiling) water. Stir until chocolate is melted. Remove from heat and stir until well blended. Add nuts and stir until all are well coated. Drop by teaspoonfuls on waxed paper-lined cookie sheet. Cool on a rack until set. (If kitchen is very warm, refrigerate.) Store in tightly-covered container in a cool place.

Georgia Peanut Commission

STRAWBERRY DIVINITY
Yield: about 5 dozen

3 cups sugar	1 3-ounce package strawberry gelatin
¾ cup light corn syrup	½ cup flaked coconut
¾ cup water	1 cup chopped pecans
2 egg whites	

Combine sugar, syrup, and water in a heavy 2-quart saucepan, and gently bring to a boil, stirring constantly. Reduce heat and continue cooking, stirring only occasionally, to hard ball stage (see **Candy Stages**) or 250 degrees to 266 degrees on candy thermometer. Remove from heat.

Beat egg whites until fluffy. Slowly add gelatin to egg whites, beating until mixture forms peaks. Pour hot syrup in a thin stream into whites, beating constantly. Beat until candy loses gloss and holds its shape. Fold in coconut and pecans. Pour into greased pan or drop by teaspoonfuls onto greased surface.

Wanda Dugger

DARIEN TAFFY

Yield: about 40 pieces

3	cups sugar	1	tablespoon butter
3	tablespoons vinegar	½	teaspoon peppermint extract
1	cup water		(optional)

Blend ingredients, except for peppermint, in a heavy saucepan. Stir over low heat until sugar dissolves. Then, cook to hard ball stage (see **Candy Stages**) or 250 degrees to 266 degrees on a candy thermometer, without stirring. Pour into a shallow buttered plate. Add peppermint, if desired. Work with the taffy, with well-buttered hands, until you can gather it up in your hands. As soon as you get it into a ball, start pulling on it, and pull it into a "rope," or until it is white and porous. Then, lay it on waxed paper, and cut it with scissors, or crack it with a knife into bite-sized pieces.

FRENCH CANDY

Take the white of an egg, the same quantity of water as the egg, (measured in half the egg shell). Stir in one and a half pounds of confectioners sugar; cook well, until it becomes like a dough. Shell one pound English walnuts. Place a half of the nut on each side of a small piece of dough, flavored to taste with vanilla. Dried figs or dates may be used in the same way.

Hints From Southern Epicures, 1890

PICKLES & RELISHES

GOOD PICKLES

There is no department of cooking more dependent on good materials than pickles. Be sure you have fresh, firm vegetables, pure, strong spices and peppers, and the best of apple vinegar. . . . Pickles are unfit for use if frozen. No care can restore them. . . . Pickles are much better, and can be kept indefinitely, by putting up in glass bottles and sealing.

House-Keeping In The Sunny South, 1885

APRICOT CHUTNEY

A delicious and welcome gift for special people.

Yield: about 3 cups

1 6-ounce package dried apricots, diced	2 garlic cloves, crushed or minced
2 tablespoons finely diced crystalized ginger, packed	1½ teaspoons ground mustard
1 cup halved seedless golden raisins	⅛ teaspoon hot pepper sauce
½ lemon, finely diced	½ cup tomato juice
¾ cup chopped onions	½ teaspoon salt
1½ cups sugar	½ teaspoon ground cinnamon
½ cup plain white wine vinegar	½ teaspoon ground cloves
	½ teaspoon ground allspice

THE SAVANNAH COTTON EXCHANGE

Symbolic of the days when cotton was king, the Savannah Cotton Exchange was completed in 1887. Using the principle of "air rights," this is the first building in the United States to be constructed completely over a public street. After serving as a visitor's center for a time, it is now the home of Solomon's Lodge.

Drawing by Jean Birnbaum

Mix all ingredients together. Bring to a boil; lower heat and cook gently to desired thickness.

Bess Jones Winburn

PICKLED BEETS

Wash them, but do not rub off any of the rootlets; boil them tender, peel them, or rub off the outside with a coarse cloth, cut them in slices, put them in a jar, cover with cold vinegar, and black pepper and ginger to taste.

Mrs. Sarah Josepha Hale,
House-Keeping In The Sunny South, *1885*

CABBAGE PICKLE

Take one quart of finely chopped onions, three tablespoonfuls each of cloves, white mustard seed, black pepper, celery seed, and ground mustard; half a pound of brown sugar; and three quarts of strong vinegar. Simmer this compound until it begins to thicken. Pour it over one gallon of finely chopped cabbage, and boil a few minutes.

Gulf City Cookbook, *1878*

EMMA'S CARROT-CURRANT RELISH

Yield: 1 quart

1	pound young carrots	1	cup plain red wine vinegar
2	cups water	½	cup diced onions
½	teaspoon salt	1	teaspoon mixed pickling
1	cup dried black currants		spice, tied in cheesecloth
1	cup sugar	½	cup water

Peel carrots. Slice into "penny" cuts about ⅛ inch thick. There should be about 3 cups. Cook in stainless steel, glass, or enameled ware, but **not** in iron or aluminum. Simmer until barely tender in 2 cups water and salt. Drain. Meanwhile, combine remaining ingredients and simmer, uncovered, for about 17 minutes. Add cooked carrots and remove from heat. Stir gently and smooth carrots down into liquid. Cover and let stand about 18 hours. Stir gently, and smooth carrots down into liquid several times. Store covered in the refrigerator.

ATLANTA CORN RELISH

Yield: about 8 pints

12	ears corn	3	tablespoons flour
1	small head cabbage	1	teaspoon ground turmeric
4	medium onions, peeled	2	cups sugar
3	sweet red peppers, halved and seeded	1	tablespoon dry mustard
3	tablespoons salt	1	quart plain white vinegar

Cook corn on the cob just enough to "set" grains, about 3 minutes. Cut from cob. Put vegetables through food chopper, using coarse blade. Combine all vegetables. Blend dry ingredients. Add vinegar gradually, stirring well. Bring vinegar mixture to a boil in a large kettle, and add vegetables. Simmer 25 to 30 minutes. Seal at once in hot sterilized jars.

Mary Beth Busbee, Atlanta, Georgia

VERY SPECIAL CRANBERRY SAUCE

Cranberries are an American product which was used by the Indians for medicinal purposes, to dye colorful robes, and for flavoring. It is said that they were also considered a symbol of peace. Cranberries may be frozen during the winter months when they are plentiful, in the same plastic bags in which they are sold. To use, shake out as many as you wish, wash, and use as you would fresh ones.

Yield: about 2 quarts

4	cups light brown sugar	2	cups dry white wine (I like Gallo Rhine Garten)
1	6-ounce can frozen orange juice, thawed and undiluted	2	pounds fresh cranberries

Place sugar, juice, and wine in a very large stainless steel pot or Dutch oven. (The berries will foam up!) Stir over low heat until sugar is dissolved. Add cranberries and boil rapidly, uncovered, until berries pop, about 7 to 10 minutes. Cool, covered, and store, covered, in the refrigerator. It's nice to take a container of this along at the holiday time when visiting friends.

Emma R. Law

Built about 1805, the Sheftall House was moved in 1970 to its present location on Columbia Square and restored by the Unitarian-Universalist Fellowship of Savannah.

Drawing by Leon Jay Meyer,
Courtesy of Unitarian-Universalist Fellowship

FAMOUS CRANBERRY CHUTNEY

Yield: 3 or 4 cups

1 pound fresh or frozen cranberries	1 teaspoon dry mustard
rind of two limes, slivered	½ teaspoon mustard seed
1 cup light brown sugar, firmly packed	dash cayenne pepper
½ cup plain red wine vinegar	½ cup dried black currants
1 cup orange juice	1 3-ounce package crystalized ginger, snipped into small pieces
1 cup diced onion	

Place all ingredients in a large saucepan. Cook over moderate heat until berries pop, about 5 minutes. Continue cooking gently, stirring often, to desired degree of thickness. (This also thickens on standing.) Store in covered jar in refrigerator to preserve the color.

Emma R. Law

CURRIED DRIED FRUIT RELISH

Yield: about 3 cups

2 6-ounce packages tenderized dried apricots	¼ teaspoon salt
1 cup dried black currants	¼ cup sugar
1 tablespoon instant minced onion	2 cups boiling water
1 tablespoon curry powder	3 tea bags
	¼ cup plain red wine vinegar

Snip apricots into little pieces in a medium bowl. Toss with currants and onion. Sprinkle with a mixture of curry powder, salt, and sugar. Meanwhile, pour boiling water over tea bags in a small bowl. Cover and brew for 5 minutes. Discard bags. Pour tea and vinegar over fruit. Cool. Marinate, covered, in refrigerator for at least 18 hours; the longer the better. Keep in refrigerator to preserve color and use as needed.

ATLANTA SPICED PEACHES

Seven pounds of peeled peaches not quite ripe; three pounds of sugar, and one quart of good vinegar; one teaspoonful each of ground cloves and cinnamon. Let the vinegar, sugar, and spices become thoroughly heated; put the peaches in and let them remain and cook until quite soft. Put up in air-tight jars. They look very pretty with three cloves through the center of each.

House-Keeping In The Sunny South, 1885

For, wherever the winds of Georgia run,
It smells of peaches long in the sun...
Oh, Georgia, Georgia, the careless yield!
The watermelons ripe in the field!
The mist in the bottoms that tastes of fever,
And the yellow river, rolling forever!

Stephen Vincent Benet,
"John Brown's Body"

Completed in 1853, the Green-Meldrim House was the home of English cotton merchant Charles Green at the time General Sherman made his headquarters there in 1864. Here was composed the famous telegram in which he offered President Abraham Lincoln the city of Savannah "as a Christmas gift." It was later the home of Judge Peter Meldrim, former mayor of Savannah and once president of the American Bar Association. It is now the Parish House of St. John's Church and is open to the public several hours each week. The Green-Meldrim House was the childhood home of Mrs. Sophie Meldrim Shonnard, several of whose family recipes appear in this book.

Drawing by Mark Lindsay,
Copyright© 1973 by The Lady Print Shop

SAVANNAH PEACH PICKLES

Yield: about 1 quart

1   cup white vinegar
1   cup sugar
½   teaspoon allspice

1   stick cinnamon
1   pound clingstone peaches
    cloves

Boil vinegar, sugar, allspice, and cinnamon together in a heavy saucepan until they begin to cook down into a syrup, about 5 minutes. Put in peeled peaches, with three whole cloves stuck in each one. Simmer, covered, until peaches are tender, about 10 to 15 minutes. Take out peaches and pack into hot, sterile jars. Continue to boil syrup, uncovered, until it is as thick as desired. Pour over peaches, and seal jars. They are better if allowed to stand 6 to 8 weeks before using.

Mrs. Sophie Meldrim Shonnard

OGEECHEE PEAR RELISH

Another traditional family recipe....

1   quart white vinegar
2   cups sugar
2   quarts raw peeled pears,
    coarsely grated
1   tablespoon salt
2   tablespoons ground turmeric

2   tablespoons mustard seed
7   cups minced onion
7   cups minced green peppers
¾   cup cornstarch
    about 1½ cups water

Heat vinegar and sugar in a large pot to the boiling point. Add all ingredients except the cornstarch and water. Bring to a boil again, then lower heat, and simmer about 20 minutes. Measure cornstarch in a quart bowl and add water gradually to make a smooth paste. Stir this mixture into the pot and continue to stir until the cornstarch is well cooked and the relish has a clear look. Fill hot, clean jars with the hot mixture and seal.

Mrs. Betty Rahn

RED PEPPER RELISH

Yield: about 1 pint

2⅓ cups coarsely ground sweet
    red peppers, or about 1¾
    pounds, with seeds, ribs, and
    stems removed
⅔   cup finely chopped onion
¾   cup sugar
⅓   cup lime or lemon juice

2   tablespoons plain white wine
    vinegar
2   teaspoons yellow mustard
    seed
½   teaspoon salt
1/16 teaspoon cayenne pepper

Place all ingredients in a 10-inch skillet. Simmer over moderate heat, stirring quite often, until very thick, about 20 minutes. Cool, cover, and store in the refrigerator.

PLANTATION PICCALILLI

Yield: about 3 pints

1	quart chopped green tomatoes	½	cup salt
1	cup chopped sweet green peppers	2	cups plain white wine vinegar
1	cup chopped sweet red peppers	2¼	cups sugar
		2	tablespoons mixed pickling spice
2	cups chopped mild onions	1	tablespoon mustard seed
2	cups chopped green cabbage	1	teaspoon celery seed

Use a stainless steel or enamel pot of at least 6- or 8-quart capacity. Mix vegetables and salt well. Let stand, covered, in refrigerator overnight. Drain well, in a colander, and press out as much liquid as possible. Add vinegar and sugar. Tie pickling spice in a cheesecloth bundle and add to mixture. Stir in mustard and celery seed. Bring to a boil, lower heat, and simmer until mixture is clear and slightly thickened. Either seal in sterilized jars or place in covered containers and refrigerate.

VIDALIA ONION RELISH

Yield: 2½ cups

⅓	cup cider vinegar	1	4-ounce can or jar whole pimientos, quartered
½	teaspoon fines herbes		
2	tablespoons sugar	1	cup thinly sliced Vidalia onions
⅔	cup water		

Combine vinegar, fine herbes, sugar, and water. Add pimientos and onion; marinate overnight in refrigerator. Drain; serve with meat.

Savannah News-Press

SWEET PUMPKIN PICKLES

Yield: about 4 pints

6	cups peeled and cubed pumpkin	2	cups sugar
2	cups cider vinegar	2	sticks whole cinnamon

Steam pumpkin in a colander just until tender, being careful not to allow water to touch the pumpkin cubes. Drain. Simmer vinegar, sugar, and cinnamon for 15 minutes. Add pumpkin cubes and simmer 5 minutes more. Set aside in refrigerator, covered, for 24 hours. Reheat and simmer 5 minutes more. Remove spices and seal in sterile jars.

SQUASH PICKLE

Yield: about 7 pints

2½	tablespoons salt	2	cups thinly sliced onions
8	cups yellow squash, thinly sliced	2	teaspoons hot peppers, seeded and coarsely chopped
2	cups sugar		
2	cups cider vinegar	¾	cup sweet peppers, seeded and coarsely chopped
2	teaspoons celery seed		
2	teaspoons mustard seed		

Sprinkle salt over squash. Put in colander and drain for one hour. Mix sugar, vinegar, celery seed, and mustard seed and bring to a boil. Set this aside while you prepare the onions and peppers. Add them to the liquid and bring to a boil again. Then add the squash, put in sterile jars, and seal.

TOMATO CATCHUP

Cut any quantity of ripe tomatoes across the middle, put them in a large porcelain kettle, and let them simmer until soft. Strain them first through a colander, then through a sieve. Boil the liquid again until the watery substance ceases to rise on the surface. To every half gallon of tomato juice, add one quart of vinegar, four tablespoonfuls of salt, two tablespoonfuls each of black pepper and dry mustard, one teaspoonful of cayenne pepper, one teaspoonful of whole cloves, and one clove of garlic. Boil again until it is thick. Cook, and seal while hot.

Gulf City Cookbook, 1878

JELLIES & PRESERVES

THE "HAUNTED" HOUSE

Built by Hampton Lillibridge about 1796, this three-story clapboard house at 507 East St. Julian Street originally stood on Bryan Street. It is not only the last eighteenth century gambrel-roofed house in the state, but is also said to be haunted. It was once "exorcised" by the Episcopal Bishop of Georgia. Privately owned, it is not open to the public.

Drawing by Charley Bland,
Copyright© 1975 by Charley Bland

JELLIES AND PRESERVES

You can preserve any fresh fruit by chopping or grinding it as you want, and then mixing a pound of fruit to a pound of sugar, and cooking until thick.

You can make any kind of fruit juice into jelly by placing the juice and sugar together in a pan, a cup of juice to a cup of sugar, and cooking together until the jelly drops in large drops from the spoon. Or, you can put a small amount in a saucer. If it jells when cool in the saucer, remove jelly from heat and pour into jelly glasses. [This is what old cook books mean by "the jelly test."] Seal with wax.

Adapted from **Ye Olde Time Salzburger Cookbook**

NUTTY APPLE BUTTER

Yield: 3 cups

1	quart canned applesauce	1	teaspoon nutmeg
1½	cups dark brown sugar, firmly packed	1	teaspoon ground cloves
		2	tablespoons butter
1	teaspoon cinnamon	½	cup finely chopped pecans

Combine all ingredients except nuts in a large saucepan. Bring to a boil and simmer uncovered over low heat for 2 hours, or until thick and dark in color. Remove from stove and cool. Stir in nuts.

Savannah News-Press

APPLE JELLY

In making jellies, the flavor and color of the fruit are best retained by boiling the juice quite a while before adding the sugar.

Let your apples be pared and cored; put them in a preserving kettle with enough water to cover, boil them quickly until quite tender, strain them through a colander, and then through a sieve. To every pint of juice, put a pound of sugar with a little lemon juice and peel. Boil gently until jellied, which will be in an hour. Take off and put in glasses while hot.

Mrs. H. N. Starnes,
House-Keeping In The Sunny South, 1885

CRANBERRY-PRUNE CONSERVE

Yield: 1½ quarts

1	pound fresh cranberries	1	cup coarsely broken walnuts
2	cups water		or pecans
4	cups sugar		
1	12-ounce package pitted prunes, cut into halves		

Combine all ingredients in a saucepan and bring to a boil. Boil gently for 10 minutes, stirring occasionally. Spoon into hot jars. Cool and seal. Store in refrigerator until needed.

Savannah News-Press

FIG PRESERVES

Yield: 8 pints

3	quarts figs	11	cups (2¾ quarts) sugar
2	cups water	4	lemons, thinly sliced

Wash figs well. Leaving stems on, cut figs in half lengthwise. In a large pot, combine water and sugar and bring to a boil. Add figs and lemon. Boil, stirring occasionally, until fruit is tender and translucent and syrup is thick. Ladle into sterilized jars.

Annual Bazaar Committee, St. John's Episcopal Church

PEACH-ORANGE HONEY

Yield: about 7 6-ounce jars

12	large peaches, peeled and seeded	2	small oranges
			sugar

Grind peaches, using coarse blade of food chopper. Quarter oranges and remove seed. Grind oranges with peel. Measure mixture by cupful, and place in heavy saucepan with equal amounts of sugar. Boil gently over low heat, stirring often, for about 25 minutes, or until it begins to thicken. Pour into hot sterile jars. It will thicken as it stands, so let it stand at least a month before using.

The Pirates' House Cook Book

The William Scarbrough House, built in 1818-19, is headquarters for the Historic Savannah Foundation.

Drawing copyright© by Pamela Lee

PEACH OR PEAR JAM

Yield: 8 6-ounce jars

1 quart fruit	5½ cups sugar
2 tablespoons lemon juice	
1 ¾-ounce package powdered pectin	

Peel fully ripe fruit. Remove seed, or core. Chop fine, or grind, and add lemon juice. Mix fruit with pectin and bring to a hard boil. Add sugar and bring to a full rolling boil. Boil hard one minute, stirring constantly. Pour into hot, sterilized jars and seal.

Margie Anderson, Savannah News-Press

PEAR HONEY

Yield: about 8 6-ounce jars

3½ cups ground pears
1 cup crushed pineapple
1 ¾-ounce package powdered fruit pectin

5 cups sugar

Bring pears and pineapple to a boil. Boil 1 minute. Add pectin and boil one minute more. Add sugar and boil 3 minutes more. Jar and seal.

Ann Card, Savannah News-Press

PEPPER JELLY

Working with peppers will "burn" your hands. Wear thin rubber or vinyl gloves. The easiest way to "grind" peppers is in a blender. I put the vinegar in the blender container and drop in the pieces of pepper. Strain and measure the pulp until you have one cup. You will end up with more liquid than just the vinegar you started with, since the peppers contain juice. Use all the liquid.

Yield: 7 4-ounce jars

enough ground bell peppers to equal 1 cup
enough ground hot peppers to equal ¼ cup (more if desired)

6½ cups sugar
1½ cups apple cider vinegar
1 6-ounce bottle liquid pectin

Combine peppers, sugar, and vinegar in a saucepan. Boil about 3 minutes, or until peppers are tender. Strain and bring juice to a full boil. Add pectin. Boil one minute by the kitchen timer; do not overboil. Pour into sterilized jars and seal. If you are using wax, this recipe requires about 3 ounces of paraffin.

Joanne Ayers, Savannah News-Press

WORMSLOE PLUM BUTTER

Yield: about 10 6-ounce jars

2 quarts fresh plums, pitted and halved

1 cup water
2 cups sugar

Wash plums well. If they have tough skins, they may be cut in pieces smaller than halves. Put them in a porcelain-lined kettle with the water, and boil until soft. Add sugar. Boil slowly for 1 hour, or until thick as desired.

TO BRANDY THE AUGUST PLUM

Select the largest and ripest plums; prick each one with a silver fork; put them in a glass jar, and cover them with brandy. Let them steep 10 days or a fortnight; then take them out of the brandy. Weigh them, and to each pound of plums, allow three-quarters of a pound of white sugar; let the plums lie on the sugar until it becomes saturated; then put all into your kettle, and boil about half an hour over a slow fire. The brandy in which the plums have been steeped makes a delightful cordial when sweetened, and a few cloves and a little cinnamon added.

House And Home, or, The Carolina Housewife,
by A Lady of Charleston, 1855

STRAWBERRY BUTTER

Delicious on hot bread…and no cooking required.

Yield: about 3½ cups

¼ pound (1 stick) butter or margarine	1 10-ounce package frozen sliced strawberries, thawed and drained
2 cups sifted confectioner's sugar	
½ teaspoon vanilla or brandy extract	

Cream butter; gradually add sugar, beating until fluffy. Blend in extract and berries. Chill before serving. Juice drained from strawberries is delicious in fruit gelatin or a fresh fruit cup.

Savannah News-Press

TOMATO JAM

Yield: about 6 6-ounce jars

2¼ pounds tomatoes	6½ cups sugar
1½ teaspoons grated lemon rind	1 6-ounce bottle liquid fruit pectin
¼ cup lemon juice	

Scald, peel, and chop fully ripe tomatoes. Simmer in a large saucepan for 10 minutes. Add lemon rind, lemon juice, and sugar. Mix well. Place over high heat, and bring to a full rolling boil. Boil 1 minute, stirring constantly. Remove from heat and stir in pectin at once. Skim off foam with a metal spoon. Stir and skim for 5 minutes to cool. Ladle into glasses, and cover with ⅛ inch hot paraffin.

Margie Anderson, Savannah News-Press

NEW VINEGAR JELLY

To each pint of the purest cider vinegar, add a pound of sugar. Tie up a little stick cinnamon, cloves, and allspice in a bag, and boil with it. When jellied, remove bag, and pour into glasses. An excellent jelly for fowls.

Mrs. E. R. Tennent,
House-Keeping In The Sunny South, 1885

WHITE BLUFF WINE JELLY

Yield: 8 8-ounce jars

4	cups red or white wine	6	cups sugar
1	6-ounce bottle liquid fruit pectin		

Pour wine into large saucepan. Add liquid fruit pectin and sugar. Bring to a full rolling boil: don't take your eyes off it! Cook one minute at a hard boil, by the kitchen timer. Skim off any froth. Pour into sterile hot glasses, and seal.

Jo Hendley

DIETER'S BERRY JAM

Yield: about 2 6-ounce jars

1	quart crushed raspberries or blackberries	8	tablespoons liquid artificial sweetener, or to taste

Measure crushed berries into a heavy saucepan. Add sweetner and stir well. Boil rapidly, stirring constantly, until mixture thickens. Fill and seal containers. One tablespoon equals 10 calories.

Savannah News-Press

LOW-CALORIE PEACH JAM

Yield: 1 pint

1	quart sliced, peeled peaches	½	teaspoon ascorbic acid
3	to 4 teaspoons liquid artificial sweetener, or to taste	1	¾-ounce package powdered fruit pectin
1	tablespoon lemon juice		

Crush peaches in a large saucepan. Stir in other ingredients. Bring to a boil; boil one minute. Remove from heat. Continue to stir for 2 minutes. Pour into clean freezer containers. Cover; freeze. Leave at least ½-inch headspace in the container before freezing to allow for expansion. Thaw in refrigerator before

273

serving and store in refrigerator after opening. One tablespoon equals 10 calories. The ascorbic acid in this recipe is to preserve the color of the fruit, which tends to discolor if frozen.

Savannah News-Press

LOW-CALORIE STRAWBERRY JAM

Yield: about 2¾ cups

1	quart cleaned strawberries	1	¾-ounce package powdered fruit pectin
3	to 4 teaspoons liquid artificial sweetener, or to taste	1	tablespoon lemon juice

Crush strawberries in a 1½-quart saucepan. Stir in artificial sweetener, pectin, and juice. Bring to a boil, and boil 1 minute. Remove from heat. Continue to stir for 2 minutes. Pour into freezer containers; cover and freeze. Thaw before serving and store in refrigerator after opening. One tablespoon equals 5 calories.

Savannah News-Press

POTPOURRI

This elegant Greek Revival terra cotta and brick home at 513 Whitaker Street was designed by G. L. Norman in 1902 for Lawrence McNeill, president of Savannah Lighting Company. It has an excellent view of the promenade and fountain in Forsyth Park. Chosen in 1977 for the first spring Designer's Showcase, it is now a private residence.

*Sketch by Mrs. Jenellen Hibbard Young,
used by permission of Mrs. Young and Scalamandre,
manufacturers of the Historic Savannah Collection*

1890 RESIDENCE

The late Helen Kehoe Crolly, from whose collection several previously unpublished recipes in this volume have been selected, grew up in this handsome 1890 Victorian house on Columbia Square. Later a business establishment, it was built for her father, William Kehoe. It has been rated notable in architectural surveys.

Drawing by Jean Birnbaum

PLANTATION POTPOURRI

In Victorian times, no parlor was complete without a mixture of dried petals and spices, with its haunting aroma of past summers. They were also collected into little cloth balls and used to scent clothing drawers. Tied with pastel velvet or satin ribbons, they were popular and sentimental gifts.

Yield: about 1 quart

6 cups dried rose petals	1 teaspoon ground cloves
1 ounce (2 tablespoons) dried rosemary	1 teaspoon allspice
1 ounce powdered orrisroot (available at some drug stores)	1 teaspoon cinnamon

When roses are at their best, pick the freshest of the petals, either all of a kind or of a variety. Separate petals and spread in single layers on a dry cloth, or in the bottom of a large, shallow box. Place in a dry, shady spot for 3 or 4 days, or until thoroughly dry, protecting them from the wind and bringing them in at night. (Don't forget them if it rains.) When very dry, combine them with the orrisroot and spices. Store for 4 or 5 weeks in a tightly-covered container, stirring every 2 or 3 days. Tie in sachet bags with pretty ribbons, or place in a container with a tight lid, and use occasionally as a room freshener. The scent is especially nice in period rooms.

Ann Seyle

A DAWFUSKIE PICNIC

I was then able to show my guests a Savannah picnic, which is an institution peculiar to the place. Leaving the city in a river steamer, our party consisting of one hundred people, after a little over an hour's sail we reached an island in the Atlantic Ocean, known as Dawfuskie, a beautiful spot on which stood a charming residence, with five acres of roses surrounding the house. The heads of families carried, each of them, huge baskets containing their dinner, and a full table service, wine, etc., for say, 10 or a dozen people.

On our arrival, all formed into groups under the trees, a cloth was laid on the ground, dishes, plates and glasses arranged on it, and the champagne at once frapped in small hand pails. There was then a dance in the open air, on a platform, and in the afternoon, with cushions as seats for the ladies, these improvised dinner-tables were filled. Each had its separate hostess; all was harmony and pleasure. As night approached, the people re-embarked on the steamer and returned home by moonlight.

Ward McAllister, **Society As I Have Found It,** 1890

CHRISTMAS WATERMELON

A unique Southern tradition. . . . When melons are in season, select a large, firm one. Remove a cone-shaped plug, (about 1½ inches wide at the top). Pour champagne into watermelon. Replace plug and cover well with melted, cooled paraffin. Store in a cool, dark place until the holiday season. Chill and serve!

Helen Kehoe Crolly

PEANUT BUTTER GRANOLA

Yield: about 2½ quarts

1 cup light brown sugar, firmly packed	1 12-ounce package mixed dried fruits, pits removed and fruit chopped
½ cup creamy peanut butter	
1 8-ounce package chopped pitted dates	5 cups quick-cooking oatmeal
	½ cup peanut oil
1½ cups shelled peanuts	1 cup wheat germ

Preheat oven to 350 degrees. Combine all ingredients, mixing until crumbly. (Use fingers if necessary.) Spread in 15-by-10-by-2-inch baking pan. Bake 20 minutes. Cool and store in a cool, dry place.

DO-IT-YOURSELF PEANUT BUTTER

Yield: about 1 cup

1 cup freshly roasted peanuts, shelled	1 or more teaspoons honey (optional)
3 tablespoons peanut oil	
½ teaspoon salt, if nuts are unsalted	

In the container of a blender, put peanuts and 1½ tablespoons peanut oil. Blend until smooth, adding rest of oil gradually, until desired consistency is reached. Add salt and honey if desired.

HOMEMADE YOGURT

It is said that Abraham in the Bible liked yogurt...and so will you!

Yield: 1 quart

1 quart skim or reconstituted nonfat dry milk	3 tablespoons plain yogurt, homemade or commercial
¼ cup dry milk solids	

Combine the liquid milk with the dry milk solids. Heat mixture in a heavy saucepan, or the top of a double boiler, until it registers 180 degrees on a thermometer. (If you don't have a thermometer, test with your finger. The milk should feel very hot, without scalding you.)

Remove from heat, cover, and let cool until lukewarm or warm to the touch, about 113 degrees. Remove scum, if any. Mix a little of the warm milk with the yogurt, and then stir this into the rest of the milk mixture. Mix well. Meanwhile, warm a quart thermos bottle. Now, pour the milk mixture into this. Set aside, undisturbed, for at least 5 hours.

At the end of that time, taste. Don't worry about bubbles on the top; they are the natural result of fermentation. Pour off the clear liquid which separates itself from the custard-like yogurt. The longer the yogurt is allowed to stand, the more sour it will become, so decide what is best for you of the 6 to 8 hours generally allowed for fermentation. To complete the job, pour into a clean refrigerator container, covered, and chill until needed.

Note: cleanliness is important in making yogurt. Fermentation is due to the action of millions of tiny harmless bacteria. More bacteria would affect the outcome. The yogurt from this batch may be used as starter in making more; however, it should not be more than 3 days old when used in a new batch.

Always allow to ferment in glass or ceramic container, never plastic or metal.

Plain yogurt is delicious flavored with honey or fresh fruit. It is delicious as a salad dressing base, with such flavorings as finely minced garlic, salt, grated cucumber, chopped onion or tomato, fresh mint, vinegar, or lemon juice.

For a fruit salad dressing, sweeten with honey, and add orange or pineapple juice, mint, and chopped dried fruits or nuts as desired. Yogurt may be used in place of mayonnaise in cole slaw, or instead of sour cream on baked potatoes and other vegetables.

FROZEN ORANGE YOGURT

A nutritious, refreshing treat in the summer is also made with yogurt.

Yield: 4 to 6 servings

½ cup sugar	¹⁄₁₆ teaspoon cream of tartar
2 cups plain yogurt	¹⁄₁₆ teaspoon salt
juice and finely grated rind of one orange or lemon	1 egg white
	¼ cup whipping cream
½ teaspoon vanilla extract	

Beat sugar into yogurt. Add rind, juice, and vanilla, and stir well. Add cream of tartar and salt to egg white, and beat until stiff, but not dry. Whip cream until stiff. Now, gently fold the egg whites, and then the whipped cream, into the yogurt. Place in a ceramic or glass (not plastic or metal) container, and freeze overnight.

Experiment with other flavors, such as blueberry or strawberry!

Honey may be used as a sweetener instead of sugar, at a ratio of 3 or 4 tablespoons of honey per pint of yogurt.

BENNE SEED TEETHING STICKS

The following recipe is adapted from *The Supermarket Handbook: Access To Whole Foods,* by Nikki and David Goldbeck.

Yield: 60

2 cups whole wheat flour	2 cups wheat germ
1¼ cups milk	1 tablespoon honey
½ cup safflower oil	½ cup **Toasted Benne Seeds**

Preheat oven to 350 degrees. Combine first 5 ingredients, knead until smooth in a large bowl, then divide dough and roll out on a floured surface into sticks ¼-inch thick and about 5 inches long. Roll in **Toasted Benne Seeds**. Place on oiled cookie sheet, and bake about 40 minutes, or until brown. These also make wholesome snacks.

SOUTHERN EGGS
Very Delicate Scrambled Eggs

Take one dozen eggs. Beat the whites and yolks separately, then together. Add a teacupful of milk in which half a teaspoon of cornstarch has been dissolved. Pour in a skillet containing hot melted butter, and stir until done.

Ham and Fried Eggs

After frying your ham, remove it, and into the ham gravy drop the eggs; turn them over once, and on each slice of ham, put an egg. They may also be fried in butter. Always pepper them.

Breakfast Dish

If you have a few bits of meat or cold fowl and two or three cold potatoes left, put some drippings in a saucepan, slice the potatoes thin, cut up the meat fine, and add salt and pepper to taste. Then beat up two or three eggs. Stir to them a cup of cream or milk and pour over the meat and potatoes. If eggs are not plentiful, use fewer eggs and more milk. If milk is scarce, add a dessert-spoonful of butter. Stir it constantly over the fire until the eggs are cooked. Do not leave it for an instant till the eggs are done, or they will burn, and ruin the whole!

Miss Jennie Mangel, **House-Keeping In The Sunny South,**
1885

FRANK'S HASH AND EGGS

Savannah artist Frank Penfold Brown says that his favorite form of entertainment (along with his annual open house at Christmas) is a brunch for out-of-town guests and local friends.

Yield: 8 servings

2 15-ounce cans corned beef hash	½ cup shredded Cheddar cheese
8 eggs	½ cup Parmesan cheese
salt and pepper to taste	paprika (optional)

Chill canned corn beef overnight, if possible, for easier handling. Slice contents of each can into 4 portions. Place each in an oiled aluminum cup (I use the kind cheese dip comes in) or a baking dish. Mash corned beef into cups, depressing center a bit to hold the egg. Now, place the cups of corned beef (without eggs, at this point) on a baking sheet. Place under the broiler, (watch them carefully!) until the corned beef is hot and sizzling.

Remove from oven and pour an egg into each cup. Season with salt and pepper. Return to broiler. Watch carefully as you cook them just until egg whites coagulate. Then, sprinkle each with some Cheddar cheese, and top with Parmesan cheese and paprika, if desired. Return to broiler, and watch carefully until cheese melts.

Of course, hash could be placed in cups ahead of time, all ready for the eggs and cheese, and refrigerated until needed, if it's easier for you to work at night than in the morning!

Frank Penfold Brown

SHRIMP AND EGGS BRUNCH

Yield: 2 servings

4 eggs, hard-cooked	½ cup dry sherry wine
mayonnaise	¾ cup shredded Cheddar cheese
curry powder	½ pound frozen shrimp, peeled
pepper and salt to taste	and deveined
(optional)	toast points
1 10¾-ounce can cream of	paprika
shrimp soup	

Halve eggs, and devil yolks with mayonnaise, ⅛ teaspoon curry powder, pepper, and salt if desired. Chill eggs, until ready to use.

Heat, but do not boil, the cream of shrimp soup. Add ¼ teaspoon curry powder, pepper, wine, and cheese. Stir constantly. Gently add deviled eggs and heat through. Add the defrosted shrimp, and cook until shrimp are pink. Serve over toast points, topped with paprika. May be doubled, or as needed.

Frank Penfold Brown

THE NEW SOUTH

Chiefest among the defects of all previous cook books stands the one glaring, unfortunate mistake that the receipts are, as a rule, costly. Necessity calls for such an adaptation as will meet the pressure of the times, and to present to the public the highest attainment of the culinary artist in a form at once tasty and inexpensive....The great majority of our receipts have been collected from private sources....Many noted housekeepers, all over the land, have contributed their tried and valued receipts....Our book is now set forth with the hope that the public may be benefited by the good it contains, and that its imperfections and omissions may be excused.

Mrs. E. R. Tennent,
House-Keeping In The Sunny South
Marietta, Georgia, Feb. 1st, 1885

ACKNOWLEDGEMENTS

In addition to individuals listed as recipe contributors, the author is grateful for those from the following sources:

Puffed Mushrooms recipe from *Holiday Inn International Cook Book* by Ruth Malone. Reprinted by permission of Mrs. Malone. Copyright© 1962 by Holiday Press.

Appetizer Ham Ball recipe from *Party Snacks Cookbook* by Jean Wickstrom. Reprinted by permission of Oxmoor House, Inc., Birmingham, Alabama. Copyright© 1974 by Oxmoor House.

Miss Edna's Seafood Bisque, Peach-Orange Honey, Chocolate Cookie Crust, Coconut Crust, Gingersnap Crust, and **Vanilla Wafer Crust** recipes from *The Pirates' House Cook Book* by Frances McGrath. Reprinted by permission of Herb Traub of the Pirates' House, Savannah. Copyright© 1964 by Frances McGrath.

Pickled Beef or **Sauerbraten and Jelly** recipe from *Ye Old Time Salzburger Cook.*

Real Chicken Pie recipe from *Treasured Georgia Recipes* by Kathryn Windham. Reprinted by permission of Mrs. Windham. Copyright© 1973 by Strode Publishers.

Classic Crab Newberg recipe from the Blue Channel Company, Port Royal, South Carolina.

Savannah Oyster Roast by Arthur Gordon and **Baked Oysters** recipe from the *Christ Church CookBook.* Reprinted by permission of Mr. Gordon and Mrs. Merritt Dixon, Jr. Copyright© 1956.

Shrimp Dejonghe recipe and **Italian Cream Cake** and **Cream Cheese Frosting** recipe from *Our Best Recipes* by Lena E. Sturges. Reprinted by permission of Oxmoor House, Inc., Birmingham, Alabama. Copyright© 1970 by Southern Living Books.

Mother's Self-Ice Cake recipe from *Outdoor Cookbook* by the Editors of Southern Living. Reprinted by permission of

Oxmoor House, Inc., Birmingham, Alabama. Copyright© 1973 by Southern Living Books.

Mrs. Wilkes Tartar Sauce and **Mrs. Wilkes Cheese Biscuits** recipes from *Famous Recipes from Mrs. Wilkes Boarding House in Historic Savannah*, by Mrs. L. H. Wilkes. Reprinted by permission of Mrs. Wilkes. Copyright© January 1976 by Mrs. Wilkes.

Gateau Cecily recipe from *Cecily Brownstone's Associated Press Cook Book* by Cecily Brownstone. Reprinted by permission of Miss Brownstone. Copyright© 1972 by the Associated Press.

Chocolate Cake with Chocolate Glaze recipe by Miss Helen McCully, former food editor, *House Beautiful Magazine*, reprinted by permission of the late Miss McCully.

Juliette Gordon Low family recipes reprinted from *Centennial Receipt Book: Juliette Gordon Low, Hostess and Homemaker, 1860 to 1960*, reprinted by permission of the Juliette Gordon Low Girl Scout National Center, Savannah. Copyright© 1960 by Girl Scouts of the U.S.A.

Georgia Nuggets recipe from Savannah Sugar Refinery, a Division of Savannah Foods and Industries, Inc. Used by permission of Mrs. Pamela B. Puckett of the Marketing/Advertising Division.

Quotations from *The Savannah Cook Book* by Harriet Ross Colquitt reprinted by permission of Anna H. Lynah, Charleston, South Carolina, Copyright© 1933 and 1960 by Harriet Ross Colquitt.

Pro Balls and other peanut recipes are reprinted by permission of the Georgia Peanut Commission, Tifton, Georgia, Mrs. Susan Avery, home economist.

Quotations from *Mrs. Rasmussen's Book of One-Arm Cookery* by Mary Lasswell, reprinted by permission of Mrs. Dudley Winn Smith, Los Alamos, California. Copyright© 1946, 1970 by Mary Lasswell.

Benne Seed Teething Sticks recipe from *The Supermarket Handbook: Access to Whole Foods*, by Nikki and David Goldbeck, copyright© 1973, 1976 by Nikki Goldbeck and David Goldbeck. Reprinted by permission of the Goldbecks.

The author is grateful to Mrs. Rita Trotz, rare books and prints specialist of The Printed Page at The Little House for the use of many of the historic cookbooks and prints used here. Also, to Jack Crolly and Ann (Mrs. Ben) Ritzert for the use of the recipes of their late mother, Mrs. Helen Kehoe Crolly; and to Mrs. Sophie Meldrim Shonnard for the use of her personal cookbook, containing many previously unpublished Georgia and South Carolina recipes.

Breakfast, Dinner and Supper, or, What To Eat, and How To Prepare it, by Maud C. Cooke, copyright© 1897, Washington, D.C., was lent the author by Mrs. Alyne Elizabeth Madden.

Desserts and Salads by Gesine Lemcke, Copyright© 1892, New York, was lent by Mrs. Jerry Downey.

Some Good Things To Eat, by Emma Rylander Lane, 1898, was lent by Emma Rylander Law. (This book was reissued in 1976, copyright© by Rebecca Parish Kelly, Clayton, Alabama.)

Vintage Cookbooks consulted included: *Housekeeping In Old Virginia,* edited by Marion Cabell Tyree, Louisville, Kentucky, 1879.

House-Keeping In The Sunny South, Mrs. E. R. Tennent, Atlanta, Georga, 1885.

Gulf City Cookbook, compiled by the Ladies of the St. Francis Street Methodist Episcopal Church South, Mobile, Alabama, 1878, revised 1911 by Aid Society.

Old London Cries, London, England, circa 1887.

House and Home; or, The Carolina Housewife, by a Lady of Charleston, Charleston, South Carolina, 1855.

The Guide to Service, London, England, 1842.

The English Cookery Book, by Frederick W. Davis, London, England, 1856.

The American Frugal Housewife: Dedicated to those who are Not Ashamed of Economy, Mrs. Child, New York, 1838.

Hints From Southern Epicures, Flower Committee of the Independent Presbyterian Church, Savannah, circa 1890, all lent by Mrs. Trotz.

The Telfair family recipes are from an original manuscript at the Georgia Historical Society, Savannah.

Favorite Recipes From Savannah Homes: Many Before Unpublished, Ladies of the Bishop Beckwith Society for the benefit of the Memorial Training School, published by the *Savannah Morning News,* 1904; from a copy in the Georgia section of the Savannah Public Library.

Also, *Society As I Have Found It,* Ward McAllister, Cassell Publishing Company, New York, 1890.

Prints and information on ships named *Savannah* from *Savannah: The River and The Port, 1900-1962,* by Master Pilot Frank W. Spencer.

Information on Savannah houses from *Sojourn In Savannah,* copyright© by Betty Rauers and Franklin Traub, 1976.

Lines quoted from *John Brown's Body* by Stephen Vincent Benet, Holt, Rinehart and Winston, Inc. (Copyright 1927, 1928 by Stephen Vincent Benet; copyright renewed 1955, 1956, by Rose-Mary Carr Benet, are used by permission of Brandt & Brandt, New York.

285

The author is especially indebted to Wallace M. Davis, Jr., Executive Editor, *Savannah News-Press*, for permission to reprint favorite Savannah recipes which have appeared over the years in the food section of the *Savannah News-Press*, and other Savannah material, such as *Poem in Praise of Practically Everything*, by Johnny Mercer, which appeared in the *Savannah Morning News*, February 12, 1958.

Food hints from *New Life Cookbook* by Marceline A. Newton, copyright© 1976 by Marceline A. Newton, used by permission of The Donning Company/Publishers, Norfolk, Virginia.

Quotation from *Lady From Savannah: The Life of Juliette Low*, by Gladys Denny Shultz and Daisy Gordon Lawrence, copyright© 1958 by Gladys Denny Shultz and Daisy Gordon Lawrence, J.P. Lippincott Co., New York.

We are grateful for the varied contributions of Savannah artists and organizations in illustrations, as noted.

Above all, the author wishes to thank Emma Rylander Law for her humor, encouragement, and expertise; all who helped test recipes; my family, for their understanding; my husband, Frank, for the indexing; and Donning Company/Publishers for having made this book possible.

INDEX

C

d

e

f

g

u

t

v